THE MARKETING AUDIT HANDBOOK

Dedication
To Mary Griffin, client, colleague, mentor – but above all, friend.

Also by Aubrey Wilson

The Changing Pattern of Distribution
Industrial Marketing Research-Management and Technique
The Marketing of Industrial Products
London's Industrial Heritage
The Assessment of Industrial Markets
The Art and Practice of Marketing
The Marketing of Professional Services
Practice Development for Professional Firms
New Directions in Marketing
Emancipating the Professions

THE MARKETING AUDIT HANDBOOK

TOOLS, TECHNIQUES & CHECKLISTS TO EXPLOIT YOUR MARKETING RESOURCES

AUBREY WILSON

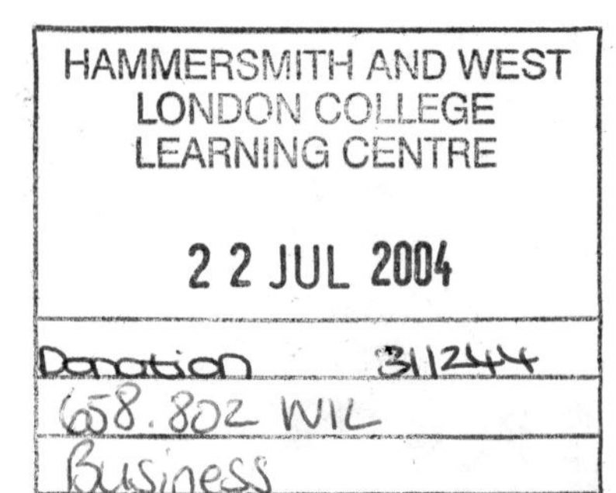

First published in 2002

Kogan Page Limited
120 Pentonville Road
London N1 9JN
UK

Kogan Page US
22 Broad Street
Milford CT 06460
USA

British Library Cataloguing in Publication Data

A CIP record for this book is available from the British Library.

ISBN 0 7494 3735 9

Typeset by Saxon Graphics Ltd, Derby
Printed and bound in Great Britain by Bell & Bain Ltd, Glasgow

Contents

Preface

Strangely, and despite the proliferation over the years of books on every conceivable aspect of marketing, there has been very little published on one of the most practical and profitable of all management tools – the marketing audit. While many texts contain check lists and 'best practice' guidelines, to my knowledge there have been no books, other than this one and its earlier manifestations, which are devoted solely to marketing.

Marketing has never experienced such turbulence and rapidity of change as is occurring now. The emergence of new media and techniques, most particularly electronic marketing, the relaxation of regulations which governed the content and targeting of promotional message, and the realities of the global market all challenge conventional and established marketing methods. As a result, checklists compiled in the last decade of the 20th century have been substantially overtaken and have important omissions. This is particularly true in information-gathering and management and, of course, the various aspects of electronic marketing.

The huge mass of information now available via the Internet is increasing geometrically every year. It has virtually eliminated most of the painstaking, time-consuming activities involved in locating information sources and accessing their contents. Similarly, although the jury is still out on the effectiveness of some forms of electronic advertising, it is nevertheless a new and important medium.

Away from electronic communications and logistics there have been important developments in relationship and affinity marketing, competitive intelligence and distribution logistics, to name just four areas. These changes require different approaches in their assessment and thus there are new questions to be asked. Consequently, this book, while retaining the core of previous editions published under the title *Marketing Audit Check Lists*, is a new work which makes the previous editions obsolete.

The turmoil in marketing is matched by turmoil in all markets. This demands that businesses monitor the effectiveness of their activities and ensure that they are fully exploiting their marketing resources. There is, in almost all organizations, a considerable marketing resource either not utilized, underutilized or utilized incorrectly. It only requires a knowledge of what is available for any sentient business person to be able to adjust his or her activities so as to exploit fully what is already possessed. However, making an inventory, mostly qualitative, is both difficult and time-consuming and, moreover, has strong internal political connotations. There is little wonder that the assessment of marketing resources and their utilization is rarely undertaken methodically. This book is an attempt to rectify such a situation.

The genesis of the technique that is described and explained in the book sprang originally from the need, at the start of a marketing research project, to establish just what data the sponsor already possessed and the degree of confidence that could be placed in their reliability. Then, as now, an inordinate amount of time and very considerable sums of money were frequently wasted on searching for information that did in fact exist but had not been extracted. Thus a list of key, if somewhat general, questions was developed for use at the beginning of any research project. However, it became increasingly obvious in studying the answers to many of the questions that most firms could materially improve their performance by a greater exploitation of both the information and the marketing resources they already possess. Consequently, the checklists, which were originally market data oriented, were considerably extended to cover all aspects of a company's marketing activities.

The answers to the questions, individually and in combination, point quickly to recommendations for a series of basic actions which can lead to impressive achievements. This approach has been described as a return to fundamentalism in marketing. Instead of theories, elegant plans, sophisticated strategies and esoteric philosophies, it produces down-to-earth practical suggestions which could, for most organizations, be implemented at once at no cost or low cost. There is no magic in this: it is simply using fully or re-deploying what a business already possesses.

The marketing resource realization technique, for that is what it is, has now been used hundreds of times and has never failed to produce operational and thus profit improvement – sometimes marginal, sometimes substantial, but always justifying the time investment in the audit.

Audit checklists all claim to be practical. None, however, seeks to provide a comprehensive model of information requirements or to formulate them in such a way that the answers suggest the courses of action to be followed. The purpose of this book is to fill this gap and provide a methodical approach to the identification, collection and evaluation of the marketing resources and strengths and weaknesses of a company; to exploit the former and avoid the latter where they cannot be corrected. It is hoped that its essential value will be the bringing together of the accumulated experiences, good and bad, of the many individuals and organizations involved in a wide range of industries and services, and with different levels of marketing and sales sophistication or primitivism with whom the author has had the privilege of working in over 30 years of intense involvement in marketing. The book has no national connotations. The technique and the questions can be (and have been) applied from Kenya to Canada and from Australia to Iceland.

One of the pleasures of composition is being able to express a public appreciation of the help, guidance, wisdom and critical support of others whose contribution is all too frequently embedded, without direct acknowledgement, in the text. I particularly want to express my gratitude for the contributions of Dr Carol O'Connor and Christopher West, who provided special lists on electronic trading, competitive intelligence and market research, areas in which they are leading experts. Their permission to mangle their text to suit my own style and the book's format has gone beyond the bounds of friendship.

Not for the first time, my particular thanks must go to Dorothy Storr – a woman of infinite patience and skill – in fact the only one who could have sorted out the complex cross-referencing. She also has a cryptographer's ability to decode and interpret my enigmatic notes and insertions and typing which gave my Spellcheck an electronic nervous breakdown. I am grateful to her for identifying errors, duplications and sometimes a less than felicitous way of formulating a question.

Again, I have an irredeemable debt to my wife Gina for her encouragement, excusing me from domestic commitments and protecting me from intrusive social demands.

At the end of every preface or introduction the author invariably offers the courtesy of exonerating all those who helped from any errors or omissions and takes on him or herself full responsibility. Never was such an inclusion more justified than for this book.

January 2002

The marketing audit

A self-administered method for identifying and realizing underutilized marketing resources

Those who have attempted to undertake a marketing audit are well aware that all too many questions asked do not of themselves yield information which will lead to practical and profitable action.

For example, the answer to the question, 'Does management recognize the importance of designing the company to serve the needs and wants of chosen markets?' is difficult to translate into immediate practical recommendations.

What this book seeks to do is to bring together the technique of the marketing audit with the technique of the checklist approach. The value of checklists is essentially threefold: 1) not to have to rethink, reorder and rewrite what has perhaps been done many times before; 2) to be able to obtain an insight into the thinking and experience of others in the same field; and 3) to ensure that no important item is forgotten. Whether a checklist is simply for packing for a holiday or is a complex one such as might be used in flying an advanced military aircraft, the advantages and uses remain the same. The checklist approach to marketing provides a reliable short-cut in assembling information and an insurance that within the broad span that comprises corporate policy, in particular marketing, no vital issue or question is omitted.

It is recognized that checklists can also inhibit original thinking and produce an unconsidered acceptance of what has been revealed. The lists that follow are only a starting point – a logical notation of aspects of the firm's operations that impact on marketing strategy and marketing actions. To be fully effective they not only require screening and reorientating; they also require expanding to meet the needs of the auditor, and the activities and aspirations of the organization.

Apart from providing clear guidelines to the actions a company might undertake to improve its position, the checklists, used correctly as an audit guide, have the inestimable advantage of identifying and utilizing marketing resources of every type. The reason these are not fully exploited is not difficult to understand. Many firms do not know what resources they own or their quality. Frequently, because of received wisdom, old practices and habits, and sometimes despair, they are constrained from introducing simple changes that would release many of the currently underexploited resources the organization possesses.

The author has found that many practical suggestions, which might be termed at no higher level than 'hot tips', will emerge from the audit. They may lack the elegance of sophisticated marketing strategies and systems, but they have the overwhelming advantage of being practical, immediate and most frequently no cost or of low cost.

That is not to suggest that marketing systems and marketing strategies are irrelevant. Nothing could be further from the truth. Indeed the random disconnected ideas that will develop might well be a test in themselves as to the practicality of the marketing systems and organizations and the marketing plan. Any recommendations that derive from the audit should be considered both on their own merit and in relation to other corporate activities – marketing and non-marketing. They form yet another usable and desirable outcome of the methodical step-by-step approach inherent in all well-composed checklists.

The marketing audit, unlike many benchmark studies, does have a value as a one-off free-standing exercise, but its greatest use is as an ongoing regular practice of the company, so that comparison can be made between the results of each audit. Very early on (List 1, 'Marketing strategy and planning') emphasis is placed on clear and agreed objectives. As the Cheshire Cat pointed out to Alice, if you do not know where you are going, 'it doesn't matter which way you go'. It will not take a marketing audit to decide if the objectives have been achieved, but the audit will show if the route chosen was the most effective and profitable. It will also indicate whether particular marketing activities should be intensified, adjusted or dropped. Attention is drawn to both the obvious and the esoteric, which will be different for each company and manager. Thus, some questions may seem simple and indeed primitive for one organization or person, while the same points in another context may represent totally new thoughts.

Not surprisingly, most marketing checklists are externally orientated. They do not take into account the strengths and weaknesses of the company or the resources available over any period of time. While this book is substantially and intentionally inward-looking, and is designed to highlight the issues specific to a company and those that impact on marketing, it has by no means ignored the external situation.

It is not suggested that most managers do not know a great deal about their company, have a lively knowledge of the immediate environment in which they work and cannot respond sensibly and effectively to change: what is frequently lacking is an understanding of what might be termed the 'outer environment', where four major forces of change are at work. These are government activities, technological change, sociological change and economic change – all irresistible forces in their own right and all interacting with each other.

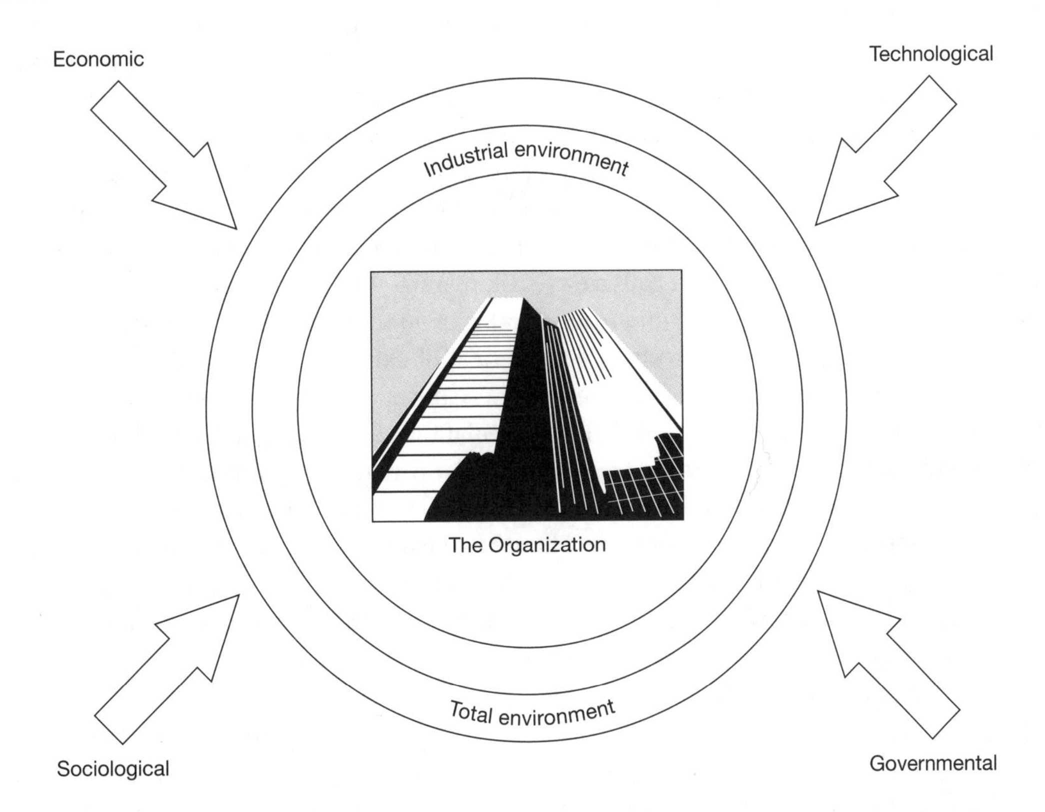

THE BUSINESS ENVIRONMENT

The impact of these forces on the outer environment must cause shock waves impacting on the business environment and in turn within the company itself. No organization is or can be insulated.

Marketing auditors, while not losing an introspective approach, must nevertheless remain firmly aware that they operate in highly volatile conditions and can control or influence only a minute proportion of them.

Turning now to the lists themselves, what has been attempted is to devise an extremely wide range of questions covering all the company's marketing activities and matters pertinent to them. The relevant questions can be selected and, hopefully, from the answers and their relationship with each other will emerge a series of marketing actions that will enable a greater exploitation of existing resources to occur. The process will indicate resources not required, and which are therefore being wasted, and also resources to be acquired.

Let us take some simple examples. There are, for most firms, about 220 selling days in a year in the United Kingdom and 365 in international markets. How many days a year is the salesforce engaged in selling, and how is the rest of the time accounted for? Is the balance of time justified by the cost of sales personnel doing something that is either not selling or not directly relevant to selling, and could it be done as effectively by someone else? How many sales calls are made each week in aggregate and individually? What is the cost per call and what are the time components of that cost, i.e. liaising within the company, preparing quotations, and the many other things a representative has to do in addition to the face-to-face sales situation, and which are so often overlooked in any assessment of the salesperson's time expenditure. Is it possible to make one more call of average quality per week? With a salesforce of ten and a typical four calls a day striking rate, this represents over 450 additional calls per year; what is the ratio of enquiries to calls; of quotations to business? Even a highly unfavourable ratio is likely to produce a great deal of extra business. How, then, can that extra call a week be achieved? The answers to these questions, all to be found in List 9, 'The salesforce and its management', will rapidly reveal if the salesforce is fully productive.

A second example can be drawn from List 13, 'Non-personal promotion: methods and media'. Many firms, but most particularly professional practices and service companies, fail to trace the source of enquiries from new clients or customers, and yet this is the only truly accurate guide as to which messages and which communication techniques are effective. It is very cheap, quick and simple to develop a tracing operation once it is appreciated how much this can contribute to profitable operations by ensuring that all promotion is concentrated on messages and methods that are seen to work.

Finally a glance at List 15, 'The buying process', will draw attention to the fact that all too few sales personnel ever look closely into the methods customers use to evaluate products or services or the criteria adopted for judging the end of the useful life of a purchase. This knowledge can sharpen the sales platform to a considerable extent by taking into account this key decision factor.

It will be seen that the basic classifications – materials, capital goods, consumer goods, operating supplies, semi-manufacturers and services[1] – have not been separated. Marketing auditors may have to adjust for the classification in which they are involved.

In using the lists it may be found that the answers to the questions in the various sections will not all be obtainable in one department or from one individual, or even within the company; therefore it would be unusual for an audit to be completed in a single session (although it is not impossible).

In my experience it is not usually necessary for each answer, particularly quantitative ones, to be provided with a high degree of precision. A phenomenon or pattern will generally be revealed by reasonable indicators. Precision should be sought only if the resulting action will be affected by the difference between an indicator and the exact position. If a market size is £50 million or £55 million, is it likely to affect the detailed, let alone the basic marketing strategy?

The order of the lists is in a sense very personal and as such idiosyncratic. Powerful arguments can be (and indeed were) made for reordering, using a different rationale – the importance of the subject, the sequence within the marketing process, alphabetical, ease of acquiring data, and so on. The continuum as presented now may appear to lack a formal logic, but it does correspond to a sequence found to work well in an actual audit. It will fit the circumstances of most organizations, but if it does not there is no reason why auditors cannot reorder the sequence to suit their own requirements.

Some questions have been repeated where they are needed in different sections, perhaps for different purposes. Where this occurs the questions have been cross-referenced to avoid having to rethink the answers. For example, Question 2.23 in List 2, 'Product/service range', on total cost analysis is repeated in List 23, 'Pricing', as Question 23.30.

Some readers may wonder why there is no section dealing specifically with the marketing message, as methods and media are covered at some length. In fact, questions relating to the marketing message, with their implications for making it more effective, will be found throughout the text: obviously in such lists as 'Product/service range' (2), 'The salesforce and its management' (9), 'Non-personal promotion: methods and media' (13), but perhaps not quite so obviously under the special circumstances of 'Non-differentiated products and commodities' (26) and 'Service businesses' (27).

Each list has a commentary, the purpose of which is to draw attention to some of the key questions and their implications and to illustrate points with short case histories. I have attempted to build into the commentaries a number of suggestions for consideration for action. In List 21, 'Physical distribution and packaging', for example, some classic failures are referred to: assuming a punctual despatch date implies a punctual receipt date and thus risking blame for late delivery; failure to design a pack that would enable distant, accurate, stock checks to be made by clear marking and 'remaining contents' indicators (where appropriate); failure to use the shipment and storage pack to carry advertising messages. In List 9, 'The salesforce and its management', an example is given of how one manufacturer managed to improve his average price obtained by sharing benefits with the sales team. Many other examples will be found throughout the book.

It is not only markets that are not homogeneous. Customers also vary widely in their needs, perceptions, policies and practices. Thus a different answer might well emerge from a number of the questions if they are applied to customers with different profiles. A practical breakdown that can be used as necessary throughout the checklists is:

- regular customers;
- sporadic customers;
- one-off customers;
- lost customers;
- prospective customers inviting quotations but not buying;
- prospects where no invitation to quote has been obtained.

An example of the use of these categorizations will be found in the Introduction to List 18, 'User industries', and the topic is also dealt with in Question 18.11.

Because the attempt has been made to cover the relevant subjects fully and make the questions as comprehensive as possible, the task of undertaking a marketing audit using the checklist approach may look daunting. It need not be so. Typically, an audit for small operations would require less than a quarter of the questions listed. It is difficult to conceive of an occasion when the entire gamut of questions would be needed.

The sectionalization of the lists enables auditors, if they so wish, to look at individual parts of the business only, as each list, while cross-referenced, is also free-standing. Thus, if an audit of the agency resources, utilization and methods is required, List 12, 'The agency system', can be completed quite independently of any other section. To obtain the maximum benefit from the compilation, the user should see it both as a whole and in its parts.

One final suggestion: marketing auditors must be totally unbiased and neutral. Internal politics have no part to play in a marketing audit, and management should not expect auditors to remain objective if they are reporting on a situation that may reflect critically on themselves, their friends, or their department. In selecting a marketing auditor this factor needs careful consideration.

The decision process in which any exchange of money for goods and services is involved has five stages, at every one of which prospective purchasers must be convinced that:

- they have a need;
- the offer is the correct one to meet the need;
- the supplier can fulfil the need;
- the price is competitive;
- they can obtain the product/service at a time and in a place they require it.

Whether these five decisions are a simple moment of truth at the checkout of a supermarket or involve investment of millions of pounds in major plant, they nevertheless occur. In business-to-business markets the decisions will be much more diffuse and for many products will occupy a lengthy time span to allow for detailed comparison, physical testing and negotiation. The end purpose of the market audit is to bring prospective customers through the five stages as quickly and profitably as possible and to leave them with the conviction that they have obtained value for money from a company who are 'nice people to do business with'.

Notes

1 Services are a minor exception in that, although they are taken into almost every section of the book, List 27, 'Service businesses', deals specifically with those aspects of marketing which are peculiar to them.

How to use the checklists

It has already been said that the use of the checklists is relatively simple. It requires only those skills that most managers would be expected to possess. They do, however, need a knowledge of the organization and its personnel as well as an ability to obtain cooperation from busy people. This is always best achieved if the purpose of the audit and the outcome are fully explained to those from whom it is sought.

The major innovation in this book, as compared to its predecessors, is one that will save a very considerable amount of time. Previously it was not practical to use the actual book to conduct the audit, so it was necessary to re-type those lists and questions to be asked, leaving enough space for answers. This can now be avoided since the lists (without the introductory sections) are to be found on the CD-ROM that accompanies the book. It is now easy to select or eliminate lists or sections, add questions and quickly follow a cross-reference by clicking on the appropriate List number and then scrolling down to the question. In practical terms, it will be found best to print out the questions to be used and to complete the answers on hard copy during the interview and then transfer them back to the computer, if necessary.

Basically three requirements exist:

- deciding which questions are relevant;
- knowing where to obtain the information;
- interpreting the answers into terms of actions to be taken.

The procedure for conducting an audit is as follows:

1. First check the documentation required for the audit. Some suggestions for the material that will be needed are given at the end of this section and on the CD-ROM. Where the

requirement for these documents arises will emerge from the lists themselves but, by way of example, 'terms of business' referred to in List 4, 'Company performance', Questions 4.42–4.44; and List 24, 'Images and perceptions', Question 24.28, will obviously need a study of the conditions. If all the documents required can be assembled before the audit begins, much time can be saved.

2. Next, decide which sections can be eliminated. A manufacturer of process plant or *haute couture* fashions will hardly need List 26, 'Non-differentiated products and commodities', or a service company List 21, 'Physical distribution and packaging'. It is wise, however, not to assume too readily from the title alone that some of the questions may not be applicable. The fact that a company does not use distributors does not necessarily imply that there are no questions within the section where the answers may not produce a reconsideration of the policy. It is always better to retain a list if any doubt exists as to its relevance.
3. The requirement now is to prune the remaining lists by deleting all questions that are not applicable or where it is known that the information is just not obtainable. An example of the first situation could come from List 7, 'Market size and structure', Questions 7.29 and 7.30, and many questions in the last part of List 11, 'Cross-selling and internal marketing', all concerning in-feeding and reciprocal trading. This will certainly not apply to the general run of companies. Similarly List 23, 'Pricing', Question 23.28; it may simply not be possible in some circumstances to ascertain just what a customer would pay to retain a particular product or service attribute.
4. Many questions have strong links with others and some will produce similar or identical answers. In List 5, 'Export Marketing', Question 5.64 on cross-licensing, the answers could be the same or closely related to those given in List 17, 'Introducing new products and services', Question 17.53. Using the hyperlinks on the CD-ROM makes it easy and quick to compare the responses, avoid duplication and establish connections.
5. Auditors will probably find that some questions and answers generate other queries and one of the skills they will rapidly develop is the ability to devise supplementary questions. These are of considerable importance and in no way should auditors stick rigidly to those listed or their formulation. They should be aware that no checklist is ever complete. Every compiler of such lists knows this. New questions always occur, and the lists grow longer and longer, both as a consequence of change within and external to the company and because of the answers to the questions themselves. The benefits and dangers of this are too obvious to need spelling out.
6. The main task starts now. Auditors should go through the remaining questions, answering all those it is within their competence to deal with and where they have confidence in responses. It will be found that the marketing ideas for actions will emerge from the answers. Here some preliminary time classifications will be required to indicate the sequence for implementation. If different colours or markings are used to indicate the completion schedule, later transfer to the action plan will be made simpler and quicker (see also 8 below).

In assembling some of the yield, auditors may well be able to take further short-cuts by the use or adaptation of some of the excellent formats developed for market planning. Examples of these are the ones at the end of this Introduction and in List 13, 'Non-personal promotion: methods and media', Question 13.3. A well laid out form can make obtaining and tabulating data much quicker and simpler and thus bring into prominence the action implications.

7. This now leaves a number of questions on which auditors must consult. They should identify those people within the organization and, if needs be, outside it whom they have to contact. If each question to be administered is marked with the respondent's initials or some identification, this will save a great deal of time and indeed some impatience at the time of the actual meeting. If the questions are submitted in writing for preliminary examination, this of course is helpful, but it does involve further loss of time. Moreover, the loss of spontaneity, particularly on qualitative aspects of the audit, may not offset the value of the prior consideration. The worst combination is to submit the questions in writing and ask for a reply in writing: the time delay will be found to be considerable, most particularly when further questions are engendered by the answers or where clarification is needed.

   Some points may be better dealt with on a consensus basis, probably using a group of informed personnel with different responsibilities and disciplines. The group approach has the advantage of the Delphi technique, which enables each member to hear the advocacy for and against a particular opinion and if need be to modify his or her views. However, while suggestions for actions should be welcomed, care must be taken not to get into the stultifying position of arguing about theory. It is the job of the auditor to decide what are the implications of the information. An action plan by a committee is going to be the antithesis of quick movement and decisiveness.

   Some recycling of both answers and action recommendations may well be needed, and the auditor should be prepared for these and be able to accommodate them. The best results will ensue if no fixed attitudes are taken or decisions adopted until all the answers are in and all the actions summarized.

   An important psychological point arises. The audit and questioning process may well disturb the respondents who may regard the whole process as a performance assessment leading perhaps to some personal disadvantage. Before any meeting takes place, or at the very beginning of a meeting, the purpose of the audit must be explained to respondents – that it is the contribution of their knowledge, experience and ideas which is sought and that the interview is not a personal appraisal. It is vital to obtain their enthusiastic cooperation. Thus the purpose and outcome of the audit need to be completely understood.

8. It is recognized that not everything can be done within the resources and time span available, so it may be necessary to place an order of priority on the introduction of changes or activities that are deemed necessary. To this end it is advisable to extract all action points for categorization into priority groups with an indication of, at the very

least, the time implied by such terms as 'at once', 'short-term', 'medium-term' and 'long-term'. On their own, time designations of this type have no real meaning.

Two other classifications are worthy of consideration. First, by likely cost implications, so that no-cost and low-cost items can be proceeded with without budget changes or authorization. This alone should ensure the removal of one possible blockage. Second, changes that will cause no disruption of normal activities and thus are most likely to be acceptable and to be implemented by those involved.

9. The last action of the audit is to place a date for initiation and completion of each activity, to decide who is responsible for carrying it through and who is to be responsible for monitoring progress and satisfactory completion. This point requires extra emphasis. Completing an audit does not automatically imply that the appropriate actions will be taken. To be certain that the marketing resources will be fully realized, it is important to ensure that every action decided upon is allocated to an individual or group, that the time for its completion is scheduled and promulgated and that someone monitors that the task is satisfactorily completed by the due date. *Allocate, schedule* and *monitor* are the key words for guaranteeing action.

The audit process can now be summarized:

- Collect documentation.
- Eliminate all non-applicable sections.
- Delete all non-relevant questions in the remaining sections.
- Answer all questions within the capability of the auditor, with recommended courses of action.
- List others who need to be consulted to complete the audit.
- Decide whether to take individual replies or work as a group.
- (for individual responses) Identify which questions will be asked of which people.
- (for individual responses) Decide how the response will be taken, eg personal interview, advance notice of questions and personal interview, written request and written response.
- Conduct interviews/inquiries.
- Write in the suggested courses of action arising from the responses.
- Extract all action points and categorize according to urgency, likely cost, ease of implementation etc.
- Allocate each task by name, schedule it by date or elapsed time, agree monitoring procedure.

Best practice shows that when it comes to initiating and carrying out agreed actions, volunteers are better than conscripts. Where possible, tasks should be allocated to those most willing to carry them out. The second rule is that peer pressure is by far the best motivator. If everyone knows what everyone else is doing then action will certainly occur, particularly if regular review meetings are held.

A format such as that given in the Appendix covers all the main issues of a marketing action plan. Everyone should receive a copy of it.

The marketing audit is *not* a substitute for action, nor should it be permitted to delay decision-taking. This should be kept foremost in mind when undertaking the audit.

DOCUMENTATION

- Organization chart (official and informal)
- Mission statement
- Corporate/market/profit plan
- Marketing job specifications
- Function specification of sales office
- Catalogues and brochures (own and competitors')
- Examples of other documentation
- Examples of press releases
- Media advertising including Web sites and direct mail material (including schedules and appropriations (own and competitors'))
- Salesforce reporting form
- Customer database
- Enquiry records
- Sales analyses (home and export)
- Salesforce/agents'/distributors' assessment forms
- New product search report and evaluations
- List of journals, etc received
- List of external statistics received regularly
- Sales contact reports
- Guarantee claim record
- Credit note analysis
- Complaints analysis
- Service record forms
- Agency agreement forms
- Terms of business
- Examples of how information on customers is kept
- Any training programmes for sales or marketing people – content, outline
- Details on any market research undertaken in the last one or two years (not the reports themselves yet).

Appendix
Format for a marketing action plan

Period Date of issue Monitored by

Target group	Actions	Objective	Budget		Person responsible	Plan completion deadline	Time schedule												Achievement
			£	Time			Jan	Feb	Mar	Apr	May	Jun	Jul	Aug	Sep	Oct	Nov	Dec	
		Total																	

List 1

Marketing strategy and planning

INTRODUCTION

The first checklist deals with the fundamental activities involved in creating a marketing strategy and implementing it. Marketing strategies and plans should be available to all managers, not just those involved in marketing. They do not have to be formal and complex, but they must be in written form.

It must be said at the outset that the marketing strategy has to be subordinate to the corporate strategy and therefore everything the marketing plan contains has to be compatible. One certain way of achieving this is to have a mission or 'vision' statement for both the organization and the marketing department. Unfortunately the value of these statements has been undermined because 'mission' and 'vision' have become favourite terms for politicians and the statements are used to express in an anodyne way party objectives. In reality the creation of a mission statement, whatever unfortunate connotations it has recently acquired, is a most valuable and practical activity.

At the corporate level, a mission statement has been described as 'an enduring statement of purpose, that distinguishes one organization from other similar enterprises and as a declaration of an organization's 'reason for being'. A mission statement is a formal expression of the vision the company has of what it wants to be and what it should be. All companies have a mission of one type or another, even if not in writing. The process of developing a written mission statement, however, forces management consciously to contemplate, debate and articulate the nature of the business, the reason for the company's existence, the customers and markets being served and those that should be served, the products/services being marketed and those that should be marketed, and the rewards and quality of life for employees. This process has an inherent risk. It can lead to disagreement and dissent among management. But the benefits of formulating a written mission statement generally outweigh the risk. A mission statement can serve as a tool that guides strategy formulation and evaluation, and unifies expectations, plans, performance evaluation criteria and corporate objectives.

Departmental mission statements serve the same purpose and face the same developmental problems as corporate mission statements. Like corporate mission statements, they serve to unify expectations, plans, goals, and performance standards. However, departmental mission statements have an additional purpose. They integrate departments (or functions) towards meeting subordinate goals. In other words, the process of formulating a departmental mission statement forces management to specify the purpose of the department, and its relationship to other functions and to the corporate mission (if one exists).

The reality is, of course, that most mission or vision statements are produced to satisfy company mores and have little practical application. This is quite wrong; the mission statement can make a great contribution to marketing success if it is followed and promoted and is not confined to vague 'motherhood' statements. Mission statements are, or should be, measurable and thus checkable against results, and qualitative but lending themselves to evaluation. By way of example, consider the mission statement shown in Figure 1.1.

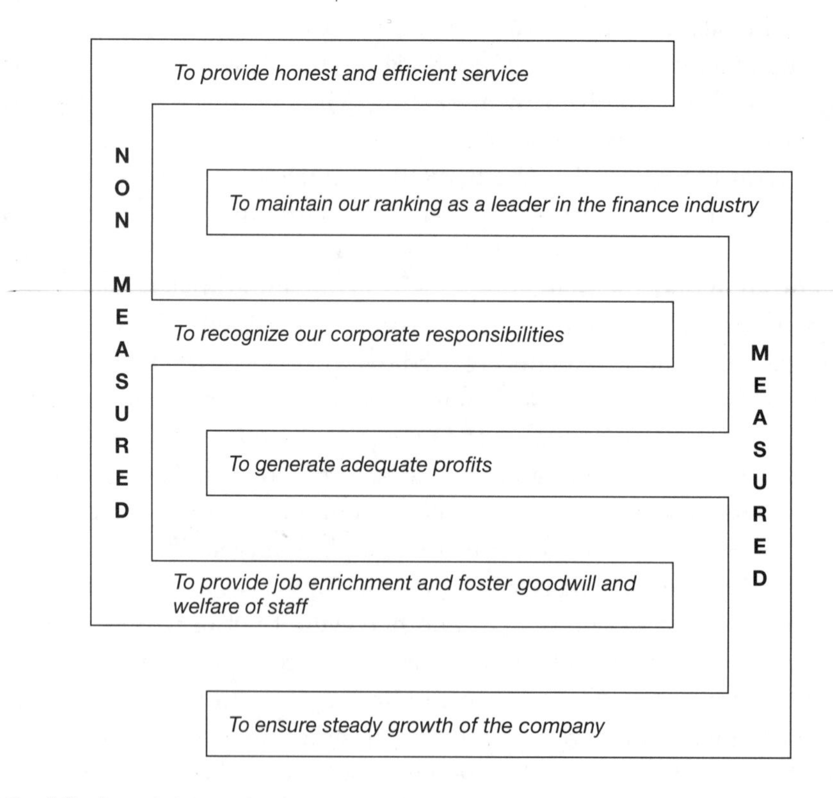

Figure 1.1 Mission statement

The plan should give the assumption on which it is based, the resources available for its implementation, a conceptualization of the market position and potential, forecasts – technical, commercial, economic, financial, and specific to the firm – threats and opportunities, courses of action and activity schedule, personnel plan, budgets, controls and monitoring. Question 1.3 implies all this.

Question 1.8 focuses on the all-important subject of objectives. It is important at the outset to check that objectives do indeed exist and are understood, that they are practical, and also that they are acceptable to those who must achieve them. It has to be seen by everyone involved that goals are compatible with the market potential and the company resources. Setting out objectives will also give a good initial indication of the strategies and tactics to be adopted. This first list is designed to ensure that elegant plans are not just documents for display. They must have action points built in with both monitoring and fail-safe facilities.

Question 1.10 on gap analysis refers to the simple technique of making a surprise-free forecast of sales or profits in the next five years – usually a straight line (momentum) projection – and comparing the position of the graph in the fifth year with the quantitative targets (see Figure 1.2). Any shortfall, which is the gap between the projection and the target set, represents the task that marketing must accomplish, which in turn will demonstrate how realistic the targets are.

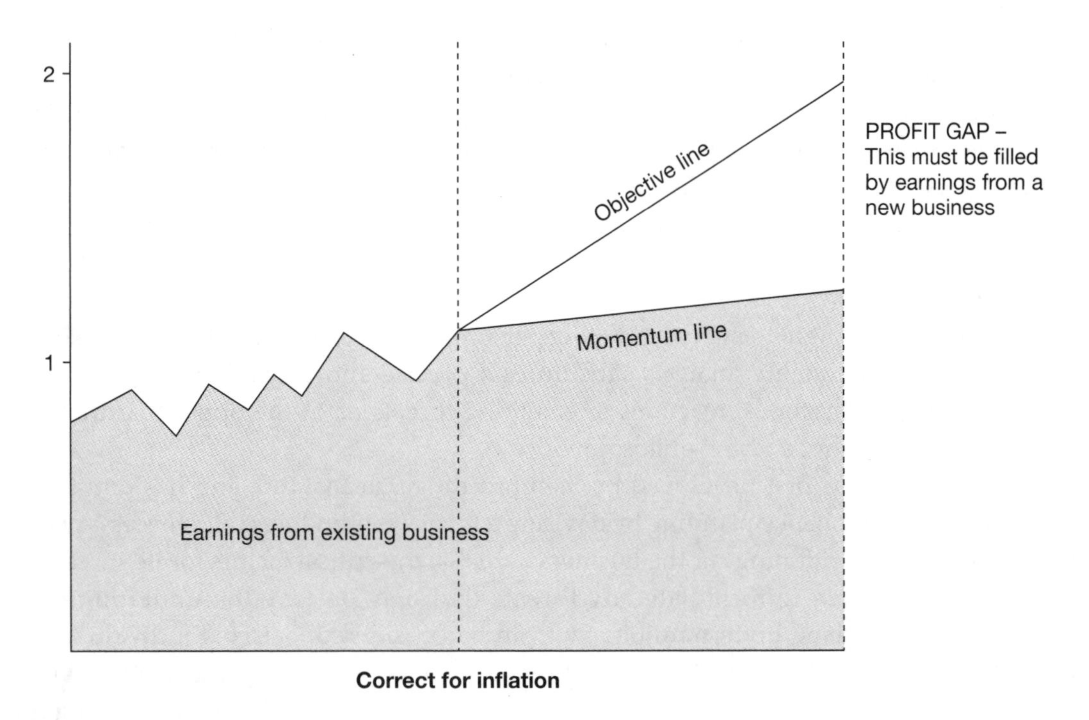

Figure 1.2 The gap analysis

Product planning is a vital part of marketing strategy although it is sometimes seen, wrongly, as completely separate. Question 1.14 asks pertinent questions of how a range is composed, and the implications for specialization and/or full-line trading are inherent.

Question 1.21 calls for a segmentation of the market. Segmentation is a vital technique in marketing, and failure to distinguish the parts from the whole can lead to massive underperformance. Few markets are wholly homogeneous. Identifying segments with common characteristics that will cause them to respond to the same marketing messages and marketing tools will enable the firm to concentrate its marketing resources in the most effective way.

There are many ways of segmenting a market. Some obvious ones are: by region, size of customer company, form of customer organization, heavy or light users, seasonal, demographic factors, psychographic factors and, a particularly interesting one, by benefit received.

Appendix 1A gives a model of this last method for a variable chamber filter. Industries appearing under the *primary impact sectors* heading in the left-hand column are obviously more likely to view the product favourably than those in the right-hand column *primary impact sectors*. The segmentation priority is obvious. For firms appearing in both central columns it is necessary to judge how far the disadvantages of the filter for their processes offset the advantages, and to decide the balance.

It is important to start any audit with an understanding of the perceived strengths and weaknesses of the business as well as of the opportunities and the threats to which it is exposed. The audit as it proceeds may cause a radical review of any profile, but this first assessment will give a useful benchmark. It will also reveal how much of the profile is based on in-company folklore and how much on the real situation. Question 1.30 deals with this key issue. Answers might well be obtained by the use of a simple form distributed to selected personnel (not necessarily only managers) and a consensus of the views taken on the major issues. It is a greatly simplified and easily adopted version of the well-known SWOT analysis – Strength, Weakness, Opportunity, Threat. The suggested content is shown in Figure 1.3.

Perhaps a new thought to many marketing personnel will be Question 1.27 on marketing vulnerability. Vulnerability analysis substitutes a precise and disciplined approach for emotional or even hysterical reactions to emerging threats or, at the opposite extreme, a 'let's not look, it might go away' philosophy.

The technique was first developed by Stanford Research Institute and has put a new discipline into contingency planning by devising a formal methodology. It is necessary first to identify the underpinnings of the business – that is, the critical factors for its successful operation – and then to formulate any threats that may destroy the underpinnings. Appendix 1C lists some underpinnings that can be considered. Selected individuals are then invited to consider each threat and to give their personal judgement on its likely impact and the chance of its occurring. A consensus is taken of each threat by grouping the judgements of the individuals involved in the exercise on to one matrix. If there are wide

THE FOLLOWING IS ONE POINT IN OUR COMPANY'S FUTURE

1. NAME__________ JOB TITLE__________

2. THESE ISSUES REFER TO A: (TICK ONE ONLY)

STRENGTH	☐	OPPORTUNITY	☐
WEAKNESS	☐	THREAT	☐

B: IN OUR COMPANY (TICK ONE ONLY)

LOCATION	☐	STAFF	☐
SYSTEMS	☐	CUSTOMERS	☐
SUPPLIERS	☐	COMPETITORS	☐
PRODUCT/SERVICE	☐	DISTRIBUTORS	☐
FACILITIES	☐	OTHER	☐
R&D	☐		

3. EXPLANATION OF STATEMENT OR ISSUE

4. SUPPORTING REFERENCES, SOURCES OR FACTS

5. RANGE OF POSSIBLE ACTION OR RESOURCE REQUIREMENTS

Figure 1.3 SWOT analysis

disparities of views, participants are invited to give the basis for the position they have allotted the threat, and, through recycling, a Delphi forecast is produced.

The same type of grid is used both for the individual personal assessments and the consensus results (see Figure 1.4).

When the vulnerability analysis process is complete, a set of priorities that can be useful to management as a basis for allocating time and resources has been established. A rough method of deciding the order in which threats should receive attention is to use the crescent shown in Figure 1.4. Clusters falling in the A band should be considered *urgent*; usually, they are already receiving some type of attention. The B crescent points up threats that should be classed as *important* and needing executive attention in the strategic plan. Action on threats falling into the C crescent can generally be postponed; such threats might be monitored for changes which could cause them to shift to a higher priority, that is, a movement to the right and/or upwards.

The arrival of video, which decimated the home movie market, and facsimile, which killed Telex, led to many desperate and failed attempts at prolonging the life of both victim products. A vulnerability exercise might well have mitigated a number of product/marketing disasters. Digital cameras have already signalled the demise of instant photography (Polaroid) and now seriously threaten chemically produced images. Will DVD spell the end of VHS? These are the types of development which would have benefited from timely vulnerability analyses.

Vulnerability analysis is a simple exercise once the underpinnings of the business are agreed and an ordered approach to the consideration of threats is substituted for hysteria or complacency.

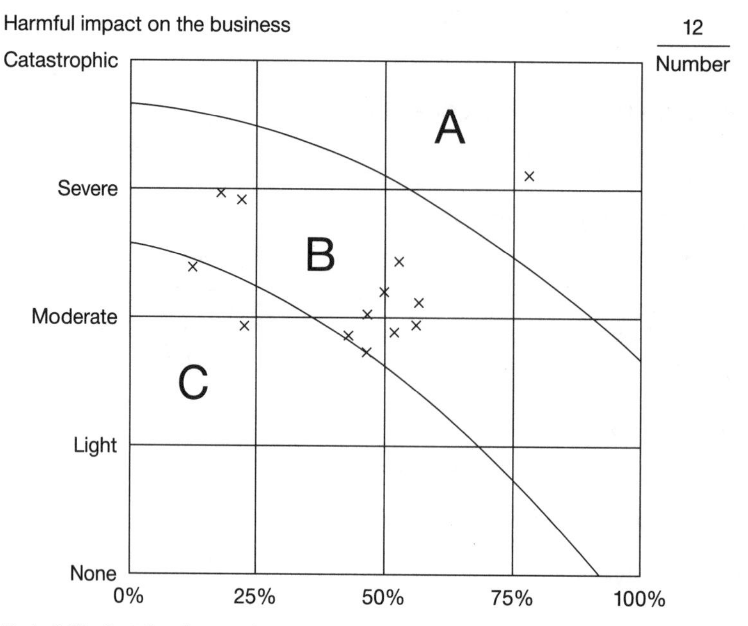

Figure 1.4 Vulnerability analysis showing composite assessments of an example threat[1]

Question 1.33 refers to a marketing tactic made possible by the great advances in data collection, analysis, communication and in production technology. The ability now exists to individualize markets through the use of constantly evolving databases. While the ultimate segmentation of *one* has not arrived, the possibility of it emerging is no longer a dream.

1.1 Do we have a formal forward marketing plan?
1.2 Is the business mission statement reflected in the marketing strategy?
1.3 Which of the following mission statement components does it incorporate?
- customers and market segments
- location – where the offer is to be marketed
- survival and growth of the company
- self-concept
- product/service
- total content of the offer
- technology involved
- philosophy

- image sensitivity
- concern for employees

1.4 What is the reason for inclusion/omission of any components?

1.5 Is the marketing plan compatible with the corporate and other operational and project plans?

1.6 What period is covered?

1.7 When was it last reviewed and revised?

1.8 Do we have agreed quantitative and qualitative objectives for the short, medium and long term? (See also List 13, 'Non-personal promotion: methods and media', Question 13.1, for communications objectives.)

- profit
- value of sales
- unit sales
- number of customers
- market share
- market penetration
- return on investment
- new products
- range coverage
- geographical coverage
- key customers[2]
- ratio of repeat to new business
- distributor density and volume
- exports
- cost of sales
- anti-cyclical products/service
- order size and drop
- value added

1.9 Is the relevance of the objectives reviewed regularly?

1.10 Have we conducted a gap analysis to appraise the nature of the marketing task and the resource requirement and, if so, how large is the gap? (See Introduction and List 17, 'Introducing new products/services', Figure 17.2, and Questions 17.41 and 17.42.)

1.11 Will the market plan, if carried out successfully, close the gap?

1.12 Do we have a complete and up-to-date resource audit?

1.13 What resources will be needed to close the gap and will they be made available?

- people – skills, qualifications, contacts
- finance
- hardware – including machine stock
- patents, licences and trade marks
- distributive network

- inventory
- customer base and customer knowledge
- range
- information
- approvals
- image
- ability to supply 'specials'
- transport
- salesforce
- contracts – leases, franchises
- intellectual property

1.14 Is there a marketing plan, by product/service? Does it include range 'mix'; 'depth', and 'width', additions and deletions? (See Introduction.)
1.15 Do all or relevant managers have copies of the marketing plan?
1.16 How and when and with what regularity is the marketing plan used by managers?
1.17 Are individual market tasks defined, allocated and scheduled, and is accomplishment monitored? (See List 25, 'Quality in marketing', question 25.19 and List 28, Appendix 28A, 'Product/service financial information'.)
1.18 Who is responsible for these tasks, ie allocating, scheduling and monitoring?
1.19 What methods exist for dealing with non-completion or unsatisfactory completion of allocated tasks?
1.20 Is there a contingency plan against failed targets?
1.21 Are market segments defined in an order of priority? (See Introduction and Appendix 1A; some suggested criteria in List 2, 'Product/service range', Question 2.2; and List 18, 'User Industries', Question 18.9.)
1.22 What criteria were adopted to identify the segment priorities?
1.23 Are they still valid?
1.24 Does the allocation of marketing resources reflect the segment priorities? (See Introduction and List 13, 'Non-personal promotion: methods and media', Question 13.13.)
1.25 Have we made an analysis of the company strengths, weaknesses, opportunities and threats? (See Introduction and List 4, 'Company performance', Question 4.1; and List 11, 'Cross-selling and internal marketing', Question 11.7.)
1.26 Does the product/service and communication 'mix' reflect the strength profile?
1.27 Have we identified major vulnerabilities, their impact, and the likelihood of their occurrence? (See Introduction and List 7, 'Market size and structure', Questions 7.18–7.20; and List 8, 'Future market', Introduction.)
1.28 Do we have a contingency plan for dealing with threats?
1.29 What actions have been taken to mitigate corporate/departmental weaknesses?

1.30 Has the SWOT analysis revealed unexploited strengths and opportunities? (See Introduction.)
1.31 Has the analysis identified any weaknesses or threats not allowed for the plan?
1.32 Has the analysis identified any strengths or opportunities not being exploited?
1.33 What role is relationship marketing allotted in the plan?
1.34 Are the three elements of strategy – segmentation, marketing 'mix' and product planning – all compatible?
1.35 Do we have a key customer strategy? (See List 19, 'Key customer marketing'.)
1.36 Is conformance with ISO 9000 or any other accreditation desirable or necessary? (See List 25, 'Quality in marketing', Question 25.23.)

Appendix 1A
Segmenting by benefit received

Secondary Impact Sectors	Primary Impact Sectors	ADVANTAGES
All Industries	Chemicals Dyestuffs Sewage	Variable cake thickness and higher throughput
Food Coal	Dyestuffs Sugar Chemicals	Facility of cake washing
All Industries	Sewage Cement Coal Chinaclay	More efficient dewatering and lower moisture content
	All Industries	Facility of cake discharge
Chemicals Dyestuffs	Food Brewing Sugar	Filter enclosed
All Industries	Trade effluent	Low-cost filter
	All Industries	Low labour requirements
	All Industries	Cycle times shortened
	Food Trade effluent	Mobility of filter
	All Industries	Automatic opening and closing

DISADVANTAGES	Primary Impact Sectors	Secondary Impact Sectors
Batch process	Brewing Sugar	All Industries
Company unknown in filter industry	All industries except dyestuffs	
Small filter area for space taken by filter	All Industries	
Corrosion of rubber diaphragm	Food Brewing Organic chemicals	All Industries
Corrosion of filter	Chemicals Dyestuffs	Food Brewing Sugar
Compressed air – safety factors and cost of air	All Industries	
Difficulty of using precoat	All Industries	
Long-term vulnerabilities, development of alternative process	Sugar Oil Ceramics	Dyestuffs Chemicals Food

Appendix 1B
Some 'friendly, sceptical' questions to appraise a strategic plan[3]

1. What special capabilities do you plan to have that your best competitors cannot match?
2. Why can't they match them?
3. What actions will you take to put these capabilities in place?
4. In what way are your investment priorities likely to be different from those of your competitors?
5. How do you know the clients will like what you're planning? What field testing have you done? What client testing have you done?
6. Who will be in charge of executing each component of the plan?
7. Who was involved in the development of this plan? Is everyone in agreement? (Who was not consulted? Do they have a role in executing the plan?)
8. On whom will you depend for the execution of this plan? Do they have sufficient incentive to do their part? Is it in their interests to do what you want?
9. Do you have to modify your reward systems to make this happen?
10. Specifically, which five or ten clients, by name, represent your most *likely* source of expanded business for the next few years? What actions do you plan to take to get closer to these clients?
11. Which new clients are at the top of your priority list? Why? What makes you think you can get their business?
12. What is the one most significant thing that each of the main competitors is doing that will affect you? What do you plan to do as a response?
13. In what way do you plan to take advantage of the firm-wide network? How do you plan to get the cooperation of others?
14. How do you plan to contribute to the firm-wide network? How will what you are doing benefit them?
15. What are the staffing implications of your plans? Where will you get the staff from?
16. What are the main assumptions on which your plan is based? Which is the most 'risky' (ie if it can go wrong, where will it go wrong)?
17. How will you know if the plan is working? What indicators can you agree on, and when will you review them?
18. What early warning signals will there be if the plan is not working? What contingencies have you put in place?

Appendix 1C
Typical business underpinnings

1. Needs and wants:	Has traditionally been applied almost exclusively to customers but necessarily must be extended to other stakeholder groups.
2. Resources:	Refers to all people, physical assets, materials and services employed in running a business.
3. Relative costs:	The relationship of a company's key cost elements with those of competitors.
4. Customer base:	This refers to the number and composition of the customer base.
5. Technology:	This refers to product and process technology.
6. Special abilities:	The ability of one company to significantly outperform its competition in certain ways.
7. Identifying symbols:	Logos and other means whereby the company's product or service are identified by the customer.
8. Artificial barriers to competition:	Various laws and regulations which help keep potential competitors out of a market.
9. Social values:	Those clusters of social values which create demand for specific products and services.
10. Sanctions and supports:	The enabling permission or public endorsement given to business by governments and other groups.
11. Integrity:	The basic trust a customer places in a product or service.
12. Complementary products:	Products and services which are essential to the performance of other products or services.

Notes

1 Source: Douglas A Hurd, *Vulnerability Analysis*, SRI, Menlo Park, California (published privately n.d.)

2 List 19, 'Key customer marketing' should be used in relation to key customer strategies and tactics.

3 David H Maister (1993) How to create a strategy, in *Managing the Professional Service Firm*, Free Press, New York.

List 2

Product/service range

INTRODUCTION

The second list brings us to the product or service to be marketed. It is appreciated that Question 2.2 could open up a huge field of enquiry for even the smallest firms. The marketing auditor must decide what is applicable and what is merely interesting. The question suggests some typical and relevant headings, but the auditor must decide which to use and any other that will throw light on the range performance.

Apart from sales analysis, there are other useful indicators, such as ratio, correlation and actuarial analyses, which can yield valuable information on both the market and on competitors, and from the firm's own records.

Question 2.3 is a signpost to indicate a common marketing trap. Low sellers may be viewed as unprofitable in terms of production runs, inventory and sales efforts, but the question seeks an answer as to whether the low sellers in fact have a marketing function far more valuable than the sales they achieve. That is, do the low sellers make a marketing contribution in a perceptual sense in that they assist the sales of other products? Do they add credibility to the company as specialists within a product group or range; do they attract business for other products/services? While a Pareto distribution (80–20 rule) is as commonplace in product sales as in customer uptakes, the temptation to drop the 80 per cent of the range that attracts little in the way of profitable sales has to be resisted until it is known with certainty whether it contributes a perceptual marketing 'plus'. A company manufacturing industrial fastenings carried a huge range of metric eyelets with minuscule sales of some sizes. However, the user industry understanding that 'if X hasn't got them they're not get-able' was a powerful promotional benefit and a high contributor to the 'visibility' of the company (see List 13, 'Non-personal promotion: methods and media', Introduction, and Figure 13.1).

Indirect marketing is an important and frequently neglected function. This is a situation where others outside the purchasing organization may have a strong or total influence over any purchase. Typical of such indirect marketing targets are OEM (original equipment manufacturers) accountants, standards institutions, trade associations, governmental and parastatal bodies, and consultants. These are as much a legitimate marketing target as the actual buying organization itself. Questions 2.13, 2.14 and 2.19–2.22 draw attention to this situation.

Question 2.23 is of particular interest and comes up again in the same or different forms in several other places in the lists. All too often a product or service is simply quoted on the basis of what the customer pays. But the real price of a product or service may be far higher or lower than the amount at the bottom of an invoice. Asking what a product really costs is important. List 23, 'Pricing', gives an example in Figure 23.1 of a 'true-price' model, where the real and hidden costs of two comparable products can be demonstrated to a customer. This can often swing the buyer to the apparently higher-priced offer when the totality of costs is known.

Question 2.27 brings in for the first time the question of 'benefits'. Selling benefits is now part of the standard approach of most firms but it is more honoured in its breach than its observance. Moreover, customers are now more sophisticated in their purchasing procedures, and it has become increasingly necessary to *prove* that benefits will in fact be received. The test as to whether the company is really marketing benefits is easily made. Take the company catalogue or brochure and underline in one colour every feature mentioned. Underline in another colour every benefit the customer obtains. For most firms the number of features far outweighs the benefits, and yet customers buy the product only for what it will do for them, not for what it is: that merely provides the proof or otherwise that they will receive the benefits. High speed to the customer may equal increased output; heavy gauge may equal safety; modularity may equal flexibility. Thus customers buy output, safety and flexibility – not speed, gauge or modularity. The fundamental question to which attention must be given is, *Do we sell what our customers buy?* (See also List 1, 'Marketing strategy and planning', Appendix 1A, which is an example of benefit segmentation.)

Completion of the model in Figure 2.1 for each product/service will provide excellent guidance for the promotional and personal selling platform.

New product/service introductions are dealt with in List 17.

Question 2.38 draws attention to a useful analysis, namely that of life cycles. If it is possible to establish a product's position in its life cycle, then it is also possible to plan to extend its life by the introduction of some new benefit or application or to plan for its replacement with a new product.

Question 2.42 identifies the old but nevertheless valid marketing approach of developing something unique in the product/service or in the cluster of surrounding benefits. Of course, a patentable innovation can achieve a USP (unique selling proposition), although it is increasingly difficult to hold a patent lead for any length of time, and in any event services are not patentable. For most companies it is usually better to seek to develop a

PRODUCT/SERVICE ______________________________

FEATURES The facts about our product, service, company, system, etc.	**FUNCTIONS** How it works Why it works How it is used	**BENEFITS** What does this mean to the customer? Be specific	**PROOF** How can we prove that the customer will receive the benefit?	**QUESTIONS** Do they need the benefit? Do they want it? (leading)

Figure 2.1 A model for personal selling and promotional platform

collection of individual benefits which on their own would not be unique but as a package offer a distinctly perceivable 'plus'. However, a benefit, unique or not, which a customer does not want is not in marketing terms a benefit. Thus in developing unique selling packages the benefits of such a package to the customer must be clear.

By way of example, using water-cooling plant, the following emerge from one supplier's offer:

Feature	**Benefit**
Totally 'packaged' product	Simplified purchasing
Longer guarantee than competitors	Cost-effective security
Twenty-four-hour manned emergency service	Peace of mind and risk reduction
No restrictive contract clauses	Certainty in commitment

While it is also true that this package of advantages cannot be held indefinitely, being first does have distinct benefits. An examination of product features and performance as well as of supporting services linked to customer needs and problems can without difficulty establish practical USPs.

Information on the perceived and actual useful life of a product, particularly if it is compared with customers' experience and view on competitor products, can give valuable product and marketing insights. The technique of actuarial analysis (probabilities of life expectancies) is a useful internal analysis tool substantially achieved by the study of service records. Question 2.45 looks into this often neglected aspect of marketing and customer relations.

2.1 List product/service ranges, including quality spread.

2.2 Analyse sales by each characteristic, application and market segment (see introduction):
- geographical
- process or application
- frequency of purchase
- benefit received
- form of customer organization
- demographic factors
- lead time required
- buyer's job function
- guarantee claims
- cost per sale
- frequency of orders
- cost per delivery
- reason for purchase
- industry or trade
- credit of requirements
- size of order
- size of customer operation
- psychographic factors
- full-line or limited purchase
- seasonal/cyclical
- servicing requirements
- order source (e.g. OEM distributor)
- value added.

(Some of this information will be required again in List 4, 'Company performance', Question 4.9; List 7, 'Market size and structure', Question 7.10; and List 11, 'Cross-selling and internal marketing', Question 11.11. Some items are repeated in List 18, 'User industries', Question 18.9.)

2.3 What justification is there for keeping low sales items in the range? (See Introduction.)
2.4 How many and which products are own developments? How many licensed? How many traded/How many franchised/How much subcontracted work? (This question is put again in List 17, 'Introducing new product services', Questions 17.5 and 17.32.)
2.5 Is this 'mix' satisfactory?
2.6 If not, what steps can we take to adjust closer to a desideratum?
2.7 List major and subsidiary uses for the products/services. (See introduction to List 7, 'Market size and structure', and Questions 7.5–7.9.)
2.8 Do existing customers know our full range and the major and subsidiary uses for the products/services?

2.9 Are our products incorporated into any other products?
2.10 Are our products identifiable as our make when incorporated into users' product or otherwise processed?
2.11 If not, can they be?
2.12 What is the form of identification? Can it be made irremovable?
2.13 Do they require, or would sales be assisted by, OEM approval for incorporation? (See Introduction.)
2.14 If we do not have all OEM approvals, what steps can we take to obtain them?
2.15 Do any of the products carry customers' or other private brands? If so, which?
2.16 What is the justification for accepting private branding? Is it still valid?
2.17 Are there any British, American, European or other standards to which the products/services must conform? (See also List 4, 'Company performance', Questions 4.27–4.29; List 25, 'Quality in marketing', Question 25.15; and List 26, 'Non-differentiated products and commodities', Questions 26.9 and 26.14.)
2.18 If not, can they be referenced to as 'above' a known standard? (See answers in List 4, 'Company performance', Questions 4.27–4.29; and List 26, 'Non-differentiated products and commodities', Questions 26–9, 26.11–26.15.)
2.19 What degree of control over specifications do customers, end customers, consultants, contractors exercise? (See Introduction List 5, 'Export marketing', Question 5.52; List 7, 'Market size and structure', Question 7.32; and List 15, 'The buying process', Question 15.2.)
2.20 How do they exercise it?
2.21 Have we identified any other influences over specifications that should be considered (e.g. government, insurance companies, financial institutions, etc)?
2.22 What steps have we taken to initiate and maintain contact with these influences?
2.23 Do our products/services have any total cost-effectiveness advantages over directly or indirectly competitive products/services? (This important topic is restated in other lists and the answers should be compared. See Introduction List 16, 'Analysing lost business'; List 18, 'User industries' Question 18.21; List 20, 'Competitive intelligence', Question 20.58; List 23, 'Pricing', Question 23.30; and List 26, 'Non-differentiated products and commodities', Questions 26.33–26.35.)
2.24 Does our promotion emphasize these?
2.25 Can we undertake a cost-effectiveness exercise for the customer?
2.26 What are the principal features of our products/services?
2.27 Have we translated these into benefits, as seen by purchasers? (See Introduction to this list and Figure 2.1, but the answers should be compared and aligned with those given to other questions. The main ones are List 13, 'Non-personal promotion: methods and media', Question 13.38; List 15, 'The buying process', Questions 15.10, 15.17 and 15.20; List 16, 'Analysing lost business', Question 16.10; and List 18, 'User industries', Questions 18.21 and 18.22.)

2.28 Does our sales and promotional platform emphasize these benefits? (This answer is required again in List 9, 'The salesforce and its management', Question 9.46; List 13, 'Non-personal promotion: methods and media', Question 13.33; and in a somewhat different form in List 23, 'Pricing', Question 23.31.)
2.29 What are the deficiencies of the products/services?
2.30 If they are not eradicable, what trade-off does the customer get?
2.31 What support do the other products/services give to the main products/services range (e.g. extending range, production or procurement advantages, selling to same buyers)? (See Introduction List 3, 'The service element in marketing'.)
2.32 Do any of our competitors specialize?
2.33 How does our own policy differ in this respect?
2.34 What is the reason for our respective policies?
2.35 Do we need to reconsider ours in the light of competitors' performances and their image?
2.36 What have been the major technological changes over the past five years in the product/service group?
2.37 Do our products/services incorporate these changes?
2.38 Would a life-cycle analysis give advance warning of product mortality? (See Introduction.)
2.39 What percentage of our business is 'specials' and what percentage 'standards'?
2.40 Do we want to shift the balance?
2.41 Does our marketing plan allow for any change in range spread?
2.42 Do we have or can we develop some unique aspect in our offering that will differentiate us favourably from competitors? (See Introduction and List 13, 'Non-personal promotion: methods and media', Question 13.39.)
2.43 Can we draw a profile of an 'ideal' product/service from the viewpoint of each major user segment? (This question reappears in a number of different contexts and the auditor should consider the answers to List 16, 'Analysing lost business', Question 16.10; List 20, 'Competitive intelligence', Question 20.58; List 23, 'Pricing', Question 23.29; List 26, 'Non-differentiated products and commodities', Questions 26.32–26.35.)
2.44 Can we list the factors that prevent us from developing our offer closer to the 'ideal'? Are they valid?
2.45 What criteria do customers use to judge the end of the useful life of our product and are they the same as those applied to competitors' products? (The question is repeated in a number of lists and is also presented with different perspectives. The auditor should consult and compare answers; List 15, 'The buying process', Question 15.42; List 16, 'Analysing lost business', Questions 16.14 and 16.15; List 18, 'User Industries', Questions 18.50 and 18.51; List 20, 'Competitive intelligence', Question 20.61; and List 23, 'Pricing', Question 23.22.)

List 3

The service element in marketing

INTRODUCTION

This section of the marketing audit checklist concerns itself with backup services (as distinct from services marketed in their own right as profit centres, dealt with in List 27, 'Service businesses') that are either vital or desirable. In many instances the quality and reliability of the service element distinguishes otherwise indistinguishable products. With products made to a standard, the marketing response tends to be on price. This is usually as wrong as it is unnecessary. A prime example of this was found in Australia, where one supplier of ready-mix concrete, a classical non-differentiated product, not only dominated a highly competitive market but did so at a marginally higher price than its competitors. The secret was the supplier's reputation for punctuality in site delivery and the employment of cooperative drivers who would place the load at precisely the point the site foreman required. The premium price was considered justified by the reduction of site problems and the improvement in labour relations. (The subject of differentiating otherwise non-distinguishable products is dealt with fully in List 26, 'Non-differentiated products and commodities'.)

The first question in this list is of great importance, since companies frequently overlook important services they should supply and retain services that are either not of real value or could more efficiently be provided by the customer. Some services are identified in Appendix 3A but they are generalized, and each company should consider specific services related to its product.

One of the greatest unexploited assets of a company may be its service backup; all too frequently customers are not aware of the range and the ignorance, strangely enough, is often matched by the organization's own personnel. Questions 3.3 and 3.4 require the most careful consideration and any answers given not too glibly accepted. The warning at the beginning of the book introducing the marketing audit technique is particularly apposite here. All answers should be considered against the background of the source of the information and its reliability. Probing will all too often reveal that customers do not in fact know *all* the services available and even sales personnel, if asked to list services, will be found not to have a complete knowledge.

Services that support the product can be of three types: profit-making in their own right, cost-recovering, and not charged. 'Free' is a misnomer; there is, as has been frequently pointed out, no such thing as a free lunch. The cost of service in the last category is part of the purchase price.

Which services shall be provided and the financial basis to be adopted is a key decision which the answers to Question 3.10 should assist in making. If the attitude of the company is that services are an unfortunate necessity, then the line of thinking must be towards developing the product to reduce service or make servicing simple and economic for the customer to undertake (eg plug-in replacement units).

A firm of manufacturers of reverse jet filters, in considering this point and the problem of servicing distant customers, redesigned the method of removing the filter elements so that it could be done in less than half the time required for conventional filters and at the same time gave more headroom for the work to be carried out. These improvements enabled customers to use less skilled and thus lower-cost labour for the maintenance, and saved the service charges. The modification was a powerful selling tool.

Improved work manuals, and indeed instruction systems on the Internet, video or multichannel programmed audio tape, can completely change the nature of servicing and the demand on service requirements from the supply firms. Time spent on producing good operating and maintenance manuals is well directed if it results, as it will, in fewer calls for service, fewer operating problems and better customer satisfaction. All manuals should be copy tested with a typical user to ensure comprehension and to avoid unnecessarily uncouth handling of equipment.

The marketing auditor must not confuse services with 'servicing'. As the list demonstrates, not all services are by any means related to servicing equipment. Services should be viewed in the widest sense and not thought of as substantially technical matters.

If, however, it is proposed to regard the service backup as either profit centres and/or marketing tools then consideration of a charging method is vital. Services can be grouped on a cost-to-the-company basis:

- services that cost nothing to provide unless/until they are used;
- services that will cost something to offer, whether they are used or not;
- services that will invoke cost to the company, plus the cost of providing them.

The position can be illustrated, but the terms 'high', 'medium' and 'low' cost in Figure 3.1 are relative and each organization must decide the financial parameters of these terms.

A	No cost unless the service is used and then:	(i) high cost (ii) medium cost (iii) low cost
B	Standing cost to offer whether used or not:	(i) high cost (ii) medium cost (iii) low cost
C	Costs to offer plus cost of providing:	(i) high cost (ii) medium cost (iii) low cost

Figure 3.1 Cost-to-the-company categories

It can be seen at once from the figure that services which fall into categories A(iii), B(iii) or C(iii) can be offered with little cost to the company and certainly should be if it will consolidate the position with existing customers and help to obtain new ones. If such services are already provided, then it is incumbent on the supplier to ensure that customers know they are getting the service as part of the offer and not let it be taken for granted. One thing can be said for certain in marketing services – lights should never be hidden under bushels.

An illustration may be helpful. A training service or an emergency service may cost nothing until it is used. When it is called for, it requires the detachment of a skilled person at what can be presumed to be a medium cost. This could either be charged at cost or at a profit or given away as a marketing input. These are categories A(ii) or A(iii). Rack jobbing (consignment stock) invokes an inventory cost whether the service is used or not. When it is called on, the cost does not increase although the company will still have the option of charging for the service. These are categories B(ii) or B(iii).

Of course, an alternative policy to be considered is whether a company should undertake any or all of the service requirements. Subcontracting or outsourcing is an option worth considering. Question 3.16 raises this point in looking at the whole complex that comprises service backup in a company.

Questions 3.20–3.22 may highlight missed opportunities. Service engineers could well be the first people to see a sales opening, since they have access to customer plant or equipment. Obviously, they should be encouraged in some tangible way to report back on such opportunities. There are many advantages to be gained from sales and service staff working closely together. It is the practice of one engineering company to ensure that sales staff make at least occasional service calls with the service engineers and that they in turn make sales calls with the salespeople. Obtaining an insight into each other's problems, working environment and situation has been found invaluable in producing a synergy that has measurable results in sales.

Many firms can provide service backup if requested but fail to see that the ready availability of these services can influence both the business obtained and good customer relations. It should be axiomatic that if services exist they should be promoted. The list is completed in Questions 3.50–3.51 by highlighting the need to include the availability of services in promotional messages. Cross-selling and internal marketing, which is the subject of List 11, becomes less than effective unless everyone in the organization knows precisely the services that are available and the charge category.

Because there will be frequent reference throughout the lists to the service backup, the various services that are referred to in the following section have been encapsulated in Appendix 3A for quick reference.

3.1 What backup services do we provide? (Use Questions 3.23, 3.28, 3.31–3.36 and 3.39–3.46 as a guide to possible services which could be offered; but see Appendix 3A for more detail.)

3.2 What criteria have been used for deciding whether to adopt or reject them? Are they still valid?

3.3 Does everyone in the company with customer contact know the full range of services available? (This answer will also be required in List 11, 'Cross-selling and internal marketing', Question 11.6.)

3.4 Do *all* our customers know *all* our services? (This topic recurs in List 11, 'Cross-selling and internal marketing', Question 11.9.)

3.5 What other services could we sensibly and profitably add?

3.6 How do we and our competitors rate on the following service aspects? (Use the checklist in Appendix 3A to ensure each individual service is considered. The question arises in a number of different forms in different lists. See specifically List 18, 'User industries', Question 18.18; List 20, 'Competitive intelligence', Question 20.20. A comparison should be made with the self-image arising from List 24, 'Images and perceptions', Question 24.8.)
- waiting time for service
- completeness of service
- skill of service personnel
- attitude and courtesy
- appearance
- response to emergencies
- accuracy in documentation
- reliability of service
- conformance with standards
- approachability and accessibility
- quality of communication
- understanding of customer needs
- equipment need
- lead time

3.7 What information do we have on customer attitudes to each service and charge method? (See below.)

3.8 Would the values that customers place on any service justify its being reclassified? (See Figure 3.1 in Introduction; Question 3.10 below; the Introduction to List 23, 'Pricing', on price and the perception of performance, and Questions 23.26–23.28.)

3.9 What is our attitude to the provision of services? Should it be changed?

3.10 Which services can be (should be) charged for? (See Introduction.)

3.11 What is the rationale for any classification adopted? (See Figure 3.1.)

3.12 How practical is it to make a charge?

3.13 What steps are required to introduce charging for what were previously non-charged services?

3.14 Do all servicing and marketing personnel know the charge category for each service?

3.15 What are our customers' views on the quality and reliability of our services? (Compare answers with those to be given to Question 3.6 and in List 25, 'Quality in marketing', Question 25.28.)

3.16 Should we consider subcontracting some or all services to an outside organization?

3.17 Are our service staff adequate in number and skills?

3.18 Do service staff appreciate their importance in projecting the image of the company? (See List 10, 'Support staff's role in marketing'; and List 24, 'Images and perceptions', Questions 24.4 and 24.8.)

3.19 Can any deficiency in service staff be remedied by training and remotivation?

3.20 Are the service staff integrated into mainstream company activity? (This question is raised again in List 11, 'Cross-selling and internal marketing', Question 11.13.)

3.21 Are service engineers and other staff motivated to seek opportunities for sales?

3.22 What liaison is there between service staff and marketing?

3.23 How quickly can our emergency services be activated?

3.24 Does our sales and promotional platform give this information?

3.25 What would it cost to shorten an emergency response time?

3.26 Are the arrangements for customers calling in emergency services satisfactory to them (eg office hours only, 24-hour manned telephone service, answering machine or service)?

3.27 Would the cost of an improved emergency service either be recoverable or significantly assist further sales and improve customer relations?

3.28 What design services are required?

3.29 Do our design staff have sufficient opportunity to meet customers and to understand their problems and aspirations?

3.30 Would it be a useful extension of services to retain freelance or independent consultants to augment the design team for design functions we cannot at present fulfil? (This question may have been partly answered in dealing with Question 3.16 above.)

3.31 What pre-start-up services are required?
3.32 What negotiation services are required?
3.33 Are customer complaints monitored to establish:

- if a repetitive pattern exists;
- how well and quickly complaints are resolved;
- post-complaint customer satisfaction;
- cost of warranty or guarantee claims;
- cost of complaint rectification outside guarantees?

(This question cross-links with a number of others which have or will provide corroborating answers, notably List 6, 'Marketing information: systems and use', Questions 6.44–6.46; List 13, 'Non-personal promotion: methods and media', Question 13.60 on guarantees; List 16, 'Analysing lost business', Question 16.39; List 23, 'Pricing', Questions 23.1 and 23.2 on costs; List 25, 'Quality in marketing', Questions 25.31–25.34; and List 28, 'Product/service financial information', Questions 28.41 and 28.52.)

3.34 What education services are required? (See List 22, 'Industry contacts', Question 22.31.)
3.35 What visiting services are required?
3.36 What maintenance and repair services are required?
3.37 Can we modify the product to reduce the number of visits required? (See Introduction.)
3.38 Can we improve our works manuals and instruction methods to enable customers to reduce service costs?
3.39 What product adaptation services are required?
3.40 What standby facilities for emergency and peak-load are required?
3.41 What consumable supplies are required?
3.42 What delivery services are needed? (See List 21, 'Physical distribution and packaging'.)
3.43 Would a marketing support service be valued by customers, eg joint promotion?
3.44 Are there any financial services that customers require and would appreciate?
3.45 What disposal services would be of value to customers?
3.46 What operating services are required?
3.47 Do we volunteer any of the services listed rather than react to requests?
3.48 Does marketing management receive service personnel reports?
3.49 Is it possible to extract market information, general and specific, from such reports? (See List 6, 'Marketing information systems and use', Question 6.11.)
3.50 Does our promotional material clearly identify all available services and, if appropriate, the charge category?
3.51 Does the sales platform ensure customers have full knowledge of the range of backup services that can be provided?

Appendix 3A
Summary of services that can comprise part of a firm's product/service up

This sub-checklist is not only intended to be an *aide-mémoire* for the consideration of services but can also be used to check customer perception of quality of services (Questions 3.4 and 3.15).

1. *Design services*
   - Physical planning
   - Pre-sale service and advice
   - Prototype fabrication
   - Equipment design and checking
   - Facilities advice
   - Packaging advice
2. *Product enhancement services*
   - Non-destructive testing
   - Certification
   - Calibration
   - Testing
   - Finishing
   - Cut to size
   - Zero defect
3. *Pre-start-up or pre-sales services*
   - Assembly
   - Installation
   - Engineering and pre-delivery inspection and testing
4. *Negotiation services*
   - Resolving complaints
   - Warranty adjustments, including exchange of product
   - Liaison between customers and production department
5. *Education services*
   - Guidance on application, use and adaptation of products to customers' needs
   - On-site demonstration, instructions, training, and in-plant lectures
   - Handling and safety advice
   - Library service

- Technical literature
- General industrial advice
- Help-lines

6. *Visiting services*
   - General and specific-purpose visits to customers' plants
   - Customer visits to service and production departments
   - On-site supervision, including the provision of special facilities, eg banking, health monitoring
7. *Maintenance and repair services*
   - Periodic testing and adjustment
   - Cleaning and repairing
   - Rehabilitation and reconditioning
   - Loan equipment availability
   - Parts stocks and repairs
8. *Product adaptation services*
   - Modifications
   - Applications research
   - Rebuild and retro-fit
9. *Emergency services*
10. *Standby services*
11. *Operating services*
    - Consumables supplies and stocks
    - Waste and packing disposal
    - Processing customers' own material
    - Notice of product/service withdrawal
12. *Delivery services*
    - Just-in-time
    - Stocks
    - Order fill
    - Van sales
    - Rack jobbing
    - Consignment (sale or return)
    - Transit quality control
    - Groupage
    - Off-loading
    - Customer collection facility
13. *Marketing services*
    - Joint promotions
    - New product or application development
    - Merchandising aids

14. *Financial services*
    - Credit
    - Lease, rent or hire
    - Buy-back or trade-in
    - Factoring
    - Discounting
15. *Disposal services*
    - Trade-in
    - Removal
    - Dismantling
    - Recycling
    - Destruction

List 4

Company performance

INTRODUCTION

This list provides an important benchmark, since it is concerned with past and present performance against which must be measured the success of any future marketing efforts. The analyses that are suggested should identify strengths and weaknesses and give a clear direction to changes that are needed.

Company performance, more than any other part of the audit, can be subjected to the most varied, complex and detailed scrutiny. There is a considerable danger of the whole audit getting mired at this stage. The questions given below should be regarded as a framework, subject to deletion and substitution. The marketing auditor must consider what other aspects of company performance are relevant and must be taken into account if they impact on the marketing performance. For example, there are no questions on staff numbers, quality, recruitment, turnover – vital in a service organization where, typically, 'people' costs represent 70 to 80 per cent of total operating costs, while the remainder are substantially people-related, eg occupational costs, insurance, office supplies.

Many of the points for consideration are subjected to further questioning in later lists. Again, by way of example, this section calls for a look at advertising expenditure but asks nothing about its effectiveness, which will emerge in List 13, 'Non-personal promotion: methods and media'.

The types of vulnerabilities that the analysis may well bring out include heavy dependence on a few customers; industries or applications that are themselves highly susceptible to the vicissitudes of an increasingly interdependent international or global business economy; and technological change, government intervention and sociological adjustment – all referred to in the book's introductory section, 'The marketing audit' and in the figure on page 3.

Question 4.1 concerns some conventional aspects of a company's operations that the auditor may wish to review in terms of performance. However, far more items are included in List 25, 'Quality in marketing', Appendix 25A, from which it is possible to pick out those issues which are of concern to the company and, more importantly, the company's customers.

The market segmentations referred to in the Introduction to List 1, 'Marketing strategy and planning', and specifically in Question 1.21, are now subject to analysis. Questions 4.4, 4.5 and 4.8–4.11 all look at the performance relative to the segment. In the case of Question 4.10, it will often be found that an apparently satisfactory figure disguises hidden potential in some areas. For example, a multi-industry or multi-application material may have a creditable performance in one segment – say, disposable workwear – but it may well not be achieving a satisfactory penetration in another segment – say, labels and packaging use.

Appendix 4A gives a format for analysis; even if the regional market sizes, user industries or applications are not known, it is often possible to complete columns such as 'number of potential accounts', which may give at least a simplistic view of whether market coverage matches apparent potential.

Questions 4.12–4.14 have interesting and practical implications. Relatively few companies examine the impact of a different sales 'mix' in their product range and order size. This analysis can be extended to include size of typical delivery 'drop'. Although small orders are usually regarded as less profitable, this is frequently a piece of business folklore that has little basis in fact. An 'ideal' product/service range and order size 'mix' takes into account not only the economies of scale and procurement, machine and skill loading, but also sales costs. A small order obtained from one department of a customer where other departments are also ordering goods or services may well be significantly more profitable than a larger order from a firm purchasing only one product or service. The permutations are many. These enquiries open the door for a new look at the firm's performance based on the current 'mix' and an ideal 'mix' to be designated.

The product life cycle, which is referred to in List 2, 'Product/service range', Question 2.38, is important in relation to Questions 4.16 and 4.17 and is concerned with product/service introductions. Reference back to the answers to Questions 2.4 on sources of new product ideas and 2.45 on life cycles should be cross-referenced with the replies to Questions 4.16 and 4.17.

The rate of new product/service introductions must vary from company to company, but certainly whatever the periodicity is, there ought to be a rhythm. The moment for feeding in a new product (or extending the life cycle of an existing one) is at some point before the growth curve plateaus ('top-out'). Unfortunately, identifying 'top-out' conditions is not easy because of managers' reluctance to believe that a product on which they have lavished much love and care, and may well have staked some element of career in the company, is experiencing a terminal decline. A plateau is often disguised as a col with swelling up-hills of continued growth beyond. This is a dangerous delusion. The warning signs of 'top-out' can sometimes be defined even before a product is introduced. If this is not possible, the marketing auditor should at the very least be sensitive to any phenomenon that might indicate the need to feed in a new product. List 17, 'Introducing new products/services', will cover this subject in more depth.

High on the list of points for consideration is that of standards covered in Questions 4.27–4.29. While accreditation such as ISO 9000 can still give a company an edge over the competition, it may well be that in future such accreditation will be a condition of business, not a bonus. However, the auditor must not confuse standards with quality or quality with value. While good in themselves, standards may be far below the quality required by customers. Similarly, high quality does not imply value in use. Few people doubt the high quality of Rolls-Royce or Mercedes cars but to use them as a builder's pick-up would hardly be value in use. The auditor should refer to List 25, 'Quality in marketing', on this issue.

Questions 4.37 and 4.41 touch on two of the only three absolutes in marketing.[1] A firm must be known to exist before buying action can occur. Question 4.37 relates to this 'visibility' and refers to the extent to which the company is known, either with aided or unaided recall, among customers and potential customers. Obtaining visibility is the vital first stage in the communication process; obtaining an understanding of the message (comprehension) and belief in the claims (conviction) are the other two steps preceding a favourable buying decision. List 13, 'Non-personal promotion: methods and media', gives a model in Figure 13.1 that illustrates the communication process. All firms should satisfy themselves that they are 'visible' to those who might influence a purchase.

It is important to trace the source of all enquiries, since this is the one certain way of knowing which methods of promotion are working. 'Working' in this context has a number of meanings. Question 4.38 requires the examination of a particularly bad omission in many companies' marketing operations. If the Internet, for example, raises enquiries but there is a low conversion rate to business as against exhibitions, which raise few enquiries but a great deal of business, it indicates that the former may be good for 'visibility' but that somewhere along the line interest is lost. This in turn could cause an examination of the communication method, the media, or perhaps the message, in that initial expectations of potential customers are not fulfilled. A system that identifies how enquiries and business originate is an extremely low-cost activity to introduce and has a value far outweighing the time and effort involved. The analyses have a great number of uses, as will be obvious throughout these lists.

Question 4.41 opens up an equally vital area. The second absolute in marketing is that there has to be a reason why customers prefer one firm to another. This reason may be trivial or fundamental, but it exists. Whatever the reason, it is a strength to be promoted to all customers of the same type. Every firm, without exception, has a differentiated advantage, but very few firms consciously or consistently search for this nugget, and even fewer exploit it when they find it. The implication of the answers to this and Question 4.37 will be obvious enough to the marketing auditor.

Questions 4.42–4.44 deal with a frequently overlooked aspect of the firm's operations that has an impact on how it is perceived. However much a company may seek to project a 'nice people to deal with' image, dictatorial pronouncements, even in faint microscopic print on the back of the order confirmations, can do considerable damage. Varying from announcing that the company is not responsible for late delivery (who is, then?) to the statement that the contract shall be interpreted under British law, the clauses are often as anachronistic as they are unreal.

That they are unreal is illustrated by the fact that few companies either choose or want to litigate with their customers. While the stated conditions of business might give them a strong legal case, if they will not be used they serve no purpose and are counter-productive in a marketing sense.

If contract terms are written by lawyers, it is not surprising that they are restrictive and comprise what it is hoped will be (but rarely is) an unanswerable case in a situation that is never going to go to court anyway. All that happens is that some potential customers who prefer to rely on protection in common law just do not buy. Every company should see if they cannot deformalize, and liberalize, contract conditions. Documentation is again referred to in List 24, 'Images and perceptions'.

The auditor is recommended to cross-check the information derived from completing this list with the questions and answers in the final List 28, 'Product/service financial information', where the call for data, usually in a slightly different form, occurs.

4.1 Grade the following (see Introduction to List 1, 'Marketing strategy and planning', Question 1.25; and List 25, 'Quality in marketing').

	STRENGTHS...........			WEAKNESSES		
	Major strength	**Significant strength**	**Average**	**Needs improving**	**Poor**	**Major weakness**
Manufacturing efficiency						
Quality and consistency						
Technical expertise (R & D, problem-solving, etc.)						
Price competitiveness						
Service						
Delivery						
Packaging						

4.1 *continued*

	STRENGTHS...........WEAKNESSES					
	Major strength	**Significant strength**	**Average**	**Needs improving**	**Poor**	**Major weakness**
Marketing (and selling) skills						
Size and/or location of operation						
Reputation						
Track record						
Financial position						
Visibility						
Links with customers or suppliers						
Industrial relations						
Other significant factors (name)						

4.2 Does our sales message and non-personal promotion emphasize our strengths and minimize our weaknesses? (The subject of strengths and weaknesses will already have been covered in answering List 1, 'Marketing strategy and planning', Questions 1.25 and 1.30, but the answer should also be compared with that for List 13, 'Non-personal promotion: methods and media', Question 13.38.)

4.3 Indicate annual sales by units and/or value and/or profitability of the products/services under review for the past three to five years. (Further information on this will be called for in List 28, 'Product/service financial information', Questions 28.3 and 28.4.)

4.4 What percentage of our output by units or value were to:

- Government ______
- Direct to end-users (broken down by industry and/or application) ______
- Sold to original equipment manufacturers (OEMs) ______
- Sold through intermediaries other than OEMs (eg merchants, distributors) ______
- Exports ______
- In-feeding (consumption or utilization of own product/service) ______

TOTAL ______

(These answers are linked with those required by List 7, 'Market size and structure', Questions 7.1 and 7.10; List 9, 'Salesforce – management', Question 9.4; List 18, 'User industries', Questions 18.1, 18.8 and 18.9; and List 26, 'Non-differentiated products and commodities, Question 26.17.)

4.5 National and regional breakdown of sales if relevant. (See Introduction and Appendix 4A.)
4.6 Do sales targets exist for the territory of each salesperson/agent/distributor? (A detailed answer to this and Questions 4.7 and 4.8 will be required in List 9, 'The salesforce and its management', for Questions 9.37–9.41; List 14, 'The distributive system', Question 14.4; and in List 18, 'User industries', Question 18.9.)
4.7 How were they arrived at? Are they still valid? (See List 9, 'The salesforce and its management', Question 9.38, which is the same point.)
4.8 Sales broken down by each sales territory against target. (List 7, 'Marketing size and structure', Question 7.10; and List 9, 'The salesforce and its management', Question 9.41, will require these same data.)

Year (or period)	Territory	Target	Achievement

4.9 Sales broken down by product/service characteristics (eg size, weight, dimensions, specifications) or any other meaningful breakdown including equipment, spares and service charges. (The answer may already have been given in Question 4.4 above or in List 2, 'Product/service range', Question 2.10; and List 9, 'The salesforce and its management', Question 9.65. They should all align, of course.)
4.10 Sales broken down by user industry/application. (See Question 4.4 above; also List 7, 'Market size and structure', Introduction and Questions 7.10 and 7.11, the former asking the same question. Comparison should also be made with List 18, 'User industries', Questions 18.7 and 18.8.)
4.11 Sales breakdown in percentage terms:

To New Users/Customers
For New Usage among Existing Customers
As Replacement Sales

TOTAL 100%

(The answer to this question will be needed for a number of other purposes in due course; List 9, 'The salesforce and its management', Question 9.97; List 17, 'Introducing new products/services', Question 17.9; List 18, 'User industries', Questions 18.6 and 18.8; List 26, 'Non-differentiated products and commodities', Question 26.17.)

4.12 What is the maximum and average order size for the products/service under review?
4.13 How does profitability vary by order size?
4.14 Based on this, can we produce a model showing the impact on profit of different products/services and order size mix to establish an optimum mix as a marketing/market target? (See List 2, 'Product/service range', Introduction and Question 2.5.)
4.15 What is the extent of our own uptake and/or reciprocal trading? State period covered. (This answer will also be required for List 7, 'Market size and structure', Question 7.29, and see the Introduction to that list; List 11, 'Cross-selling and internal marketing', concentrates on these activities.)
4.16 Percentage of sales on products introduced in the last:
- one year;
- two years;
- three years;
- more than three years.

(Compare answer with those to List 2, 'Product/service range', Question 2.4; and List 17, 'Introducing new products/services', Questions 17.1 and 17.32.)

4.17 Is the rate of successful introductions comparable to the industry standard? Does it suggest that a change is needed?
4.18 What is the explanation for the performance figures shown?
4.19 What market weaknesses does it indicate (eg too heavily weighted in any particular area, or sector, or customer; new/repeat business ratio; inadequate geographic or industry coverage; lack of counter-cyclical business)?
4.20 What is the proportion of new customers to repeat business (eg numbers, volume, value)? (See List 9, 'The salesforce and its management', Questions 9.96 and 9.97, relative to this and the previous question; and also the answer to Question 4.10 in this list.)
4.21 What are the safe limits (eg 40–60 per cent)?
4.22 Does the analysis indicate that a change is required in product/service range composition, selling or promotional methods and/or message, segmentation priorities, customer types, distribution methods, etc?
4.23 What is, or should be, the normal lead time (period from receipt of order to customer's receipt of goods) and/or start-up offered? (See also List 14, 'The distributive system', Questions 14.45 and 14.49; and List 18, 'User industries', Introduction.)
4.24 What is our conversion ratio of enquiries to quotations? (See also List 13, 'Non-personal promotion: methods and media', Introduction and Question 13.22.)
4.25 What is our conversion ratio of enquiries to orders? (These last two very important questions are asked again in List 9, 'The salesforce and its management', Questions 9.49–9.51.)

4.26 What does the average quotation cost us to prepare?
4.27 Do adequate or officially recognized standards for products/services/administration/information/product introductions, etc exist? (See List 2, 'Product/service range', Question 2.18; and List 25, 'Quality in marketing', Question 25.14.)
4.28 How is 'adequate' judged?
4.29 Is ISO 9000 or Baldrige in the USA or any other accreditation necessary or desirable? (See List 25, 'Quality in marketing', Questions 25.23 and 25.24.)
4.30 What proportion of our business is transacted through distributors? (A more detailed answer will be sought in List 14, 'The distributive system', Questions 14.4 and 14.31.)
4.31 Has this varied over the last three to five years?
4.32 What is the explanation for this variation?
4.33 Does the explanation call for changes in distribution methods, distributors, marketing, markets or products?
4.34 How does profitability on distributor sales compare with profitability on direct sales?
4.35 How do sales costs to distributors compare with sales costs for direct customers?
4.36 What would be the effect in both profit and marketing terms of increasing/decreasing distributor support? (This and the previous six questions should be used in conjunction with List 14, 'The distributive system'.)
4.37 How 'visible' is the company and/or its brands? (See Introduction. This answer is also required in List 13, 'Non-personal promotion: methods and media', Question 13.58; and in List 24, 'Images and perceptions', Question 24.14.)
4.38 What system exists for tracing sources of enquiries? (See Introduction.)
4.39 Are all members of the firm who receive enquiries required to probe and report on product/supplier information sources used by potential clients?
4.40 If these data exist, how are they circulated and used?
4.41 Why do our customers buy from us? What are our differentiating advantages? (See Introduction and general comments on differentiation in List 26, 'Non-differentiated products and commodities'.)
4.42 Are our terms of business too demanding, restrictive or disliked? (This question arises in a number of different contexts. The auditor should consult and compare answers given in List 9, 'The salesforce and its management', Question 9.117; List 24, 'Images and perceptions', Question 24.28, which sets out the components of quality in documentation; List 25, 'Quality in marketing', Question 25.36.)
4.43 Which of our terms of business would we be prepared to litigate on?
4.44 What would be the risks and benefits of de-formalizing business terms? (See Introduction relative to these last three questions; and List 24, 'Images and perceptions', Question 24.28.)
4.45 Do we have a policy on 'own brand' supply and how do we justify it? (See also List 14, 'The distributive system', Question 14.76.)

4.46 Can we benchmark aspects of our performance with appropriate organizations who are judged as 'best in class'?

The final questions below should be considered in conjunction with List 11, 'Cross-selling and internal marketing', where the answers will be required again in one form or another.

4.47 Do all of our customers know about all our products/services? (This topic will have been covered in List 3, 'The service element in marketing', Question 3.4.)
4.48 What products/services do our customers buy that they do not buy from us but which we could provide profitably?
4.49 Does cross-selling occur? (See List 11, 'Cross-selling and internal marketing'.)
4.50 How much of our own output do we consume?
4.51 Could it (should it) be increased/decreased?

Appendix 4
Market share by territory, user industry or applications

Area Territory User Industry or Applications	Market Units and/or Value	Market Share	Total Competitive Volume and/or Value	Existing Number of Accounts	Number of Potential Accounts

Notes

1 The third will be found in List 15, 'The buying process'.

List 5

Export marketing

INTRODUCTION

Checklists have an unfortunate proclivity to spawn sub-checklists – something that this book for the most part attempts to avoid. However, in the case of exporting, so much is involved that the rule has to be bent, most particularly in regard to choice of territories. Throughout industry, export markets tend to be of the Topsy school ('just grow'd'), the result of an approach from the market or else a selection on the most arbitrary basis: senior management like the country or speak the language, or have relations and friends there. This is not an exaggeration. In making a decision on territories there are more than 100 separate factors to consider, and perhaps as many countries to choose from. Because markets are as much a part of the firm's resources as its machinery, materials, staff and money, their selection and nurturing is part of marketing resource realization.

There are many aids for exporting, some of them heavily subsidized by government, and it would be a very foolish marketing department that did not make it its business to be fully appraised of what is available. Question 5.6 should direct the auditor to governmental and trade or professional association aids. Large organizations should also check if any part of the company has used any particular assistance and with what difficulties and what success.

The choice of markets depends on a knowledge of very many factors, as Question 5.24 implies. The complexity of the task of choosing which territory to target and the way that it is serviced is so daunting that most firms totally ignore the problem and operate on a reactive or historical basis. What is required is a methodology for acquiring, analysing and interpreting a mass of material concerning a large number of territories. One such approach has been included as Appendix 5A. The auditor should examine the questions in the screening list, even if they do not use it, since many will be relevant to a decision whether or not to enter a market. The inclusion of 90+ questions within the main list would be more confusing than helpful. Nevertheless, their relegation to an appendix is not intended as a comment on their significance.

It is of particular importance, because of the complications of communication, to ensure that, whatever form of representation is chosen, representatives are aware of what is expected of them or their company and their suppliers are equally aware of what they in turn are supposed to do. Question 5.34 and Stage 6 of Appendix 5A cover this. The cost of appointing distributors and servicing them is high and a loss of a distributor serious. Most losses that are not caused by bad appointments in the first place are the result of neglect, not underperformance. Appointing distributors and agents should receive the same care as appointing any senior staff. Induction is equally important.

In many territories the choice of agent/distributor is very narrow and may in fact be the decision of the distributor rather than the supplier. The loss of a distributor under these circumstances can equate with the loss of the market. Increasingly, good distributors are being tied in with good suppliers, leaving the less successful as the only choice. This is a situation that can be avoided.

Inevitably, in looking at the potential of export markets, a posture will have to be taken on the use of agents or other representatives. The questions in this list are augmented in List 12, 'The agency system'. If the incorporation of agents in the export marketing effort is an option then the auditor would be better to work from List 12 in regard to representation and ignore those questions relating to agents in this list.

Non-tariff barriers are among the most difficult constraints to identify and circumvent, since they are often unofficial and frequently impossible to thwart. Japan, for example, has been successful in maintaining a wide range of these defensive measures while continuing, despite international pressure, to deny both their existence and that they are in fact barriers. To some exporters the American product liability requirements are also seen as non-tariff barriers. The mass of European Union regulations could also be interpreted by those outside the Union as non-tariff barriers. The existence of such blockages needs careful appraisal because they can easily eliminate what on the face of it seems to be an excellent market opportunity. Behind Question 5.56 may lie the decision of whether to attempt to penetrate any particular market.

The checklist steps onto forbidden ground with Question 5.57, which deals with bribery. It is useless to pretend that this in not a method of doing business in many markets. The checklist takes no moral attitude on what a company does when approached for an inducement or in volunteering such inducements. Each organization must decide for itself and, more importantly, must be sure that those who represent it understand and comply with the policy. If the kitchen is too hot....

Finally, the checklist touches on a frequently overlooked opportunity for companies, especially in geographical areas where market penetration is difficult or impossible. This is licensing. For many companies licensing is not necessarily a simple or indeed cheap method of operation. Questions 5.60–5.71 pose some key issues in considering what and how to license. Every company should look to their skills and resources to ensure that they are not in fact missing what could be a useful way of generating new revenues.

5.1 Are our products/services capable of meeting an export demand?
5.2 On what information is the answer based? Is it recent?
5.3 What changes would be needed in (a) product or range, (b) facilities in destination market, (c) representation, (d) pricing, to meet an export demand? (See List 28, 'Product/service financial information'; Question 28.36.)
5.4 If our products/services are exportable, what reasons exist for not seeking export markets?
5.5 Are the reasons valid under present conditions?
5.6 Do we have full knowledge of the various government schemes and organizations giving financial aid and/or advice and information to assist market research or market entry? (See Introduction and List 6, 'Marketing information: systems and use', Question 6.29.)
5.7 Do we have information on professional, commercial and trade association services to aid export performances? (See also answer to List 6, 'Marketing information: systems and use', Questions 6.29 and 6.32, relative to market information; and List 22, 'Industry contacts', Questions 22.5 and 22.8.)
5.8 What percentage of our output is exported and to which regions?

		Value/unit	
Country/region	**Year 1**	**Year 2**	**Year 3**
European Union			
Rest of Western Europe			
Eastern Europe			
North America			
Central and South America			
Africa			
Middle East			
Australasia			
South-East Asia			
Far East			
Others (specify)			

5.9 What are the barriers to improving this performance?
5.10 Which of these areas offer (a) greatest opportunity for increased profitable business, (b) greatest stability in demand?
5.11 What actions are needed to exploit any untapped potential identified?
5.12 Which are presently the top three export countries? Indicate product(s)/services.

5.13 How can we account for this performance?
5.14 On what basis were the territories originally selected? (Compare with answer to Question 5.33.)
5.15 Was the basis for selection sound, and is it still valid?
5.16 Did we develop the market or were we approached?
5.17 What marketing actions did we take?
5.18 How successful were they?
5.19 In which of the countries to which we are currently exporting is turnover expected to increase significantly over the next two to three years? (This answer should align with that to List 8, 'Future market', Question 8.25.)
5.20 How far will such an increase be the result of our efforts?
5.21 Could our efforts significantly change the position?
5.22 Indicate additional countries for which export markets are (or will be) sought.
5.23 Why these countries? (See Appendix 5A.)
5.24 What are our information needs for each market? (The contents page of the book gives headings for virtually all information sectors which are likely to be needed.)
- market size
- market structure
- opportunity for profit
- market trends
- climate of competition
- economic climate

5.25 How can we obtain this information?
5.26 What is the minimum information requirement for a go/no-go decision? (See List 6, 'Market information: systems and use'.)
5.27 What are the critical factors for success in each territory?
- product compatibility with existing or proposed production methods
- size/growth of demand
- availability of finance to purchase
- climate of competition
- availability of operating skills in destination country
- visibility and credibility of our company/product/service/branch
- attitude to new technologies/products/service
- requirement for customized products/service
- customer appreciation of benefit received from the product/service
- business climate within the prospect industries
- language capability
- cost of sales
- availability of service backing and/or suitable distributors
- distributor/agent availability

5.28 Can our present organizational structure undertake export marketing or expand export marketing effort successfully?
5.29 If not, what changes are required?
5.30 Can we introduce the necessary changes?
5.31 How are present export markets served?

	Proportion of Total Export Sales (%)
Own company in territory	
Direct representation (full-time representative in domicile)	
Regular visits by home-based staff	
Distributor (acting as principal and carrying stocks)	
Agent selling on our behalf	
Franchise agreement outlets	
Joint venture	
Licence	
Federated marketing[1]	

5.32 Which form of representation is preferred and why?
5.33 What factors were considered in the selection of representation, and was each significant factor correctly weighted? (See Introduction, Question 5.14 and Appendix 5A.)
5.34 Are territory performances evaluated regularly, and by what criteria? (See Appendix 5A, Stages 6 and 8.)
5.35 What happens in an underperformance situation?

The answers to the next five questions should be compared with those in List 12, 'The agency system'.

5.36 Are there formal agreements and contracts with agents/distributors?
5.37 How will intermediaries not selling in their own right be rewarded – retainer + commission, commission only, salary with or without bonus etc?
5.38 Have we listed the major performance and commercial clauses for any agreement, and do they contain safeguards for us and the agent/distributor?
- sales performance
- exclusivity
- provision of services
- minimum stock levels
- extent of marketing effort
- length of contract
- language capability

5.39 What direct knowledge (ie not through the distributor/agent) do we have of the market?
5.40 What is the source of that knowledge?
5.41 How are enquiries/orders generated in the territories concerned (eg electronic marketing, personal selling, advertising, public relations, sales visits, not known)? (See Introduction.)
5.42 When were the territories last visited?
5.43 By whom?
5.44 Is the managerial rank of the visitor commensurate with the market potential of the territory? (The question is repeated in different contexts in List 9, 'The salesforce and its management', Questions 9.6 and 9.103; List 12, 'The agency system', Question 12.55; List 14, 'The distributive system', Question 14.72; and List 19, 'Key customer marketing', Question 19.21.)
5.45 When are the next visits planned?
5.46 Have the agents/distributors been invited to visit us?
5.47 If not, why not?
5.48 If so, have they accepted? If not, why not?
5.49 How much of our business is indirect exports?
5.50 What form does it take (main customers and types)?
5.51 Can this type of business be stimulated by marketing in the ultimate country of destination?
5.52 How important are consultants and/or buying agents for direct and indirect exports? (See Introduction to List 2, 'Product/service range', and answers to Questions 2.19–2.22; and List 7, 'Market size and structure', Question 7.32.)
5.53 Does our marketing to consultants/buying agents reflect their importance? (See Introduction to List 2, 'Product/service range', on indirect marketing.)
5.54 How important are government and para-statal bodies in decision making?
5.55 Are our contacts with government at the right level?
5.56 What non-tariff barriers exist? (See Introduction.)
5.57 How endemic are bribery and other inducements in influencing business?
5.58 What is our policy on this?
5.59 Are all members of the firm informed of this policy?

(The answers to Questions 5.60–5.71 should be cross-checked with those in List 17, 'Introducing new products/services', Questions 17.54–17.60.)

5.60 Is it possible to license any of our products, our production methods, application know-how, patents, trade names, or designs?
5.61 Would licensing offer improved opportunities for:
- increased earnings
- entry into difficult markets

- facilitating low- (or lower) cost production
- meeting local supply preferences
- improving installation or maintenance services
- eliminating high transport cost and shipping delays
- releasing investment for other developments?

5.62 Do we have some unique or unusual aspect related to our operations which is superior to the competition and which we could license?

- manufacturing process
- application
- raw material blending
- design
- packaging
- product performance
- procurement
- finance
- logistics
- servicing

5.63 Can we export the high-technology components of our product(s) and license less critical assemblies?

5.64 Are there opportunities for cross-licensing that would provide new products for home or export markets? (See answer to List 17, 'Introducing new products/services', Questions 17.53–17.60.)

5.65 What factors must exist to make a licence arrangement profitable (eg high transport costs, trade barriers, lack of marketing and financial resource, lack of territorial knowledge, inability to provide back-up services, market preference for indigenous or favoured nation suppliers)?

5.66 What conditions will we attach to our licence (eg minimum sales or royalty payments, down-payment, territorial limitations, access to production methods, access to accounts, no marketing of competitive licensed or merchanted products?)

5.67 Does the licensing agreement cover the following points and specifications?

- parties to the agreement
- territory
- details of the licence and backup
- basis for remuneration
- duration
- arbitration provisions
- (for trade marks only) goods for which it may be used
- conditions for transfer to third party
- reporting procedures and frequency
- stock levels

5.68 How big must the local market be to justify granting a licence? (See List 7, 'Market size and structure'.)
5.69 How will we police licence agreements?
5.70 Can we prevent the licensee from re-selling the licence to third countries without our knowledge or agreement?
5.71 Can we develop a form of licence agreement that is comprehensive, practical and legally acceptable in the countries of the licensees, but is not so restrictive as to deter would-be licensees? (See Introduction and List 4, 'Company performance', Questions 4.42–4.44.)
5.72 Are patents, copyrights, intellectual property and brands respected and controlled in the destination country?
5.73 What development/internationally funded aid schemes are taking place or are planned that will affect demand for the product and affect business conditions in general?
5.74 Do physical conditions call for product and packaging modifications?
5.75 Is local participation legally required or desirable?

Appendix 5A
A method for the selection of export territories and export representation[2]

INTRODUCTION

Marketing – business-to-business or consumer – does not differ in its basic approach in any country of the world, but the variations involved in meeting the unique conditions of each market are as numerous as the markets themselves. Different messages, different tools, different media – indeed, different human beings – may well be critical for achieving success. The danger of assuming that a successful marketing system or approach in the home market will be equally successful in a foreign market is too obvious to need stating, and yet this is precisely what many companies attempting export markets in fact assume.

Success in export markets depends heavily on a company's willingness to adjust to the market's needs in terms of products and the market's receptivity in terms of communication methods and message. Culture clash, differences in levels of sophistication and business literacy, and confusion of the relationship of marketing response with marketing effort can lead to underachievement on a massive scale.

Thus, in the study of export markets it is necessary to have a real understanding of the markets, which, in the final analysis, even with business-to-business products, comprise people rather than things. Moreover, since all companies have limited resources for marketing, it is even more vital to select only the number of markets that can be successfully penetrated with the appropriations available.

Any decision to export involving the choice of a territory and the appointment of a foreign representative or agent pre-empts an important step, which is to have a long hard look at what the company has to offer the market (see Questions 5.1–5.5). Is the product suitable? Will the price be competitive? Can the company provide the backup service and sales support that will be needed? What, if any, minimum stock levels will be required? What payment terms are reasonable and how do they compare with the competition? Are resources available to allow the territory selected to be visited regularly? Answers to all these questions were called for in the list. Of equal importance is how much the appointed representative can reasonably be expected to earn, and whether it would be commensurate with the time investment (and possibly money), allowing for the build-up and consolidation period. The representative will certainly ask, either as an individual or corporately, 'What's in it for me?' and the company must have the answer and be sure that an alternative use of the representative's time and money would not be more profitable for him or her. The representative with a long list of principals, of which only the profitable few receive attention, is an all too common feature of the export scene.

Thus a decision on representation must be preceded by an evaluation of the company's products, the agency agreement, the terms of trade, etc., aimed at making the representation attractive and profitable both for the principal and for the representative.

STAGE 1 TO EXPORT OR NOT TO EXPORT

It may be that a company does not believe that it has an exportable product. Clearly, in those circumstances the decision is obvious, but the facts leading to that conclusion should nevertheless be marshalled and double-checked.

In contra-distinction, some markets offer such obvious and substantial possibilities that there is little point in undertaking the screening exercise that follows. Developments within a territory – the discovery of a basic raw material, the construction of a new type of plant such as water distillation, or the injection of foreign aid funds for specific projects – may produce what is called an 'availability effect', that is, to make the creation of other industries feasible and viable. This in turn may open up substantial and obvious opportunities. In these circumstances the territorial decision is again pre-empted.

STAGE 2 WHICH TERRITORY?

Having made a decision to export, given that neither of the two pre-emptions referred to above applies, then the question to be decided is which territory or territories represent the best potential market. Questions 5.19, 5.22 and 5.23 refer to this point.

The decision is not an easy one and most certainly will differ for each company. An export screen is shown on pages 65–67 which aims to provide management with some guidelines to the relative attractiveness of various territories; this screen can be reused when reviewing the factors affecting the achieved performance in a particular territory.

Screen 1 is concerned with non-controllable external factors which might eliminate a country that could otherwise appear to be satisfactory on the many points in Screen 2. An example of this would be alcoholic drinks to some Muslim countries. Thus, Screen 1 is intended to remove countries that would not warrant deeper examination before any further investigation takes place.

Screen 3 is also an eliminating grid but, unlike Screen 1, is intended to be specific to the company making the analysis. In contra-distinction to Screen 1, the company may well have some control over the items involved if it so chooses. The suggested items for consideration are no more than examples of the sort of issues that ought to be considered. Each company must develop its own factors for Screen 3.

The point about Screens 1 and 3 is that, no matter how heavily they are weighted and rated on the system described below, they might still not be sufficiently depressed to eliminate a territory automatically. These two screens, 1 and 3, are used to ensure that any extra heavy impact of the aspects listed is not accidentally diffused in the main screen. Where Screen 2 indicates an otherwise favourable territory situation, the company may wish to consider adjustments to the factors in Screen 3 that might otherwise eliminate a market.

As for Screen 2, a good deal of the information required can be obtained from source books and the Internet. Note that all the open-ended questions seek an answer as to whether the subject of the question is favourable for the exporting company in that destination country. Thus, in answering Factor 2, which refers to the development plan of a country, the question means 'does it favour the company's product?' As an example, if the territory had a large offshore oil search programme, it would probably be a plan that would encourage a turbine or open steel flooring manufacturing company. An opposite situation might occur. If labour is desperately short, any indication in a forward plan of immigration restrictions would signal an unfavourable position to any labour-intensive activity.

Many questions can be safely deleted. For example, a service company could ignore Factors 37 and 38 regarding ports. If the decision about the form of representation does not involve setting up a local company with premises, then factors like 49, cost of land, can be deleted as well as Factors 50–62.

Hence this screen is not quite so formidable when the inapplicable factors are deleted.

Weighing and rating

The next step is to decide on the weight of any one factor in relation to others, and it is recommended to use a single 1–2–3 basis: 3 is important and 1 is unimportant. Any finer scale will only tend to confuse the issue. Thus, for example, the gross national product and growth rate (Factor 1) would be rated 3 (important) by most companies, as would Factor 10, size of market. Price levels, Factor 15, would perhaps be 2, and Factor 6, balance of payments outlook, 1.

Taking the first four factors as an example, the weightings might appear as follows:

3 for GNP growth
2 for nature of development plan
3 for resistance to recession
1 for relative dependence on imports/exports

After the weighting comes the rating, which aims to decide how the individual country rates on the point under consideration. Here it is important to use a negative and positive scale, usually +2 to –2. If 'positive only' scales are used, a heavily *weighted* factor multiplies up to a low *rated* factor to a better position. For example, take weighting 3 on a very poor rating 1: using only a positive scale (where 'bad' is rated 1) gives 3 1 = 3, while on the + and – scale a heavy weighting on a bad rating gives 3 –2 = –6, providing an appropriately low position. Thus the scales might be:

+2 excellent
+1 good
0 acceptable
–1 poor
–2 bad

Thus the ratings on the first four questions might look like this:

Question	Territory Rating					
	A	B	C	D	E	F
1	+2	0	+1	–2	+1	+1
2	0	–1	–2	0	+1	–1
3	+2	+1	–2	0	–2	+2
4	+1	+1	0	+2	–1	+2

Now if the weights are applied, they total like this:

Question	**Weighting**	Territory Weighted Ratings					
		A	B	C	D	E	F
1	3	+6	0	+3	–6	+3	+3
2	2	0	–2	–4	0	+2	–2
3	3	+6	+3	–6	0	–6	+6
4	1	+1	+1	0	+2	–1	+2
	Totals	+13	+2	–7	–4	–2	+9

From this analysis, on the first four questions territory 'A' looks best. The system continues to the end and the final totals are compared. It is emphasized that a difference of two or three points in the total is not significant. What the screen aims to do is to separate the excellent from the average or poor – not much more.

For Screens 1 and 3 much heavier weightings will be needed for factors which on their own do not indicate the elimination of a country (eg political barriers). Here, numerical weightings perhaps as high or higher than +10 to –10 may be needed.

Screen 1 having been applied before using Screen 2, the first eliminations will have taken place. If the top-scoring territories in Screen 2 are now final-checked against Screen 3, the best territories for further consideration or action will be clearly seen.

STAGE 3 FORM OF REPRESENTATION

The next step after the selection of the territory is to decide what form of representation to use. To some extent, the choice of territory will also govern the form of representation. For example, no agents are currently permitted to operate in Algeria; Indonesia demands full local participation; suitable local representatives may just not exist in some Gulf states. Question 5.31 gave the major alternatives for consideration, which are:

- own company in territory;
- home-based representatives travelling to the territory;
- directly employed representatives residing in the territory;
- local agents;
- distributor representation;
- regular visits by home-based staff;
- forming, acquiring, licensing, or franchising a foreign individual or organization;
- joint venture;
- federation.

STAGE 4 PROFILING THE OPTIMUM REPRESENTATIVE (OR ORGANIZATION)

Criteria will be necessary to assist in the decision as to what type of representation will be adopted. For example, if there is a need to hold minimum stock levels in the territory this will almost certainly eliminate an agency arrangement in favour of a distributor; the requirement for frequent end-customer contact at technical level will imply the use of directly employed local resident representatives. Quite obviously, the development of these criteria needs careful thought to ensure that all facets of the exporting trading activity are listed and considered. List 12, 'The agency system', includes questions covering all these aspects.

STAGE 5 SCREENING THE CANDIDATES

The next step is to devise a screen through which all representation candidates/organizations are passed in order to aid the selection of the best one. Again, the factors to be considered require development within the exporting company, and the need for product training and level of marketing/sales support should not be overlooked.

As with the country selection, a system of weighting and rating is recommended so that each candidate is considered on a quantified merit basis and comparisons are thus reasonably accurate. (Tangentially, designing a screen of this type assists considerably in constructing a structured and disciplined interview with each candidate and in asking them appropriate questions.)

The use of any screen, of course, ignores the question of whether the representation will be attractive enough to tempt the candidate who comes out top of the rating. Even when looking at the problem substantially from the exporting company's point of view, the attraction of their offer to the potential representative is not a factor to be ignored.

STAGE 6 PERFORMANCE STANDARDS

It is desirable to develop quantified performance standards and operational procedures with representatives at the time of their initial appointment, or at the very least to agree that standards of performance will be devised as the relationship develops, and that achievement of these standards and conformance with procedures will be critical in the annual review on which continuation or severance of the arrangement will be based. Question 5.34 focuses on this topic. In setting standards, the candidates must agree that they are reasonable and the exporting company will need to be certain that the minimum standard they set will justify their investment in time and money in servicing the representation.

STAGE 7 LOCATING CANDIDATES: SOURCES OF INFORMATION

Clearly, the greater the number of potential representatives for consideration, the greater the chance of locating one close to the criteria established. Thus, multiple sources of information need to be approached. A number of suggested sources, including advertising, are listed below, but each company should seek to add to the list:

- Chamber of Commerce – home, foreign-joint, local in the selected territory;
- exhibitions;
- visiting trade missions;
- customers;
- advertising in local and foreign journals read in the territory;
- marketing and management associations in the territory;
- other agents,[3] commercial departments of embassies and high commissions;
- trade associations – home and in the territory;
- foreign embassies;
- Internet;
- banks and financial institutions;
- associations of agents or distributors;
- airline and hotel business centres.

Screening potential export territories

Screen 1 Eliminating factors

Unacceptable product	(Standards, safety, socio-cultural factors)
Political barriers	(Boycotts, sanctions, local participation, state monopolies)
Economic	(Non-transferability of funds, barter trading, price levels)
Legal	(Anti-trust legislation, labour laws, patents, environmental control)
Supply	(Shortage of labour/materials, distributors/servicing)
Concentration of demand	(Too few buyers)

Screen 2 General influencing factors

Individual Countries

Group	Factor	Weighting	A		B		C		D	
			Rating	Total	Rating	Total	Rating	Total	Rating	Total
Economic	1 Size of GNP and rate of growth									
	2 Nature of development plan									
	3 Resistance to recession									
	4 Relative dependence on imports and exports									
	5 Foreign exchange position									
	6 Balance of payments outlook									
	7 Stability of currency, convertibility									
	8 Remittance and repatriation regulations									
	9 Balance of economy (industry–agriculture–trade)									
	10 Size of market for products; rate of growth									
	11 Size of population; rate of growth									
	12 *Per capita* income; rate of growth									
	13 Income distribution									
	14 Current or prospective membership in a customs union									
	15 Price levels; rate of inflation									
Political	16 Stability of government; its form									
	17 Presence or absence of class antagonism									
	18 Special political, ethnic and social problems									
	19 Attitude towards private and foreign investment									
	20 Acceptability of foreign investment by government									
	21 Acceptability of foreign investment by customers and competitors									
	22 Presence or absence of nationalization threat									
	23 Presence or absence of state industries									
	24 Do state industries receive favoured treatment?									
	25 Concentration of influence in small groups									
	26 'Most favoured nation' treatment availability									
Government	27 Fiscal and monetary policies									
	28 Extent of bureaucratic interference and administration									
	29 Fairness and honesty of administrative procedures									
	30 Degree of anti-foreign discrimination									
	31 Fairness of courts									
	32 Clear and modern corporate investment laws									
	33 Patentability of product									
	34 Presence or absence of price controls									
	35 Restriction on complete or majority ownership									

Group	Factor	Weighting	Individual Countries A		B		C		D	
			Rating	Total	Rating	Total	Rating	Total	Rating	Total
Geographic	36 Efficiency of transport system and methods									
	37 Port facilities*									
	38 Free ports, free zones, bonded warehouses*									
	39 Proximity to export markets									
	40 Proximity to suppliers, customers									
	41 Proximity to raw materials sources									
	42 Existing supporting industry									
	43 Availability of local raw material									
	44 Availability of power, water, gas									
	45 Reliability of utilities									
	46 Waste disposal facilities									
	47 Ease of exporting									
	48 Ease of importing									
	49 Cost of suitable land									
Labour	50 Availability of managerial, technical personnel									
	51 Availability of skilled labour									
	52 Availability of semi-skilled and unskilled labour									
	53 Level of worker productivity									
	54 Training facilities									
	55 Outlook for increase in labour supply									
	56 Degree of skill and discipline at all levels									
	57 Climate of labour relations									
	58 Degree of labour involvement in management									
	59 Compulsory and voluntary fringe benefits									
	60 Social security taxes									
	61 Total cost of labour, including fringe benefits									
	62 Compulsory or customary profit-sharing									
Tax	63 Tax rates (corporate and personal income, capital, withholding, turnover, VAT, excise, payroll, capital gains, customs, other indirect, and local taxes)									
	64 General tax morality									
	65 Fairness and incorruptibility of tax authorities									
	66 Long-term trend for taxes									
	67 Taxation of export income earned abroad									
	68 Tax incentives for new business									
	69 Depreciation rates									
	70 Tax loss carry forward and back									
	71 Joint tax treaties									
	72 Duty and tax drawbacks									
	73 Availability of tariff protection									
Capital	74 Availability of local capital									
	75 Costs of local borrowing									
	76 Normal terms for local borrowing									
	77 Availability of convertible currencies locally									
	78 Efficiency of banking system									
	79 Government credit aids to new business									
	80 Availability and cost of export financing including insurance									
	81 Do normal loan sources (US, European, Japanese, international agencies) favour investment?									

* And level of costs.

Group	Factor	Weighting	A Rating	A Total	B Rating	B Total	C Rating	C Total	D Rating	D Total
			Individual Countries							
Business methods	82 General business morality 83 State of development of marketing and distribution system 84 Normal profit margins, for industry concerned 85 Climate of competition 86 Anti-trust and restrictive practices laws 87 Quality of life for expatriate staff									

Screen 3 Specific influencing factors (for the individual company)

Group	Factor	Weighting	A Rating	A Total	B Rating	B Total	C Rating	C Total	D Rating	D Total
			Individual Countries							
	Company and trade mark must be well known. A good geographical network or distributor/service companies must exist. No conflict must occur with corporate development elsewhere in company's markets. Reasonable level of local management sophistication. Must not compete with company's customers also exporting/producing in the area. Internal transportation capable of handling products.									
	Score:									

In addition, the use of press releases in the territory could engender enquiries for handling the representation; eg the announcement of a new product or product availability and a statement that the company is seeking representatives in the territory have been found to stimulate responses.

STAGE 8 MONITORING PERFORMANCE

The final step is the development of an evaluation procedure to enable performance to be monitored and to ensure that the minimum performance standards are in keeping with any change in the exporting company, with new opportunities in the territory, and with other influencing factors that will legitimately increase or decrease the targeted performance (Question 5.34).

It is vital that every effort should be made to avoid losses of representatives since the cost of appointment and lost opportunities is considerable. Reasons for less than satisfactory performance should be analysed, and only if the position is unlikely to be improved should termination by either side be considered. Any breakdown in relationships must be detected in time to enable the reasons for disenchantment to be analysed and corrective action taken where possible. There is a world shortage of competent representatives, and those that a company has appointed should be nurtured and motivated so that their activities will be mutually profitable.

The discipline of a formal and regular agency/distributor review meeting which looks beyond immediate activities or enquiries, quotations and contracts and considers the performance and relationship in depth is most likely to produce ideas that will improve the total export performance of a company.

CONCLUSION

The level of company resources will, of course, dictate the degree of sophistication that can be employed in the development of an export strategy and exporting objectives. It appears to be well proven that the highest rewards follow a policy of concentration and the avoidance of any attempt to spread the total marketing management and its resources too thinly over too many territories.

Notes

1 Federated marketing comprises the setting up an overseas facility by a group of suppliers in the exporting country who sell broadly to the same customers. The costs and risks of market entry are shared and partly underwritten. There appears to be no recent examination of Federated Marketing, although it is known to be working successfully. However, a full explanation with case studies will be found in the old, but still valid, Christopher Claxton (1980) *The Industrial Challenge*, Associated Business Press, London.

2 The terms 'representative' and 'agent' are used interchangeably, but it should be noted that in some territories they have distinctive meanings. 'Representative' can imply a full-time direct employee of the exporting company, and 'agent' a freelance person or organization, usually rewarded on a commission basis.

3 This group subdivides: (a) Agents approached but who are not appointed, because of either their lack of interest or their unsuitability; (b) other existing agents (particularly within the organizations that have different operating companies) covering the same territories.

List 6

Marketing information: systems and use

INTRODUCTION

This list, perhaps like the ones concerned with company performance, sales, and other financial analyses, is the most difficult to contain in length since information is the key to profitable action and there is an insatiable demand for more information. That is not to say that the information gathered is always used or, if used, used well. On the contrary: it has long been recognized that an appeal for more information is about the best excuse to postpone a decision, and market research the best reason ever devised for not making a decision at all. The litmus test must be 'need to know', not 'want to know'.

Marketing research has been revolutionized by the development of the Internet. Information that previously might have involved days of painstaking work can now be obtained in a few minutes at the press of a few keys. The volume of information is vast and expanding daily. While it has become easier to collect, the danger of information overload has hugely increased. Now, more than ever, researcher and auditor need a firm and disciplined approach to ensure that inquiries are confined to the information objectives and they are not diverted by the volume and inherently interesting content of so much of the information which is available.[1]

It is a mistake, however, to believe that the Internet can provide all the secondary research that is needed and is a complete substitute for the older methods. It has many weaknesses. Among these are: market size figures not usually available, coverage is of necessity patchy, there is most frequently an absence of penetration figures and demographics and data often lack authority and, for non-Americans, the emphasis is often strongly US orientated.

The whole self-conducted market audit fails if there is not the information to answer the questions posed, so in a sense this section is a key to the success of the technique. Indeed, many auditors may well want to make this section the first. That it is not was deliberate, however. The interface between perceiving the need for information and the gathering, disseminating and action process is best appreciated if 'need' is demonstrated, as has been attempted in the previous five sections, before methodology.

Information can be divided into two groups: desk or secondary research, and original field research. In the former group is the information already inside the company, or that already exists elsewhere, although not perhaps in an immediately usable form. Secondary research can be assisted by making use of organizations that provide free and paid-for information and assistance based on desk research. For example, The British Library offers up to 15 minutes uncharged time for information on companies, markets and products. The Internet will provide lists of other sources of free and paid-for secondary research and of published market research which is available for purchase.

Field research comprises inquiries and surveys which have to be made externally, usually by different forms of interviewing and observations. Too many companies rush into fieldwork without adequate examination of what can be obtained quickly and cheaply internally, which frequently gives data with a far higher degree of accuracy than can be derived from other sources.

One of the most neglected sources of internal information is salespeople's reports. Individually, in aggregate, and over time, they can yield extremely valuable evidence on market conditions and trends. To tap into this rich potential, it is necessary in the first instance to ensure that the report format provides a disciplined approach notably lacking in narrative-type reports, and that it does not encourage such blanket responses for failure as 'price'. Time devoted to developing an easily completed but fully informative reporting form and in encouraging sales representatives to complete them is always well invested. One possible format is shown in List 9, 'The salesforce and its management', Appendix 9A.

None of this is to imply that the sales personnel should be used for market research. This is quite wrong. They are trained to persuade, not to report objectively, but they can and should be motivated to be forward listening posts of the company. By demonstrating the value of the information, both to the firm and to their own activities, it is not difficult to persuade salespeople to provide data not easily obtainable elsewhere and certainly not at such low cost.

From internal records it is usually possible to carry out a number of practical analyses. Ratio, correlation and actuarial analyses referred to in List 4, 'Company performance', permit reliable appraisals to be made of, for example, competitors' position and markets. There are many excellent books on desk research, and particularly internal research, and on the technique for developing and using different types of analyses. These should be consulted if the auditor feels at a loss to undertake the study required to answer questions that require sales analyses.

So far as external market research is concerned, this checklist is confined to questions relating to doing or commissioning research and evaluating the results, and not to the questions that the researchers must ask. However, in order to assist the marketing auditor, two subsidiary checklists have been added to this section relative to external marketing research.

The first subsidiary list, Appendix 6A, is a guide to factors for consideration when choosing an outside agency to undertake the research. In many countries there is a bewildering choice of organizations with widely varying specializations and approaches. This second list suggests some of the operational and resource aspects that ought to be taken into account when making a choice of agency. Appendix 6B relates to Question 6.15 and is an assessment to determine if the research has achieved its purpose. In order to put some methodology into the search, a standard operating procedure might make a useful starting point.[2]

Underlying every question is the need to ensure that responsibility is designated for deciding what information is needed, that the task of finding and disseminating it is allocated, and above all, for ensuring that the data gathered are used quickly and effectively. Without this control, information gathering is either a waste of time or an underutilized resource. Questions 6.4, 6.5 and 6.27 identify whether the situation is satisfactory.

In relation to Question 6.23, again the Internet will provide many sources of published information, but it is always worthwhile inviting major marketing research agencies to place the company on their mailing lists to be kept informed of multi-client studies available or being undertaken.

Question 6.29 seeks to identify a frequently overlooked source of market opportunity identification. Most of the international agencies provide, on request, information on projects under consideration at every stage from pre-feasibility to commissioning. All companies should ensure that they receive regular notification of the activities of all agencies and governmental and non-governmental bodies that might imply a business opportunity.

By way of example, the European Regional Development Fund in 2001 had over €200 billion available as grants or 'soft loans' for aid projects ranging from new airports to the equipment for new science technology centres. Awarding and spending these monies creates a large number of business opportunities for firms who monitor the market position.

Another invaluable source of information is abstracting services. These scan hundreds of newspapers, and trade, professional and technical journals, and issue frequent 10–15 line abstracts. Most will then provide tearsheets or electronic copies of the full articles on request.

A frequent cause of waste is the large number of journals, technical publications and books that a company buys or subscribes to and which never get read. A full listing of who receives what will quickly identify material that ought to be read as well as received and what publications are superfluous to the organization's needs. Answering Questions 6.38–6.43 will quickly show how efficient and cost-effective the publications subscription list is.

The last questions deal with one of the oldest and most revered maxims in marketing – 'know your customer'. The majority of companies, and most particularly the salesforce, gather but fail to record personal information concerning contacts in the customer companies. Yet everyone responds favourably to any demonstration of knowledge or interest in both the individual and their company. The customer database, which usually only contains details of business transacted, can easily be adapted to include information on personal interests and family. Used carefully and with discretion, personal information can cement relationships in a way that must favour the supplier.

6.1 Are our financial records in a form that permits important and regular sales analyses? (For requirements see questions in List 4, 'Comparing performance', and List 28, 'Product/service financial information'.)
6.2 What adjustments could reasonably be incorporated in record keeping in order to obtain key performance data in relation to markets and marketing?
6.3 What internal and external market and marketing surveillance systems exist? (See also Questions 6.20, 6.23 and 6.29; and List 9, 'The salesforce and its management', Questions 9.118–9.122.)
6.4 Who in the organization is responsible for collection and dissemination of information?
6.5 Does any system exist to check (a) efficiency of collection, (b) accuracy of dissemination, (c) extent of utilization? (See also answers to Questions 6.17, 6.21 and 6.28.)
6.6 What constraints prevent greater exploitation of available information?
6.7 What constraints prevent gathering of more information?
6.8 Do the sales personnel's reporting forms encourage collection and dissemination of market information? (See Introduction and List 9, 'The salesforce and its management', Questions 9.118–9.119, 9.123 and Appendix 9C.)
6.9 How are sales calls reports used and with what frequency?
6.10 Do we feed back use of sales calls reports to the individuals reporting? (The question is repeated in List 9, 'The salesforce and its management', Question 9.45.)
6.11 Do sales calls provide information on market and individual customer sales opportunities? (See List 3, 'The service element in marketing', Question 3.49.)
6.12 Is responsibility for analysing reports clearly assigned, and do instructions exist as to the people who are to receive the information derived?
6.13 What marketing research – internal and external – has been undertaken?
6.14 What factors were considered when deciding to undertake the research internally or externally?
- special skill requirements
- need for anonymity

- total objectivity
- existence of special resources or experience
- knowledge of company and/or its markets
- product/service knowledge
- nature of research problem
- advantage of cross-industry fertilization
- cost
- timing
- location

6.15 Was the research judged to be successful and profitable? (See Appendix 6B.)
6.16 If not, what should have been done, or not have been done, to make it successful?
6.17 How were the marketing research data utilized?
6.18 How does marketing research expenditure compare with competitors' expenditure?
6.19 Can we justify any differences?
6.20 Does the firm have a central source of market and marketing information?
6.21 If so, to what extent is it utilized and does this justify the cost of its maintenance?
6.22 If there is no internal information service, would it be cost-effective to provide one?
6.23 Do we monitor multi-client studies being made available or encourage agencies to undertake the examination of subjects of interest to us? (See Introduction and List 5, 'Export marketing', Question 5.7.)
6.24 Is there a precise specification of the information to be collected regularly?
6.25 How is market information fed into the system?
6.26 Is it disseminated and used quickly?
6.27 Who in the organization receives the information?
6.28 What knowledge and experience do we have of its utilization? (See also answers to Questions 6.5 and 6.17.)
6.29 Do we possess a comprehensive list of regular market information and market opportunity reports? (This question may already have been partially answered as a result of consideration of List 5, 'Export marketing', Question 5.7.)
6.30 Which reports do we subscribe to?
6.31 Have we evaluated their worth to the company by checking what actions and results have occurred through using them?
6.32 What information does our trade or professional association supply? (See also List 22, 'Industry contacts', Questions 22.1–22.8.)
6.33 Can we persuade them to initiate a market information service for our industry or to improve any data they already provide? (See List 22, 'Industry contacts', Questions 22.5 and 22.8.)
6.34 Would a benchmarking study assist us in evaluating our performance against an industry norm?

6.35 What trend information do we have, and how well is it disseminated and used? (This answer should be used in conjunction with List 8, 'Future market'.)
6.36 What variance information do we have, and how well is it disseminated and used? (Compare answers with those in List 28, 'Product/service financial information', Questions 28.16–28.25.)
6.37 Are there any lead or lag indicators that signal future developments and opportunities? (This question is repeated in List 8, 'Future market', Question 8.1.)
6.38 What journals and subscription services are taken by the company?
6.39 Who receives them?
6.40 What evidence do we have that they are (a) read and (b) used?
6.41 Do they cover all areas and markets of interest to the company?
6.42 Can a formal system of reading and reporting be adopted?
6.43 Does a method exist to monitor action on important information circulated?
6.44 Should we (do we) undertake customer satisfaction surveys? (This question links closely with a number of others and the answers if cross-checked will provide corroborating evidence. The auditor should consult answers given in the following sections: List 3, 'The service element in marketing', Question 3.33, concerning complaint rectification; List 13, 'Non-personal promotion: methods and media', Question 13.60 on guarantees; List 16, 'Analysing lost business', Questions 16.14 and 16.39, on researching dissatisfied customers; List 23, 'Pricing', Questions 23.1 and 23.2, on relative cost of complaint rectification; List 25, 'Quality in marketing', Questions 25.31–25.34, on quality aspects; List 27, 'Service businesses', Question 27.38; and List 28, 'Product/service financial information', Questions 28.41 and 28.52, concerning reasons for guarantee and warranty claims.)
6.45 Are results monitored by an allocated person?
6.46 Have they authority to act on the results?
6.47 Do we have personal information on individuals in the decision-making unit and those who influence them?
6.48 How is it gathered?
6.49 Who uses it?
6.50 Who ought to use it?
6.51 How is it used?
6.52 How is it updated and with what frequency?

Appendix 6A
Choosing the right research organization

The following checklist may be helpful in selecting the research organization best suited to particular needs. It covers the salient points on which a firm should satisfy itself in short-listing and selecting a marketing research company to conduct a project. It is rarely helpful to consider more than three companies in detail.

A rating method applied to each factor is usually most effective if the number of points can be limited. A suggestion is:

Very good	+2
Good	+1
Acceptable	0
Poor	–1
Very poor	–2

However, not all the factors are of equal importance and will require weighting to be sure that each one considered is given its due significance; for example, in most circumstances, numbers of full-time professional staff will be less important than research capability in the area under consideration. If both are very good (ie +2 each), the factor total would be 4. This would not make the needed distinction. By weighting 'number of full-time professional staff' by 1 and 'research capability in the subject' by 2, a distinction is achieved which recognizes the importance of the second factor ('numbers of full-time professional staff' $+2 \times 1 = +2$; 'capability in area researched' $+2 \times 2 = +4$).

A suggested weighting is:

3	very important
2	important
1	of moderate significance

The ratings and weightings system is similar to that in the market selection procedure in List 5, 'Export marketing', Appendix 5A.

Points to be evaluated

The weightings given are suggestions only but will be applicable for the majority of firms without internal marketing research facilities and who are seeking outside services.

Company A Name ....

Company B Name ....

Company C Name ....

	Suggested Weighting	Company A	Company B	Company C
A Reputation				
1 Reputation of the agency in general	3			
2 Reputation of firm in our industry or industry to be investigated	2			
3 Reputation of individual members of the agency	1			
4 Agency's clients' evaluation of their ability and capability	2			
5 Evaluation of their ability and capability by agency's clients in our own field	2			
6 Professional and other non-commercial bodies' approval	2			
7 Number and types of the agency's clients in our own field	1			
8 Financial strength	2			
B Organization				
1 Links with other organizations	2			
2 Method of overseas operation	2			
3 Directors' other interests	2			
4 Extent of use of external advisers or associates	2			
5 Terms of business (payment method, etc)	1			
C Capability and experience				
1 Length of time established	1			
2 Degree of specialization in marketing research	3			
3 Degree of specialization in our field or the field to be investigated	2			
4 Degree of specialization in techniques	1			
5 Conformity of completed projects with our special interests	1			
6 Links with learned institutions and/or universities	2			
7 Understanding of problem	3			
8 Unambiguous research design – clarity and detail	3			
	TOTAL c/f			

	Suggested Weighting	Company A	Company B	Company C
TOTAL b/f				
D Qualifications and proof of professional ability				
1 Types of research staff used and conformity to our requirements	3			
2 Qualifications of research staff	3			
3 Extent of repeat business	2			
4 Fields in which technical expertise is claimed	2			
5 Any client recommendations or references	2			
6 Staff membership of professional organizations and societies	1			
E Evidence of professional leadership				
1 Publications	1			
2 Academic contributions	1			
3 New technique developments	2			
4 Non-sponsored research into techniques and practices	2			
5 Agency's contributions to state-of-the-art of marketing research	1			
F Resources				
(I) *Staff*				
Number of full-time qualified professional staff	1			
Number of part-time professional staff	2			
Number of support staff	2			
Interview force (permanent)	3			
Interview force (part-time)	2			
(II) *Directors*				
Qualifications and experience in market research	3			
Involvement in preparing projects	2			
Involvement in undertaking projects	1			
Involvement in presentation of projects and follow-up	2			
Extent of directorial responsibility for projects	3			
(III) *Premises*				
Location	1			
Size	2			
Adequacy and conditions	2			
Equipment	1			
	TOTAL			

Appendix 6B
Evaluating research

- What were the research objectives?
- Is there a sufficient number of facts and are they satisfactorily validated?
- Was the methodology correct?
- Did the research succeed or fail in its objectives?
- How 'hedged' was the reporting?
- What degree of confidence can be placed on the results?
- How far do the final results depart from the agreed research design?
- Are the reasons for any departures valid?
- Could they have been foreseen before the research began?
- Were the researchers suitably qualified and experienced to carry out the project?
- How much reliance can be placed on their judgement?
- Is the report intended to inform? Does it do this?
- How far is the report an explanation or a plea? Are these justified?
- Has the research coverage been adequate?
- Have all secondary sources of information been consulted?
- Is the research taken to the most recent date possible?
- Is the project logical, complete and well designed?
- Are the conclusions justified by the facts?
- Are the recommendations practical and do they take account of internal factors?
- Is the reasoning correct and without fallacies?

Notes

1 An excellent text dealing with all aspects of marketing research and information gathering, including electronic surveys and using the Internet for research, is Christopher West's (1999) *Marketing Research*, Macmillan, Basingstoke.

2 Christopher West (2001) 'Market Research', in *Encyclopedia of Marketing*, ed M Baker, pp 265–7, Thomson Business Press, London, or online http://www.iebm-on-line.com

List 7

Market size and structure

INTRODUCTION

The size and configuration of a market are almost invariably the first questions asked in either appraising an existing market or product/service or considering new products or marketing, and certainly these are highly important factors in the internal marketing audit. However, market size and structure are not necessarily the most important issues. For example, the size of the market for digital multimeters could be described as 'big enough', but for one consumer electronics manufacturer the critical factor for success was the need for acceptance as a committed supplier of professional instruments rather than as a firm selling DIY products through retail chains.

Having said that, however, it would be an odd marketing audit that did not attempt to make some estimate of its current and potential market and then compare the company's performance with the position as revealed. A firm's markets are as much part of its resources as are the factory, offices, machinery, staff and know-how.

In basing market action on assessments, it is necessary to have a realistic view of their validity. Where market estimates and their breakdowns are not derived from research, official, or trade association statistics, they tend to take on the aspects of the children's game of Chinese Whispers. They become distorted and exaggerated, and then hallowed by repetition. In arriving at an estimate, great care should be taken to examine the facts and if possible the sources that led to the conclusions drawn. It is crucial to consult all useful sources within the company (see List 4, 'Company performance', and List 6, 'Marketing information: systems and use') and to check contact reports with other personnel whose performance is not judged by the apparent market size and their share of it.

There is no real substitute for research, but it is recognized that for the marketing audit purpose it may not be cost-effective. Therefore best judgement, perhaps compiled on a Delphi basis, must substitute, but the market auditor should always be aware of possible deficiencies in the estimates and should attempt to place some degree of confidence on each one.

The answer to Question 7.1 is of course the uptake, not the production, of the product/service in the country under review. To arrive at this figure it is necessary to add imports to domestic production and deduct exports to obtain the net market figure. These amendments should not be omitted.

It will be found that this list gives some very clear guidelines as to actions required in specific market situations. The second question, for example, directs attention to a hidden trap in many markets. Research and other methods of market assessment often fail to take account of the difference between the uptake of a product or service and that which is bought in the open market. For example, one section of the hydraulic cylinder market is reduced by almost 15 per cent when business never available to an outside supplier is removed. That is not to say that in-fed markets cannot be successfully penetrated, only that they set the marketer a particularly difficult task that is best not attempted if there are other 'softer' markets to go for.

Question 7.3 looks at market share. It is always important to ask 'share of what'? By way of an example, and to show how misleading market share can be as an indication of performance, it is worth quoting the case of an asthma-relieving drug. In this multi-million pound market one firm had a 20 per cent share of the market but 30 per cent in terms of prescriptions issued. However, this represented the prescribing of only 18 per cent of all doctors, although 40 per cent of sufferers were using the brand. This study pointed out that 30 per cent of all prescriptions issued for asthma relief drugs of this category was good news, but that only 18 per cent of doctors prescribing was bad news. These four different ways of looking at market share in this case illustrate how deceptive such figures might be unless the key question, 'share of what?', is answered first.

Questions 7.18–7.22 are best dealt with as vulnerability analysis which is explained in the Introduction to List 1, 'Marketing strategy and planning'.

A caveat is needed concerning competition, although this will be dealt with in greater depth in List 20, 'Competitive intelligence'. Competition should not be judged too narrowly. It is not just directly comparable products/services, but must include different products/services that will achieve the same end or benefits for the user. Here products and services can compete head-on: laundry versus disposable workwear, contract cleaners versus cleaning suppliers and equipment. Similarly, in identifying competitors it is as well to include significant importers or distributors, or, in the case of distributor competitors, direct trading manufacturers.

The early questions on the current market, both as it is now constituted and as the 'fairy tale' absolute total market (if everyone who could use the product/service actually used it), point to a marketing direction and to activities that also involve other parts of the firm. A simple question, all too often overlooked, as to what changes in the product/service ranges offered, in commercial terms and operational aspects, would open up new segments, is formulated in 7.25. There is an example of a spring balancer used for holding spot welding guns. Looking at it not as an ancillary for a machine tool, but as a piece of equipment that permitted something to be turned through 360 degrees and lifted or lowered and then left in the chosen attitude, it was found there were applications in meat preparation, paint spraying, tanneries and many craft industries. The modification to the balancer was minor, the new market openings huge.

The positioning map in the penultimate question is a valuable exercise. It is often found that, despite reports (usually from the sales representatives) that the market is cut-throat, the bulk of the market is held by firms whose price is relatively high. In open steel flooring, for example, well over 60 per cent of the market is in the hands of companies whose price is in the high quartile, and this despite the existence of low-price flooring.

This checklist links with a number of previous and later ones. In particular, the marketing auditor is advised to use the answers to questions completed in List 4, 'Company performance'.

7.1 What is the size of the total market for our product/service as presently used? (See Introduction and compare answer with List 4, 'Company performance', Questions 4.3–4.5; and List 18, 'User industries', Question 18.1.)
7.2 How much of the market is subject to in-feeding and reciprocal trading arrangements? (See Introduction and List 18, 'User industries', Question 18.39.)
7.3 What is our market share? (See Introduction.)
7.4 How was the figure calculated and what degree of accuracy can we ascribe to it?
7.5 What would the size (units/value) of the market be if our product/service were to be used in all possible applications? (See answer to List 8, 'Future market', Question 8.23. Part of the answer to this and the next two questions may make a contribution to List 20, 'Competitive intelligence', Question 20.2.)
7.6 What is the total number of establishments that could use our product/service in its present application?
7.7 What is the total number of establishments that could use our product/service if it were purchased for all possible applications? (This answer will be required again in List 18, 'User industries', Question 18.7.)
7.8 How many of these establishments are currently customers?
7.9 How many of these establishments are regularly contacted?
7.10 Breakdown of the total market by:
- end use or application
- OEM industries
- products

- dimensions
- price
- handling method
- territory or region
- imports/exports
- retrofit
- replacement
- through distributors
- quality range
- size of orders
- frequency of orders
- seasonal
- performance requirements

(See answer in List 2, 'Product/service range', Question 2.2; List 4, 'Company performance', Questions 4.8–4.10; and List 18, 'User industries', Question 18.9.)

7.11 Breakdown of sales by each member of the salesforce or agent. (See answer in List 4, 'Company performance', Question 4.8. Note that sales into territory do not necessarily equate with sales representative or agent performance.)
7.12 Who are main domestic and foreign direct competitors?
7.13 Who are the main indirect competitors? (See Introduction and List 20, 'Competitive intelligence'.)
7.14 Can we assess our competitors' market share? What reliability can we place on any estimate? (See Introduction; this information will also be needed for List 20, 'Competitive intelligence', Question 20.3.)
7.15 How have these varied over the last three to five years?
7.16 How can we account for competitor market share and variations? (This information will be sought again in List 20, 'Competitive intelligence', Question 20.6 and Appendix 20A.)
7.17 How durable is the market? (The answer to this and Questions 7.18–7.26 should align with List 18, 'User industries', Questions 18.44 and 18.45.)
7.18 What factors threaten the market? (See List 1, 'Marketing strategy and planning', Introduction and Question 1.27, on vulnerability analysis; and List 8, 'Future market', Question 8.33, in relation to this and the next two questions.)
7.19 What would be the impact of these threats on the firm and the market? (This information will be needed for List 8, 'Future market', Question 8.11.)
7.20 What is the likelihood of the threat occurring?
7.21 What control and influence do we have over the threats?
7.22 What steps can be taken to avert the threat and on what time-scale?
7.23 What factors will stimulate the market?

7.24 What actions can we take to encourage any favourable trends?

7.25 What changes in product/service, the ranges offered, commercial terms, and other operational aspects would widen the market? (See Introduction and compare answers with Questions 7.5 and 7.7; and List 18, 'User industries', Question 18.6.)

7.26 How feasible are such changes?

7.27 On what information are our answers to Questions 7.25 and 7.26 based?

7.28 How reliable and recent is it?

7.29 What is the extent of own uptake of the specified products/services? (The answer to List 4, 'Company performance', Question 4.15; and List 11, 'Cross-selling and internal marketing' includes these activities.)

7.30 What is the extent of our sales to suppliers on a reciprocal trading basis? (Compare answer with Question 7.2.)

7.31 Do we want to increase/decrease either own uptake or reciprocal trading?

7.32 How much business stems from organizations or individuals who influence/advise on the use of products/services (eg consultants, architects, accountants)? (See List 2, 'Product/service range', Questions 2.19 and 2.21; and List 5, 'Export marketing', Questions 5.52 and 5.53.) There is also a link between this question and those referring to networking in List 27, 'Service businesses', Questions 27.32–27.35.

7.33 If the market is cyclical, what is the periodicity? What causes it?

7.34 How great are sales variations between peaks and troughs?

7.35 Can we develop anti-cyclical products or services? (See List 17, 'Introducing new products/services', Question 17.15.)

7.36 Relate market share to price on the positioning map. (See Introduction and cross-reference with the positioning maps in List 18, 'User industries', Question 18.57, and List 23, 'Pricing', Question 23.5.)

(Auditors should indicate on the vertical scale either an accurate or perceived price level of their own and major competitors' prices and on the horizontal scale the actual or estimated market shares. This will clearly indicate the price–market relationship.)

7.37 How will developments in electronic trading change the extent, type and fulfilment of demand on our product/services?

List 8

Future market

INTRODUCTION

'The only good thing about the future,' said Herman Khan, 'is that it comes one day at a time.' True as this may be, the nature of business demands that the future be under constant review and, equally, that plans for the future also be under constant review and always contain a contingency element. Markets are perhaps one of the most hazardous of all areas to forecast, the variables being as great as in any other discipline and the movements perhaps more volatile and unpredictable than most. Nevertheless, the difficulty of the task is not a reason for not undertaking it in a methodical manner and applying best judgement to situations that defy stricter analysis.

Perhaps above all else the auditor and researcher would like to know how future changes in the market will manifest themselves. This can never be known with any exactitude, but at least information on the many strands which impact on the market will remove or reduce the grosser errors.

Forecasting, more than any other aspect of marketing audits, requires detailed, recent and accurate information, and much that is included in List 6, 'Marketing information: systems and use', is directed to producing a relatively high confidence level in prognostications.

A great deal of the raw data required for forecasting can be obtained from many official, semi-official and unofficial sources, specialist organizations, data books of various types, and of course the Internet. A week rarely passes without some prestigious organization prognosticating on economic, market, technological or social futures. Some of these bear the stamp of genuine scholarship and authenticity while others may well be more political statements than objective assessments. The auditor must take the greatest care before accepting any external forecast.

Most commercial or specialist libraries and the Internet can provide useful bibliographies, but the auditor must again be warned against becoming diverted by information-gathering and sophisticated analytical techniques at the expense of the interpretation.

For marketing audit purposes qualitative assessment is as important as numerical precision, and the views of those in the market and competitors is as significant a contribution as industry output data.

It is necessary in dealing with forecasting for marketing auditors to make their own decision as to what data give a reliable guide to future requirements. The questions provide a framework within which, and from which, the final lists can be developed.

For forecasts to be useful they require constant surveillance. As the events of the past two decades have shown, the hypotheses on which medium-term forecasts are based are highly unlikely to remain valid through the period. It is only necessary to look at the volatility of oil prices, unemployment, inflation, interest rates and Eastern Europe and China as markets in the past few years to see how violently forecasts can differ from ultimate reality. Even short-term forecasts have proved to be hazardous. The destruction of the World Trade Center impacted within days, if not hours, on economies throughout the world and on whole trade sectors such as air travel and tourism and those industries that supply them.

One possible way to mitigate the problem is to state clearly the hypothesis upon which a forecast is based and to have a series of contingency plans which can be triggered if there is a significant variation in the forecast as a result of changes in the factors on which it was based. That is not to say the market plan should be adjusted for every variation that occurs. There is a world of difference between a touch on the tiller and a mad grab at the wheel.

The most useful first step is to decide which business indicators are significant. For most companies the major economic indicators are useful only in a macro-sense and the individual organization or company requires micro-forecasting. There are, however, well-accepted and thoroughly reliable economic lead–lag indicators which can be applied to the individual company: and, oddly enough, there are also corporate indicators that can be used to forecast national economic trends. It is well known that employment agency services feel the shock waves of recession long before any official statistics reveal the position. An early task for the auditor is to identify those external lead–lag indicators which have a meaning for the company and the internal ones which historically lead to a given situation. The answers to Question 8.1 for perhaps the more fortunate company may be a wholly reliable forecast in themselves. For the less closely correlated situations they will make a significant contribution to the forecast.

However, as with other types of information, it is important to emphasize again that receiving data for forecasting or the actual forecasts themselves is not a substitute for action. Questions 8.3 and 8.4 are a very adequate test as to whether information, perhaps laboriously and expensively gathered, is in fact fully utilized.

Question 8.6 has a particular significance if any part of the market is likely to grow or decline faster than others. The danger of regarding a market that is in fact the aggregate of a number of disparate parts as homogeneous is obvious. The question breaks down global into segment expectations. The market for air conditioning equipment may have an overall growth rate of 5 per cent, but the hospital sector could show nil growth, while the hotel demand might well be in excess of 10 per cent. This illustrates the importance of forecasting segment change.

Another danger to be avoided, which Question 8.21 touches on, is the failure to distinguish between what the market would like and what it has the resources to purchase. Nowhere is this better or more tragically illustrated than demand for many products – most of them basic – from Third World countries, but lacking resources to purchase.

Attention is drawn to Question 8.24 for the many firms whose products or services, or indeed marketing methods, might be favourably or adversely affected by legislation. If increasing public pressure for higher standards of restaurant hygiene leads to greater regulation and control then a demand will be engendered, not only for cleaning equipment and services, but also for products and materials that are easier to maintain or handle. Deregulation of the professions, while not creating a huge surge in the demand for marketing services, certainly produced a small but valuable market for public relations skills, advertising and print.

Legislation proposed or even enacted is still fraught with dangers for forecasting purposes. There was a considerable delay between the time that EU law demanded the use of tachometers in commercial vehicles and its full implementation. The opposition of drivers and their unions succeeded in holding back the latent demand for a number of years. There is a lesson here: proposed legislation may vary significantly from the original proposals, may not be enacted at all or, if enacted, not implemented.

Forecasting the future without using the information in some practical way is an interesting but, on its own, substantially useless exercise. The whole point of forecasting is to be able to make plans to avert threats and to exploit opportunities that arise. The vulnerability analysis method set out in the Introduction to List 1, 'Marketing strategy and planning', will be found to be a very useful tool for micro-forecasting.

It is obvious, of course, that the company's marketing can have a strong influence on the way a market will go. The impact of any marketing plans ought to be considered in the forecast. At the same time, it is as well to ensure that the forecast does not become a self-fulfilling prophecy. Both factors will be considered automatically in answering Question 8.32.

It is recognized that the following checklist has many shortcomings. This one, more than most others, is intended to give starting torque to the forecasters and is by no means the last word on the subject.

8.1 Which economic/industry/social (lead–lag) indicators have a significance for us? (This question will have been answered in List 6, 'Marketing information: systems and use', Question 6.37.)
- levels of employment
- inflation
- population trends

- credit availability and restrictions
- hire-purchase debt
- export trends
- changes in corporate taxation
- rates of personal taxation
- wholesale/retail prices
- levels of production
- personal savings
- climatic conditions
- levels of income
- level of investment
- level of profits
- social and political factors
- import trends
- balance of payments
- non-tariff barriers
- consumers' expenditure
- interest rates

8.2 Who in our organization receives them?

8.3 What procedures are followed in their use?

8.4 What actions have been taken in the past as a result of using market forecasts?

8.5 Estimate the annual average growth rate for the market for our products/services for the next five years. (Distinguish between the market at constant values and any changes that are due to inflation. If possible, 'units' or 'volume' should be used to avoid the problem of high and changing inflation or exchange rates.)

8.6 Can the 'global' forecast be broken down into significant segments? (For some suggested segmentation criteria refer to List 2, 'Product/service range', Question 2.2.)

8.7 Do we have agreed plans for the method of operation in the selected segment/target areas?

8.8 What hypotheses are the 'global' and segment forecasts based on?

8.9 Indicate any market segment for our products/services growing faster/slower than the total.

8.10 What reasons can we attribute for the growth/decline? (See List 7, 'Market size and structure', Introduction and Questions 7.17–7.19 and 7.23.)

8.11 What opportunities or threats does this imply for us? (See List 7, 'Market size and structure', Questions 7.19 and 7.24.)

8.12 Will changes in materials, production, communication or delivery methods impact on the need for our products/services?

8.13 Does our R&D and new product/service programme reflect these expected changes?

8.14 Do we understand the reasons for any changes?

8.15 What are the implications for us?
8.16 What technical developments in our own and our competitors' products/services/ production methods/materials used/commercial practices are taking place or expected to take place in the future? (See List 20, 'Competitive intelligence'.)
8.17 Do these changes imply a compatibility with the changes referred to in the earlier Questions 8.12 and 8.13?
8.18 What trends are likely to increase/reduce the number of competitors in the market?
8.19 What new products/services are likely to emerge that may impact on our markets?
8.20 What time span is likely to be involved?
8.21 Is there likely to be any difference in the forecast period between market requirements and its ability to purchase? (See Introduction.)
8.22 Will economic, social or political changes provide us with new opportunities or create new threats and new entrants over the next five years? (The answers to this and the previous three questions should be compared with those given in List 17, 'Introducing new products/services', Question 17.37.)
8.23 Are any present non-users likely to take up the product/service in the next five years? (See List 7, 'Market size and structure', Introduction, and Questions 7.5 and 7.7.)
8.24 Is proposed legislation, domestic, EU or international, likely to affect either demand or the structure of the market? (See Introduction.)
8.25 What changes are likely to occur that will restrict or liberalize trading in our major export customers? (See answers in List 5, 'Export marketing', to Questions 5.19 and 5.22.)
8.26 How will price change over the forecast period? (See answers in List 23, 'Pricing', Questions 23.35 and 23.36.)
8.27 Which customers and which competitor companies (by name) do we think are likely to enter or leave the market over the next five years? (Compare with answers to Questions 8.18 and 8.32; and see List 20, 'Competitive intelligence', Question 20.7.)
8.28 What are the reasons?
8.29 What changes in the structure of the market are foreseen (distributors and other intermediaries, buying influences, imports/exports)?
8.30 How accurate have previous forecasts been?
8.31 In what way could we improve accuracy?
8.32 Has the impact of our own, and our competitors', marketing strategies and ambitions been taken into account in arriving at the forecasts? (See Introduction and List 20, 'Competitive intelligence', Question 20.56)
8.33 Would a vulnerability analysis exercise enable us to identify threats with greater accuracy? (See Introduction to List 1, 'Marketing strategy and planning', and Question 1.27; and List 7, 'Market size and structure', Questions 7.18–7.22.)

List 9

The salesforce and its management

INTRODUCTION

This checklist is substantially about selling activities but must inevitably involve sales management. That 'there is no such thing as a bad salesperson, only bad sales managers' is the belief of many marketing directors. While not wholly true, this is uncomfortably close to the position found in many companies.

Marketing auditors may well want to enquire if their sales managers have also asked the questions listed and if the answers have been used to improve sales performance. Thus what follows could have the treble purpose of forming part of the total marketing audit, an audit of sales efficiency, and a sub-audit of sales management effectiveness.

It has been estimated that in, for example, the professional and commercial service industries the cost of a sales call is a phenomenal £200–£300 and the cost of an order or contract £500–£800, these figures including support staff costs as well as the sales team. Given these very high costs it is obvious that increased productivity of the salesforce requires close and frequent attention.

While most checklists, as has been pointed out, have an in-built danger of encouraging the demand for more information and analysis than can profitably be used in an internal marketing audit, this one on selling tempts the compiler to extend the question almost indefinitely, because there is so much that can be asked and so much that can be actioned in the majority of sales organizations. Indeed, this list might well have been subtitled 'One hundred questions every good sales manager should ask' (although there are in fact over 130 questions).

Underlying many of the points is the query whether the reasons that account for present organization and methods are still valid. Too many sales operations are based on history and have not reacted to the rapid changes in market conditions and marketing techniques that have typified the last decade.

Questions 9.15, 9.28 and 9.44 open up the often neglected aspect of salesforce rewards. Commissions often induce price-cutting. Given a 5 per cent commission, a salesperson offering a reduction in price of 10 per cent means a loss of 0.5 per cent commission but a much greater certainty of getting business. It must be asked who would not rather have 4.5 per cent of something than 5 per cent of nothing. Moreover, in getting the order, even at a sub-standard or unprofitable price, it is a fact of life that the seller receives the approval of superiors, the regard of peers and the admiration of subordinates. No wonder price-cutting is as often the result of the representatives' offers as of buyers' demands.

An interesting illustration of this phenomenon is provided by a firm of electrical insulation material suppliers. The sales team were given a list price and a minimum price they could negotiate down to. Not surprisingly, prices were invariably nearer the bottom of the range, since the difference in commission between top and bottom prices was marginal to the salesperson and the chance of the order much higher at the lower price. The company adopted a system of dividing equally with the salesforce the incremental price over the set minimum. Within weeks, the average price obtained had risen 28 per cent above the minimum, giving the firm an extra 14 per cent and the salesperson a substantially higher income.

Throughout the list runs a strong emphasis on examining factors that generate sales motivation. Questions 9.15–9.28 all have strong implications relative to motivation, while Questions 9.23, 9.25–9.28 and 9.44 deal directly with this subject. It is recognized that different things motivate different people, and a mechanistic approach is unlikely to be successful across the whole salesforce. Some selling requirements are socially and domestically destructive. Where a representative is subjected to this type of domestic disruption, there ought to be some compensating factor, an important motivational point that is referred to in some detail later when Questions 9.92 and 9.93 are reached.

Question 9.45 focuses on a common – indeed almost universal – omission in sales management. While it is expected that the representative will report to the company, most companies fail to report to the individuals. Such a report can be a very valuable motivational tool. In Appendix 9B will be found a model of a report-back system. It is interesting to note that even the socially and domestically destructive elements in a schedule, already referred to, are considered in the performance comparison analysis.

The link with salesforce rewards and giving salespeople price variation authority will be seen to have its dangers. The other positive aspect is that it enhances the role and status of the salespeople in the eyes of the customer. This is a trade-off to be considered in making such a decision. Question 9.47 raises the issue.

Question 9.63 may seem a little obscure in its shortened form. There are many ways of selling. Sometimes a company sells the product or service concept on the basis that once this is sold they will obtain their share of orders. The task of some salesforces is to 'sell' a demonstration, not a product. One manufacturer of mixing equipment had not realized that his 80 per cent conversion rate of demonstrations to orders clearly implied that the task was to 'sell' demonstrations, which is easier to accomplish than a direct sale. Some potential suppliers will leave a demonstration model with the customer for a period of time to enable them to experience its performance and benefits. This too yields a high conversion rate. Related to this is the sales technique of loaning equipment of a higher quality or with greater capabilities than products being repaired or serviced. This frequently leads to a sale of a higher-grade machine.

In a number of industries the customer only requires the supplier to put a price on a specification. On the face of it, this leaves little opportunity to apply selling skills. The task is to try to change customers' approach to their buying. Thus the question calls on the marketing auditor to decide how the product/service is sold and whether there might not be an alternative and better way. Both tendering and referential bids are the subject of comment and questions in the Introduction to List 23, 'Pricing'.

'Cost per call', if it can be calculated, is a valuable control tool. Where the cost is high there is clearly a need for greater sales productivity. The prompts in Question 9.62 will have identified some issues for consideration and the importance of doing so may be inherent in the answers to Questions 9.67 and the many that follow.

This book's introductory section, 'The marketing audit', illustrated one of the great weaknesses often found in salesforces: the difference between available selling days and days actually spent in the field. It cannot be right for personnel with selling skills to be devoting time to tasks that could be done as well, or indeed better, by others, and Questions 9.68–9.73 consider this point.

An examination of the time expenditure of an export salesforce of three people based in the UK headquarters of a manufacturer of fast patrol vessels showed that fewer than 125 days a year were spent in the field – the remainder being justified as 'factory liaison', 'quotation preparation' and other non-selling activities. An increase to a still low figure of 175 days produced an additional half-year of selling days for the company. This very simple analysis is one that ought not to be missed by any organization. Tangentially, it is worth commenting that technology and rapid liaison enables the mechanization of quotation preparation. This alone can significantly increase selling availability for field, as opposed to office, work.

Question 9.91 is deceptively simple and frequently produces a conditioned response. After all, to question whether representatives know their territory is criticism of the most severe type. Yet, where a product/service has a multi-industry application – for example, office equipment, janitorial supplies, space heating systems, telecoms – virtually every establishment is a potential customer. The salesperson must distinguish between worthwhile and other calls, which is not always easy to do, by judging the factory by size and activity or the shop from its fascia board. There are, however, excellent commercial services, most available on the Internet, which can provide data on individual establishments, from the name of the buyer or works manager to whether they have a staff canteen or a forklift truck.

The concept of customer profiling in Question 9.100 needs some explanation. This is a simple analytical system for tabulating the major characteristics of good, regular customers – eg size of company, method of operation, type of activity, form of purchasing organization, or whatever characteristics are appropriate. The profile is then applied to 'prospect' firms so that those conforming most closely to the 'best customer' profile can be identified and made priority targets. Experience has shown that it is one of the most simple and practical analyses that can be undertaken by a company. Appendix C gives a list of the most frequently used characteristics.

Documentation, which has been described as a leading-edge marketing tool, is a most neglected area and yet holds out the promise of substantial rewards. Question 9.117 identifies the key considerations in the preparation of proposals or offers but the question of documentation as support for the salesforce does require careful consideration and action.

As has been noted in List 6, 'Market Information', sales contact reports are an extremely valuable source of market and client information. Questions 9.118–9.123 examine this issue and Appendix 9A is an example of one such form which is easy to complete and easy to analyse.

Questions 9.128 and 9.129 can highlight another area of weakness which may be far from obvious. A superbly operating salesforce and excellent non-personal promotion can do nothing to obviate incompetent and clumsy processing of enquiries and orders received directly by e-mail, post, telephone or personal calls. The routing of enquiries from the mailroom, switchboard or reception can be the first weak link in a weak chain, followed by the use of low-level clerical staff to handle what might be important actual or potential customers. Getting enquiries or orders wrong, failing to pass on messages, telephone back or write are common errors that do untold damage. The whole system of internal handling of enquiries/orders received direct should always be examined critically, reviewed frequently, and monitored constantly.

The marketing auditor must never lose sight of the fact that the whole company is a selling organism, not just those who have the word 'sales' in their job title. Apart from reception and telephone, which are obvious, the auditor must question whether the accounts department staff, for example, are pleasant and efficient even if the firm is pressing for settlement of overdue accounts and whether service personnel visiting customers are acceptable to them in their work, appearance and manner. All these aspects and many others are as much part of the sales process as the sales team's calls.

9.1 Is the sales director or manager a leader and motivator as well as a skilled salesperson?
9.2 Does sales management have a product or market orientation and how is the orientation demonstrated?
9.3 How recently has the sales manager received updating training?

- leadership and motivation
- performance assessment
- marketing
- training
- mentoring
- control
- counselling
- induction
- recruitment

9.4 What segmentation criteria have we and our competitors adopted?

- geography
- process or application
- frequency of purchase
- benefit received
- form of customer organization
- demographic factors
- buyer's job function
- servicing requirements
- value added
- credit requirements
- price levels
- size of customer company
- size of order
- psychographic factors
- full-line or limited-range purchase
- seasonal
- order source (eg OEM, distributor)
- guarantee claims
- cost per sale
- cost per delivery
- industry or trade

(Other versions of this will be found in List 2, 'Product/service range', Question 2.2; List 4, 'Company performance', Question 4.4; List 7, 'Market size and structure', Question 7.10; and List 18, 'User industries', Question 18.9.)

9.5 Is there an effective control system for routing, visits, enquiries, orders?

9.6 How much time does the sales manager spend with the salesforce and in visiting customers? (The question has already been asked in a different context in List 5, 'Export marketing', Question 5.44; and will occur again in List 12, 'The agency system', Question 12.55; List 14, 'The distributive system', Question 14.27; and List 19, 'Key customer marketing', Question 19.21.)

9.7 How many sales personnel do we have/need?

9.8 What would be the effect on sales of cutting/increasing the salesforce?

9.9 How are they organized? By region, by industry/application, by type of customer, by product/service, etc?

9.10 Are the reasons for this form of organization still valid?

9.11 Is the salesforce technically qualified in our product or in the customer industries, or not at all? (See also Question 9.125.)

9.12 What are the customer preferences in this respect?

9.13 How do we know? (The answer to this and the two previous questions will also be required for List 20, 'Competitive intelligence', Question 20.46.)

9.14 Would meeting the customer preference be incompatible with our needs?

9.15 What method of remuneration are we using? (Questions 9.15–9.28 are commented on in the Introduction.)

9.16 How does it differ from previous methods?

9.17 Why were the present methods adopted?

9.18 What proof do we have that it provides strong motivation?

9.19 How does our remuneration method compare with competitors?

9.20 Can we justify any differences?

9.21 Have we considered alternative methods?

9.22 What were the criteria for rejection? Are they still valid?

9.23 What other benefits do our salesforce get?

9.24 Are the benefits actually earned, or do they form part of the salary package?

9.25 Would there be a stronger/weaker motivation if benefits were related to performance?

9.26 How are house accounts and direct orders treated in terms of remuneration and performance appraisal? (See also Questions 9.107 and 9.108; and List 14, 'The distributive system', Question 14.40.)

9.27 Does the remuneration policy encourage price-cutting by the sales team? (See Introduction; List 26, 'Non-differentiated products and commodities', Introduction. The same answer will be required for Question 26.8.)

9.28 Would any change in the remuneration policy improve/reduce representatives' motivation and thus affect performance?

9.29 Rate the motivation of each member of the sales team: high, moderate, low.

9.30 What major factors motivate each person?

9.31 Are these emphasized in sales training and induction?

9.32 How are sales personnel recruited?

9.33 What is the record of salesforce turnover?

9.34 How does it compare with the standard for the industry?

9.35 What is the major cause of losses?

9.36 How far can losses be attributed to poor recruitment criteria and methods, poor induction, inadequate training, supervision or encouragement?
9.37 What sales target does each individual have? (See List 4, 'Company performance', Question 4.6.)
9.38 How are they devised?
9.39 Are they reached in agreement with the individual?
9.40 If not, is the method of arriving at a target explained to the sales personnel?
9.41 How does each salesperson perform against target? (Use answers to List 4, 'Company performance', Questions 4.5 and 4.8.)
9.42 How is constant underperformance dealt with?
9.43 Is the method effective?
9.44 What rewards or acknowledgements do individual members of the salesforce receive for passing targets?
9.45 Is there a report-back system so that comparisons can be made with performance of others or with the best and with the company's progress as a whole? (See Introduction and Appendix 9B, but this question will have been answered in List 6, 'Marketing information: systems and use', Question 6.10.)
9.46 What is the sales platform (features/benefits)? (List 2, 'Product/service range', Introduction, Figure 2.1 and Questions 2.26–2.28 cross-reference with this point; and List 24, 'Images and perceptions', Introduction.)
9.47 Does the salesforce have authority to vary price? (This question raises the issue of negotiating skills as well as pricing. List 19, 'Key customer marketing', Questions 19.47–19.56; and List 23, 'Pricing', Questions 23.9, 23.12, are concerned with this topic.)
9.48 Is the product/service sold as a concept, by demonstration, on quotation, or by attribute? (See Introduction.)
9.49 What is the proportion of sales calls to enquiries received?
9.50 What is the proportion of enquiries to quotations?
9.51 What is the proportion of quotations to orders obtained? (The answers to the last two questions should have been given in List 4, 'Company performance', Questions 4.24 and 4.25.)
9.52 How does it vary between individuals/products/territories?
9.53 What is the cause of any variation?
9.54 Is it justified by circumstances?
9.55 Can favourable variation factors be transferred to other salespeople?
9.56 Does each member of the sales team have individual job specifications?
9.57 Are they regularly reviewed?
9.58 What criteria are used for performance evaluation and how frequently is an evaluation made?
9.59 Does the salesforce know and understand the criteria used for judging performance?
9.60 Are the criteria valid in today's conditions?

9.61 How does each member of the sales team rate on issues of knowledge, attitude and skills?

Knowledge of:	**Attitude**	**Skill in:**
territory	positiveness	planning
company policies and procedures	determination and perseverance	image creation
product/service and applications	self-development	asking questions and listening to answers
key accounts	cooperation	opening sales discussions
own strengths and weaknesses	sustained enthusiasm	translating technical facts into buyer benefits
		using visual aids
		overcoming objections
		problem solving
		report writing and providing meaningful feedback
		closing

9.62 What steps can we take to eliminate poor performance?

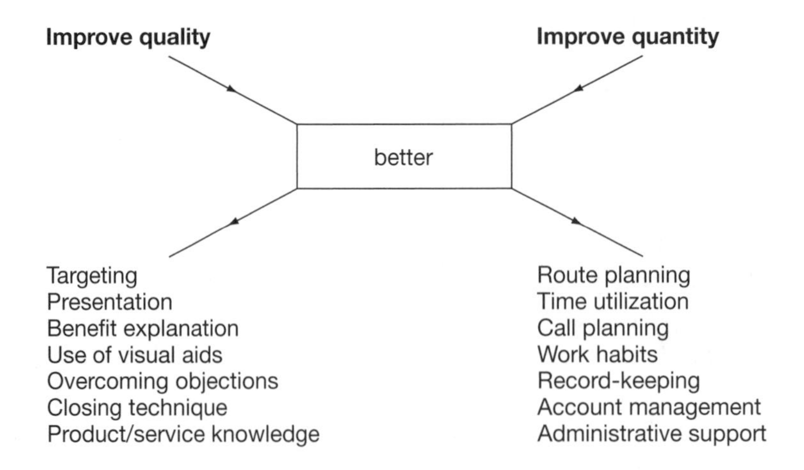

9.63 Are intrinsic or extrinsic approaches used? ('Intrinsic' concentrates on the prospect's substantive needs or problems; 'extrinsic' emphasizes the attributes of the firm or product/service without relating it to the customer needs – see Introduction.)

9.64 Is the emphasis on the product/service, reputation of the company, or successes they have achieved? Are these approaches suitable and effective? (See List 27, 'Service businesses', Introduction, and Question 27.43. Although this refers specifically to services selling, it has direct implication in product selling.)

9.65 What are the individual's performances broken down by industry, application, type or size of company or other breakdowns? (See List 2, 'Product/service range', Question 2.2, which suggests some headings for analysis, and compare answers with List 4, 'Company performance', Questions 4.8 and 4.9.)

9.66 Does this analysis indicate that some members of the salesforce might be better committed to a specialization rather than a territory?

9.67 What is the cost per call? (See Introduction.)

	(£)
Recruitment	
Remuneration	
Company vehicle	
Other expenses	
Sales manager (including secretarial expenses and overheads)	
Area manager (including expenses and overheads)	
Communications	
Reporting and administration	
Support staff (including overheads)	
Print and stationery	
Training	
TOTAL	

Calls per day
Orders per day
Working days per annum
Total calls per annum
Total orders per annum
Sales cost per call: cost ÷ calls
Sales cost per order: cost ÷ orders

9.68 How many active selling days are there in a year (as compared with total of approximately 222 in the UK)? (See Introduction.)

9.69 Can the difference between days in the field and days available be justified?

9.70 What steps can be taken to reduce non-selling days?

9.71 Do representatives prepare their own quotations or tenders?

9.72 Could this work be wholly or partially standardized, simplified, handled by non-selling personnel, or undertaken electronically? (This answer will be required again in List 28, 'Product/service financial information', Question 28.57.)

9.73 What is the average number of calls each day?

9.74 How does this compare between sellers (allowing for different territorial distribution of customers)?

9.75 Is personal route planning mandatory?
9.76 Does a system exist for supervising and ensuring compliance with route plans?
9.77 How does this compare on an 'all-industry' basis?
9.78 Could the call rate be improved by better call cycle planning? (See Question 9.62.)
9.79 Could call frequency rate be reduced with no risk to volume or quality of orders?
9.80 Could some field calls be handled as well by telephone?
9.81 Are any accounts uneconomic to service, even by telephone, and hold nil further potential? (The auditor should consult the Introduction to List 28, 'Product/service financial information', concerning customer value analysis, and the answer to Question 28.1.)
9.82 Do the sales personnel or sales office tend to overreact to a customer's telephone call or fax, and abandon a carefully constructed schedule in order to make previously unscheduled calls?
9.83 How much off-territory mileage is there during selling time?
9.84 Can some calls be made at 'unconventional' times?
9.85 Is driving considered to be 'part of the job' which must be done during normal working hours?
9.86 Are the journey plans maximizing coverage of the territory with minimum driving?
9.87 Is there a geographically organized record system?
9.88 What is the average length of calls?
9.89 Would there be a material improvement in performance if call length were increased/decreased?
9.90 If so, how can the change be achieved?
9.91 Are all prospects on routes and off-routes known?
9.92 How frequently are members of the sales teams required to spend nights or weekends away from home? (See Introduction and the 'Personal sacrifice' item in the report-back form given as Appendix 9B.)
9.93 Are they compensated additionally for this?
9.94 Does the salesforce know which accounts are key customers? (See List 19, 'Key customer marketing'.)
9.95 Are they fully briefed on policy for key customer handling?
9.96 What proportion of total calls are committed to existing customers? (See List 4, 'Company performance', Questions 4.11 and 4.20.)
9.97 Does the analysis in List 4, 'Company performance', Question 4.11, and the answers to Questions 4.19 and 4.20, indicate that the proportion is correct/incorrect?
9.98 What steps can be taken to bring about any changes needed?
9.99 How many calls are dedicated to seeking new business? (See List 4, 'Company performance', Questions 4.11 and 4.20.)
9.100 Has any attempt been made to profile prospects with a high business possibility? (See Introduction, Appendix 9C and List 15, 'The buying process', Questions 15.44–15.46.)

9.101 Is there a prospect grading system, similar to a customer grading system, which helps formulate a target priority plan over each territory?
9.102 How many first approaches does it take, on average, to develop a meaningful dialogue?
9.103 How frequently do top management accompany salespeople on calls? (See also List 5, 'Export marketing', Question 5.44.)
9.104 How frequently does top management meet customers visiting the plant or office?
9.105 To what extent is telephone selling used?
9.106 Could the sales effort be supported by telephone selling?
9.107 What is the procedure for handling direct enquiries/orders? (See also Questions 9.26 and 9.126.)
9.108 Is it formal, understood, and complied with?
9.109 What are the salesforce's views on the internal handling of direct enquiries/orders?
9.110 What are the customers' views on the handling of direct enquiries/orders?
9.111 What changes are required to allow for any sales personnel's or customers' expressed needs and criticisms for direct enquiries and order handling?
9.112 Is there any history of mishandled direct enquiries/orders? (Compare answer with List 10, 'Customer care and support staff's role in marketing', Question 10.7, and List 16, 'Analysing lost business', particularly Question 16.30.)
9.113 What steps have been taken to prevent recurrence? (See Introduction relating to the above seven questions.)
9.114 How is the sales team notified of direct enquiries from their territory? (Compare answer with Questions 9.26 and 9.107; but it should be noted that the issue is just as important in relation to agents. See List 12, 'The agency system', Questions 12.80 and 12.81.)
9.115 Is the sales team notified of deliveries into their territory? (This and the preceding question should be taken together with List 14, 'The distributive system', Question 14.40, where a dual system of selling exists, ie direct and indirect.)
9.116 Are sellers notified of any change in status of their customers, particularly credit rating? (See List 28, 'Product/service financial information', Question 28.44.)
9.117 How does the documentation of company and individual sales representatives rate on the following aspects?
- aesthetics – appearance, quality
- content – all the information the customer needs
- finality – enables the customer to order against it
- protection – guarantees, type/extent of liability

(This question arises in a number of different contexts. The auditor should consult, compare and align answers given in List 4, 'Company performance', Questions 4.42–4.44; List 16, 'Analysing lost business', Questions 16.40 and 16.41; List 24, 'Images and perceptions', Question 24.28, where a compilation of quality factors in documentation is given; and List 25, 'Quality in marketing', Question 25.36.)

9.118 Do the individuals provide a full report on their activities? (See Appendix 6A. List 6, 'Marketing information: systems and use', Question 6.3, also deals with this topic.)
9.119 Is it a narrative report or a formal document? (See Appendix 9A.)
9.120 Does the reporting system yield market information? (See Introduction to List 6, 'Marketing information: systems and use', and Question 6.8.)
9.121 Does the reporting system require reasons for lost business to be given? (See List 16, 'Analysing lost business'.)
9.122 Does the reporting system encourage 'price' as a reason? (Compare with answer to List 16, 'Analysing lost business', Question 16.2.)
9.123 Is a 'price' response probed?
9.124 What support and sales aids are provided for the salesforce?
- advertising
- give-aways
- catalogues
- samples
- Web sites
- point-of-sale display
- technical data sheets
- drawings
- educational slides or film/video

9.125 Does the salesforce receive new product training? (See List 17, 'Introducing new products/services', Questions 17.43 and 17.44.)
9.126 Is the performance of the sales/order office monitored?
9.127 Is the salesforce encouraged to report back on how their enquiries and orders are handled internally? (See answers to related questions 9.26, 9.107 and 9.126.)
9.128 Is the role of the sales/order office to receive orders and/or handle enquiries? (The question is restated in List 13, 'Non-personal promotion: methods and media', Question 13.76.)
9.129 Could their role be expanded by proactive selling?
- increase order size
- sell other products
- improve range spread
- least-cost routing for delivery
- larger delivery 'drops'
- compatible order and lead times and frequencies

9.130 What encouragement does the salesforce receive to cross-sell?
9.131 What benefits do they receive from cross-selling?
9.132 What are the constraints to cross-selling?

(The above three questions will be subject to further probing in List 11, 'Cross-selling and internal marketing'.)

Appendix 9A
Model contact form

MODEL CONTACT FORM							
Client name		Client address		Business activity		Telephone Fax	Client status Key . . . . Regular . . . . Sporadic . . . . One-off . . . . Lost . . . . Failed quote . . . . No invitation to quote . . . .
CONTACTS Name		Titles		Product/services purchased			
Date of visit	Who seen	Topic	Length of meeting	Next vist	Who to act	When	Monitor
Client organizations			Business lost		Competitors		
t/o	staff	branches	to whom	why			
Ownership			Previous business				
Subsidiaries			Services	Value	Completion date		
Next							

Appendix 9B
Model for company report-back system

Sales representative: ____________________ Region: ____________________

	September 200?	Six months cumulative	Best salesperson cumulative
	£	£	£
Volume sales			
Institutional			
Commercial			
Total sales			
Budgeted sales			

	Monthly sales	Budget GP	Cumulative sales	Actual cumulative GP	Cumulative sales	Actual cumulative GP
	£	%	£	£	£	£
Product mix						
Sensitized paper						
Tracing paper						
Drafting machines						
Printing machines						
Ancillaries						
Job printing						

	On budgeted sales at budgeted percentages	Actual GP	Budgeted GP on budgeted sales	Actual GP
Gross profit				

	Budgeted	Actual	Budgeted	Actual
Expenses (cumulative)				
Your selling expenses				
400% regional overheads				
Total cumulative expenses				
Attributable to your sales				
Net profit				

	Yours monthly	Yours cumulative	Best salesperson's cumulative
Personal statistics			
Total orders booked (no.)			
Total calls made (no.)			
Reports submitted (no.)			
Days worked in the field (days)			
Time spent with customers (hrs.)			
New prospects (no.)			
Number of orders cancelled			
Value of orders cancelled			
Advertisements discussed on calls			
Your efficiency index			
Calls per day			
Percentage of orders to calls			
Average value of order			
Personal sacrifice			
Nights spent away from home			
Your cumulative commission			
1½% sensitized and tracing paper			
2% job printing			
½% rest			
TOTAL			

Your all-England ranking	1. A. Green	2. F. Brown	3. S.Patel	4. J. Smith
Branch ranking	1. West	2. East	3. South	4. North

Appendix 9C
Possible factors for inclusion in a profiling exercise to identify non-clients with similar characteristics to those of regular clients

These are just some suggestions and many will not apply or cannot be ascertained. Each firm should develop its own list using this as an aide-mémoire. *The list focuses on business-to-business organizations but many of the questions will apply to private customers.*

1. Size of company by any or all of the following:
   - turnover
   - profit
   - assets employed
   - numbers employed
   - number of establishments
   - size of establishments
   - ROI
   - other
2. Form of organization:
   - owner-managed
   - limited company
   - international/multinational/local/regional/national
   - extent of verticalization
   - cooperative
   - voluntary purchasing group
   - other
3. Extent of specialization:
   - full line
   - associated products
   - complementary products
   - general suppliers
4. Type of distributor:
   - retailer
   - wholesaler
   - cash and carry
   - merchants
   - factor

- dealer
- agent
- importers
- exporters
- stock holder
- rack jobber
- voluntary group
- mail order
- fulfilment house

5. Buying organization:
   - central purchasing
   - central selection – local ordering
   - local autonomy
   - purchasing officer
   - committee purchasing
   - stringent product testing
   - approval body
   - susceptibility to inducements (above and below the line)
6. Activity:
   - construction
   - manufacture (by SIC) (including energy)
   - consultants
   - service company
   - educational
   - defence
   - research
   - other institutional
   - transport
   - energy
   - importers
   - exporters
   - professional services
   - industrial/commercial services
   - commission packing
   - jobbing
7. Psychographic factors:
   - ultra-modern
   - modern
   - contemporary
   - old-fashioned

- receptivity to new products and designs
- sensitivity to other aesthetic factors
- changing requirements
- static requirements
- transitional

8. Reason for purchase:
   - resale
   - resale and install
   - appearance
   - wear/resistance
   - safety
   - compatibility with existing installation
   - incorporation into own product
   - first installation
   - repair
   - extension
   - retrofit
   - replacement
   - improved performance
   - insurance/security
   - full-line availability
   - legal requirement
   - lack of appropriate skills or capacity
9. Contact method:
   - salesperson
   - area manager
   - sales manager
   - director
   - chief executive
10. Source of information:
    - salespeople
    - advertisements
    - exhibition
    - editorial
    - direct mail (including E-mail)
    - Internet
    - telephone selling
    - referral
    - other

11. Seasonality of demand:
    - nil
    - moderate
    - total
12. Types of usage:
    - heavy
    - medium
    - light
    - clean environment
    - aggressive environment
    - abrasive environment
    - wet/damp environment
    - regular movement pattern
    - irregular movement pattern
    - mechanical (vehicle, ie trolleys, forklift trucks)
    - cleaning method
    - vibration and movement
    - unfavourable climate
13. Purchasing decision basis:
    - performance
    - backing services
    - resale
    - in-feeding
    - quality
    - safety
    - full-line availability
    - compatibility with existing installation/equipment
    - trial purchase
    - lead time offered
    - physical dimensions and properties
14. Service purchasing reasons:
    - R&D assistance
    - production problems
    - storage problems
    - new product requirements
    - litigation
    - adaptation advice
    - testing
    - new material appraisal
    - compliance
    - others

15. Other:
    - geographical location
    - frequency/regularity of purchasing
    - benefit received
    - size of contract

It is suggested that the exercise begins with the 'best customer' only profile: that is, those in the first group below. It can then be extended to the other categorizations given.

- regular customers;
- sporadic customers;
- one-off;
- discontinued;
- failed quotation;
- non-invitation to quote.

List 10

Customer care and support staff's role in marketing

INTRODUCTION

Care of the customer and awareness of customer's needs is a major issue for all organizations. 'Customer care', like 'quality' and 'zero defect', is among a number of fashionable management phrases honoured more in their omission than commission. To be customer orientated, a number of important and highly practical steps must be accomplished:

- *Understanding the customers and what they expect from the company.* This understanding is not just at top management level or in the marketing/sales department, but includes every employee, whether they have direct dealings with the customer or not.
- *Establishing methods of measuring the standards of service quality provided.* What gets measured gets done.
- *Involvement.* All employees must be involved in both setting and constantly improving standards of service quality – there has to be an acceptance at all levels that today's top quality is tomorrow's average quality.
- *Development.* Creating systems, organizational structures and styles of management that enable people at the customer interface to take customer care decisions on their own initiative (empowerment).
- *Communication.* The tying together all of these elements is the quality of the organizations' communications, both internal and external, vertical and horizontal. Communication must be frequent, consistent and involve everyone in the company.

The foundation of every customer-driven business is person-to-person contact with the customer. But this is all too frequently eroded, not just by those charged with the task of marketing (and within marketing, selling) the company's offering but by others in the organization who have the customer contact but unfortunately do not regard 'customer care' as their responsibility. The not inconsiderable efforts which have been made in consumer markets to promote the principles, activities and motivation involved in customer care have not been wholly effective, but few industrial and commercial companies have even attempted to apply them at all. Training in marketing and customer care is just as applicable in business-to-business markets as in consumer markets. Support staff have to be seen and treated as part of the marketing team. They represent a potential fund of goodwill and talent, albeit of a non-technical and non-marketing nature, which can be effectively used to improve customer relations and enhance the business and image of the enterprise.

Many organizations are surprised, when they come to audit the range and nature of customer contact, just how many people in the company do at some time or another interface with customers. Question 10.1 begins the list with a consideration of this topic, but obviously it needs to be adjusted and augmented for each business. The sub-list omits those functions where the principal contact is for sales purposes.

In general, the term 'customer care' is used very loosely and consequently has many meanings. To complicate the issue further, while there are some elements which are fundamental to all customer contacts, eg courtesy, concern, responsiveness, accessibility, there are others which are specific to job function. Question 10.3 leads to the recommendation that every job specification should set out clearly the customer-care aspects – that is, what the customer expects of staff and what the organization expects of them. These must be clear, concise, observable and realistic.

Because the support staff function is by definition people-based, and because people are not machines but will vary considerably from time to time and from situation to situation, it is necessary to monitor performance both by observation and by customer response. Questions 10.10–10.12 identify the need for constant monitoring and where necessary for a system to be devised to identify signs of deterioration before it becomes serious and the trigger for issues which might lead to poor performance. Some of the answers to the questions in List 16, 'Analysing lost business', may well throw some light on the quality of staff activities and attitudes. However, the danger which must be avoided is using the monitoring system as a vehicle to criticize and cast blame instead of using it positively to identify and reinforce desirable behaviour. Monitoring should be devised to measure how well personnel are doing, not how poorly. The answer to the questions will indicate if it is necessary to adjust any system to avoid this particular problem.

Questions 10.15–10.17 deal with the subject of acknowledging high-quality service. Acknowledgement can of course come in many forms, from monetary reward to work ambience. It can also include corporate recognition, opportunity for promotion or greater responsibility, job content, or education and training to improve skills.

Everyone involved in customer care recognizes the need for training but its half-life can be very short. Retraining is as important as training, particularly where changes in the programme content and method are made. Question 10.18 forces consideration of this issue.

It has been said that behaviour breeds behaviour – the way people behave towards one another engenders reciprocal attitudes. To be a customer-centred company there must be a mutual interdependence among all levels and between staff and management. Thus the manager or supervisor has to command a number of skills. The four central ones for marketing are *communication, monitoring, supporting* and *delegating*. Some of the characteristics of a good team-builder and manager are listed in Question 10.25. None is genetic – all can be acquired.

Customer care is highly dynamic and no system, management or administration will remain relevant indefinitely. The development of a really effective structure depends on constant adjustment which encourages ongoing identification of the need for changes and can comfortably embrace and welcome them. Question 10.27 identifies those factors which influence the creation of an internal ambience that will deliver high-quality customer care at all times through the involvement of support staff.

There is little doubt that personal attitudes will mirror those of top management and only if top management is completely committed to a policy of customer care and customer caring will this filter down throughout the organization. An ingenious solution to maintaining standards adopted by one company was to set aside a sum of money to compensate dissatisfied customers. Any money left in the fund at the end of the year was distributed to customer contact staff. The impact of this highly motivational technique for monitoring standards has been impressive.

Most customer care campaigns have three things in common. They are launched in a blaze of publicity, they exhort employees to pay attention to customer needs, they all have a short-term effect and lapse. This is because they concentrate on fault finding, not cause elimination, customer care is seen as the role of managers appointed to supervise quality and whose job is to find fault, failure to improve customer care is perceived as a point-of-contact problem only, and organizations do not enter into the campaign with full appreciation of and commitment to the scale of change that was required. In short, there is usually no fundamental change in the way organizations operate.

It has been well said that 'People don't care how much you know until they know how much you care'.

10.1 Which departments and staff have customer contact?
- reception
- telephone
- messengers
- drivers

- security
- service
- accounts
- technical advice
- customer help-lines
- library
- R&D
- market research
- order office
- order fulfilment
- credit control

10.2 Does each member of support staff understand the customer-care element in their work? (See List 25, 'Quality in marketing', Appendix 25A.)

10.3 Have the customer-care standards relevant to each support staff function been set out clearly in job specifications?

10.4 Does each person in the organization appreciate the importance to the company of customer care?

10.5 Is each person's role thoroughly explained?
- most important duties
- secondary duties
- frequency of performance
- range, scope and limitations in personal decision-making

(Align answers with that of List 11, 'Cross-selling and internal marketing', Question 11.13.)

10.6 Is each person aware of how their job relates to others – the internal supply chain?

10.7 Do all staff know what the customer expects of them and what the company expects of them?
- timing – speed of response or completion
- accessibility – in place and time
- flexibility – meeting customers' needs
- anticipation – delivering services without reminder or request
- communication – comprehensive, accurate, timely
- feedback – encouraging customers to comment routinely and in specific instances
- organization and supervision – co-ordinating, zero defect approach

(See answer to List 9, 'The salesforce and its management', Question 9.112; List 16, 'Analysing lost business', Questions 16.30 and 16.31; and List 27, 'Service businesses', Question 27.11.)

10.8 How do personal standards match up to required standards?
- appearance
- attentiveness
- guidance
- body language and voice tone
- tact
- problem solving

10.9 Is customer care and sensitivity part of the individual performance appraisal?
10.10 What system exists for identifying substandard performance?
10.11 Is the monitoring system structured in such a way that it only encourages criticism?
10.12 Can it be adjusted to encourage desirable behaviour?
10.13 Are customer complaints analysed to identify underperformance by staff? (See List 16, 'Analysing lost business', Questions 16.35–16.37.)
10.14 Does a method exist to encourage customers to comment on support staff cooperation and service?
10.15 Is good performance by support staff acknowledged? (See Introduction.)
10.16 If so, in what way?
10.17 Does the form of internal acknowledgement and recognition act as a motivator for the recipient and for others?
10.18 Is there a formal training programme appropriate to each job function?
- on induction
- on job/customer change
- refresher

10.19 Are the effectiveness and relevance of the training programme checked at regular intervals?
10.20 How is this done?
10.21 What mechanism exists for adjustment?
10.22 Are staff members who have already been trained retrained or updated?
10.23 Are managers and supervisors fully aware of their role in ensuring their subordinates maintain a high quality of customer contact?
10.24 Should we introduce a formal mentoring policy?
10.25 Are managers and supervisors good communicators with their own staff?
- keep subordinates informed
- listen well
- create and maintain a cohesive structure
- admit mistakes
- generate an energetic ambience
- express themselves clearly
- encourage upward communication
- use authority with sensitivity

- consult others before decision-taking
- build a feeling of pride in the team

10.26 What steps are (can be) taken to encourage staff to identify customer problems and to suggest solutions? (See List 27, 'Service businesses', Questions 27.18–27.21.)

10.27 Is the internal climate conducive to customer service problem-solving? (See Introduction and List 27, 'Service businesses', Question 27.20.)

- with staff themselves diagnosing service problems
- involving staff in suggesting improvements
- working towards solutions that reduce present job burdens
- supporting solutions that are consistent with organizational values and culture
- implementing solutions gradually or incrementally
- maintaining flexibility during implementation process
- encouraging feedback and flow of information
- promoting a climate of acceptance, support and trust between management and support staff

10.28 Which of the following factors can we/do we use to assess quality of customer care? (See List 16, 'Analysing cost business', Question 16.39.)

- customer satisfaction/evaluation
- accessibility of staff
- attitude of all personnel
- number of errors, freedom from errors
- repeat business
- benchmark against competitors
- completeness of service
- waiting time, delays, lead times
- number of complaints/claims and reworking
- adherence to timetables, schedules
- management involvement
- extent of customer participation in service
- cost of service
- efficiency of communication
- service utilization
- supplier evaluation
- reliability/safety measures
- time taken to resolve complaints
- accurate documentation

10.29 Would it be possible to benchmark our customer care performance?

List 11

Cross-selling and internal marketing

INTRODUCTION

Two neglected aspects of most companies' operations are, first, the failure to maximize the potential locked up in the customer base – that is, seeking to increase sales to existing customers – and, second, to utilize fully their own resources for internal supply.

It is generally accepted that it costs between five and seven times as much to obtain a customer as to retain one, and this fact alone should make the marketing of the full product/service range to the existing customer base a high priority.

Multi-product, multi-brand and multi-departmental companies all too frequently fail to exploit their most valuable asset – customers. Asking the very simple question, 'What do our customers buy that they don't buy from us but which we could profitably supply?', not only leads to new product/service development at a very low cost, but also reveals where the supply company already has an offer which will meet a customer need. Box 3 in Figure 17.1, 'Product matrix', List 17, 'Introducing new products/services', illustrates this point.

It is not only those involved in marketing and selling who are capable of contributing towards obtaining sales across the company's full range. Functional departments can also make a measurable contribution. The servicing department in particular could easily be the first to identify a sales opportunity.

There are, however, very real barriers to cross-selling. First among these is a lack of trust. Those involved in servicing customers may, indeed usually, have in-built reservations about exposing their customers to other parts of the company that may not perform to what they regard as a sufficiently high standard and thus possibly even lose the customer for the introducer. Second, there is usually little or no reward for the individual or team in cross-selling. Their first priority is to meet their own quotas, not someone else's, and to service their own customers to the best of their ability. Internal rivalry for promotion and its associated rewards can well militate against enhancing an internal competitors' performance even when it would be for the overall good of the organization. One other pervasive, but often overlooked, reason why cross-selling fails is that customers see no benefit in transferring additional business to the firm.

These and other barriers, while illustrating the difficulty of building an effective cross-selling structure, are all surmountable by internal marketing. Questions 11.1–11.5 concern the problem of barriers.

A precondition for successful cross-selling has to be an audit of the company's resources along with a customer audit to see if a match can be made between what is available (or could be made available) and what the customer needs (or could be shown to need). Questions 11.6–11.9 are relevant, but the apparent naivety of Question 11.6 ought not to disguise the need for ensuring that everyone knows everything that is available. On probing this point, a glib response will often reveal that full knowledge is lacking, most particularly when the customer contacts are not from the marketing team, ie servicing personnel or senior management. Auditors can prove this for themselves by using List 3, 'The service element in marketing', Appendix 3A, and seeing how many people can identify those services (and others) which are available in their own company.

An internal audit of a major engineering component manufacturer revealed some 23 services available, but on average the sales team could list only 14 or 15, while those members of the firm not involved in marketing were able to name only about 10. Clearly, if the supplier's personnel do not know all the services available (and it might be deduced that many would not know the full product range either), it is not likely the customer knowledge would be any greater.

The second neglected aspect is that of the opportunities offered for self-consumption of products and services. Companies embarking on cost-reduction campaigns often decide that it is better to buy in products and, in particular, services rather than provide them themselves. The decision is not of course a purely financial one. There can be good strategic reasons for keeping a purchase in-house – security of supplies, quality control and trade secrets are examples – but the decision should be based on a broad-ranging consideration of all the issues involved, as Question 11.22 suggests.

All too frequently the comparison of the cost-effectiveness of internal and outsourced supply is less than objective because of different ways of arriving at cost. How are overheads to be allocated? Is time costed on a realistic basis? Answering Questions 11.26–11.30 will provide a realistic basis for comparison. List 23 on 'Pricing' gives in Figure 23.1 in the Introduction a checklist of some of the elements of cost to be considered.

Internal marketing is more than a change of emphasis, it is a substantial change of attitude. Psychologically, the removal of corporate protection – in the sense that internal customers *had* to use internal products/services or, at the very least, give every opportunity to compete with external suppliers – and the move to a situation in which, in many cases, the internal customer does not even have to short-list the internal supplier, are cathartic.

Cross-selling and internal marketing have resulted in new criteria emerging for assessing managers' performance which were never previously part of the job specification. Managers who pride themselves on the skills with which they practise their individual disciplines and expertise – engineering, finance, operational research, information technology and many others – now have to add marketing skills and, more important and much more difficult to achieve, marketing motivation.

The new task is to achieve close internal working relationships which are based on a genuine mutual interest. Adversarial patterns of the past have to be broken. Negotiating skills are badly needed, something few managers of internal departments have been taught. Improved coordination is required and the in-built assumption that the customers' needs are known removed. Internal coordination involves more than the personnel actually delivering the product/service. It extends to the most junior members of the unit. Everyone has to be customer-centred. The summary at the end of the Introduction to List 19, 'Key customer marketing', is as applicable to internal marketing as to external marketing.

Images, as List 24, 'Images and perceptions', clearly shows, are a vital component of decision making. The fact that the supplier is in-house does not make the need to achieve an internally acceptable image any less important than when seeking external customers. The last series of questions, 11.33–11.36, concentrates on this important internal marketing factor.

Appendix 11A provides a practical guide to the actions which a company can follow to improve the exploitation of its customer base.

Every auditor should seek to establish the potential demand for additional business from existing customers. With the help of their salesforce and the customer database, the format in Appendix 11B should be completed as far as possible. This will quickly identify opportunities available to the company.

11.1 What constraints militate against cross-selling? (See Introduction.)

- customer 'hugging'
- transfer pricing mechanisms
- lack of incentives
- interpersonal friction or rivalry
- lack of motivation
- customers see no benefit
- organizational barriers
- internal policies
- missing marketing skills
- managerial career competition
- lack of mutual trust
- setting unreasonable standards

11.2 Could barriers be reduced or removed? (See Appendix 11A for a summary of techniques.)

11.3 What incentive exists for cross-selling to occur?

11.4 What are the risks involved in cross-selling as perceived by the salesforce and other members of the company?

11.5 Can they be eliminated or reduced?

11.6 Is everyone in the company with customer contact aware of all the products and services we can offer? (This question will have been answered in List 3, 'The service element in marketing', Question 3.3; and compare with Appendix 11B if/when it is completed.)

11.7 Do we have a complete up-to-date register of staff qualifications, experience and capabilities? (This information may already have been revealed by the answer to List 1, 'Marketing strategy and planning', Question 1.25. There is also a link between the answer to this question and List 10, 'Customer care and the support staff's role in marketing', Questions 10.1–10.5.)

11.8 Do we have a complete and up-to-date register of other resources, eg machine stock?

- hardware
- software
- systems
- distribution network
- stocks
- finance
- transport
- track record
- special skills (including languages)
- information
- salesforce
- R&D
- new product introductions
- image
- technical advice
- customer database
- logistics
- brands and intellectual property

11.9 Are all our customers and potential customers aware of all the products and services we can offer? (At least part of this question will have been answered in List 3, 'The service element in marketing', Question 3.4.)

11.10 Is it possible to bolt together relevant product/service offers which meet an actual or client latent need (proactive marketing)?

11.11 How is marketing structured? (See also List 2, 'Product/service range', Question 2.2; and List 18, 'User industries', Question 18.9.)
- product/service
- industry
- application
- customer
- geographical
- value added

11.12 Would a better range spread of sales by cross-selling be achieved by a different structure? (The answers to List 9, 'The salesforce and its management', Questions 9.130–9.132 will also have provided information on this topic.)
11.13 Is there a role for non-marketing personnel to encourage cross-selling, eg servicing, order office? (See List 3, 'The service element in marketing', Questions 3.20 and 3.21; and List 10, 'Customer care and support staff's role in marketing', Question 10.5.)
11.14 Are there any motivational factors that would encourage them to do so?
11.15 Will the present methods of internal/external communication be effective for cross-selling?
11.16 If not, in what way are they deficient?
11.17 What steps must be taken to adjust them for a cross-selling strategy?

The following questions refer largely to meeting requirements from internal sources.

11.18 What products/services do we already supply from internal sources?
11.19 What products/services could we supply from internal resources? (See also answers to Questions 11.6–11.8.)
11.20 Is internal purchase mandatory or competitive?
11.21 What is the basis for such a policy?
11.22 If internal supply is mandatory, what are the reasons?
- cost-effectiveness
- quality, reliability or consistency of supply
- own purchase conditions
- JIT or other delivery systems
- strategic supplies
- trade secrets
- external suppliers' conditions of business
- procurement advantages

11.23 Are they valid in today's conditions?
11.24 Where there is freedom to purchase internally or outsource, is the internal supplier given a second opportunity to requote?
11.25 If 'no', should they be?

11.26 How are internally supplied products/services costed?
11.27 Does the method reflect corporate objectives?
11.28 Is the comparison based on a fair internal allocation of costs? (See List 23, 'Pricing', Figure 23.1; and List 28, 'Product/service financial information', Appendix 28A.)
11.29 Are our costings a reliable basis for comparison against outsourced purchases?
11.30 Does the costing/charging *method* vary between different product/services?
11.31 What is the basis for any variation?
11.32 Is any variation valid under present conditions?
11.33 What image do internal clients have of the internally provided product/services? (See List 24, 'Images and perceptions', for breakdown of image questions to be asked.)
11.34 How far does the image align with reality?
11.35 Is an internal image correction or improvement campaign required for internal supply and suppliers?
11.36 How does the internal image compare with that of external suppliers of similar products/services?

Appendix 11A
Tactics to achieve network benefits and collaboration

- Combined customer visits
- Cross-staffing – quotations and bids
- Rotation of staff
- Generating integrated customer work
- Company-level funding of collaborative marketing activities ('free resources')
- Appointment system of cross-boundary 'customer relationship managers'
- Introduce customers to the managers and marketing personnel in other departments and SBUs
- Appointment of coordinators
- Reorganize around people we want to collaborate more
- Reward collaboration in compensation system
- Joint training
- Joint committees
- Transfer payments and other accounting devices
- Information sharing and technology backup
- Wide database availability to facilitate access to information
- Ensure awareness on skill and resources available
- Customer files to contain information on other products/services purchased and this information to be widely available
- Internal brochures, newsletters and directories (who does what, where etc)
- Feedback – promotion of successful cross-reference
- Change of working/office structures for easier internal contact
- Encouragement of cross-company social involvements with customers
- Contribute to induction programmes
- Support staff inter-departmental meetings and social events

(This appendix is developed from the original work of David Maister.)

Appendix 11B
Client potential evaluation

Supply level (tick) / Significant clients	We supply **all** their product/service needs	We supply **some** of their product/service needs	Competitors supply **part** of their product/service needs	Opportunities exist for new products/services we could provide profitably
1				
2				
3				
4				
5				
6				
7				
8				
9				
10				
11				
12				
13				
14				
15				
16				
Total				

List 12

The agency system

INTRODUCTION

Attitudes towards the use of agents tend to polarize between those firms who operate totally with agents, most particularly overseas, and those who prefer not to have any at all. 'Agents,' it is argued, 'sell what's selling.' 'They carry so many lines that they are not interested in any of them.' 'The agent is in business for himself, not us.' All are frequently heard typical comments. In fact, agents do have a role to play, and it is wrong to take up rigid attitudes based on history or hearsay without a real consideration of the 'pluses' and 'minuses' of using agents.

The first and overriding point to be considered is that, despite the fact they operate on what is called a 'contingency pay pricing' (payment by results) basis, they cost money to acquire and maintain. Samples, catalogues, brochures, visits, stocks, correspondence, post, fax, telephone calls, training, etc – all take time, and all cost the firm something. It is important, therefore, that their performance not only justifies the investment the principal makes in them, but shows a *pro rata* profit commensurate both to that produced by the directly employed salesforce and relative to the cost of maintaining the agent.

It is possible, of course, to run an agency system with minimum costs. However, this usually produces a high turnover of agents and a low input of orders. The rule must be that, if agents are to be used, they should be supported in every way and used well. They must be made to feel part of the company, not outsiders. As with directly employed sales personnel, motivation is vital, and as with the principal's sales personnel, motivation is not simply a question of money.

The major problem with agents is finding them. Good agents, particularly overseas, are few and far between, and generally speaking are not 'hungry' for new lines and new principals.

There has to be something about the company and its offerings to tempt them. There is as much a marketing job to be done in acquiring agents as in disposing of a firm's output. List 5, 'Export marketing', Appendix 5A, gives a staged process for obtaining and monitoring agents. It should be studied in conjunction with this list because of the similarity of the problems and tasks involved.

One major international manufacturer of automotive batteries found that his sales organization was disintegrating, with an ageing agency force. Replacement from conventional sources was proving impossible. He decided therefore that if agents did not exist he would have to create them, which he proceeded to do with great success by converting many of his directly employed salespeople to agents, assisting them with extended credit, occasionally some capital, and other forms of financial and non-financial support. The system was rebuilt successfully within two years.

This checklist can be extended by many of the questions in List 9, 'The salesforce and its management', and should certainly be completed in conjunction with List 5, 'Export marketing'.

Two very important questions are posed at the outset. Question 12.6 looks at what an agency must be or not be before its appointment would be considered. The first bullet point is critical. There are many ways in which agents can be remunerated, from a straight commission on sales to complex arrangements which include incremental increases for additional or different types of sales or customers, retainers, special incentives for new accounts, regular basic payments with or without claw-back, and others. Obviously the financial returns and the principal's ability to provide the right 'mix' and level of reward will be the key decision factors in agreeing to take up an agency or in appointing one. Question 12.12 also deals with this topic.

Too often, where a mixed system of direct sales and agents is used, responsibility for agents within the company is diffused and in any event is a marginal activity. Question 12.9 calls for a closer look at this situation, particularly when the high cost (in every respect) of recruitment is considered. In far too many cases agents are appointed informally, usually because of the mistaken belief referred to above that 'agents cost nothing'.

It is to the total benefit of both parties that agency agreements should be detailed and unambiguous while not being so restrictive as to demotivate the agent. Questions 12.15–12.30 cover the major aspects of contract contents and the auditor should ensure that all agreements, including existing ones or where no formal agreement governs the relationship, deal with these issues.

Performance is indeed the outcome of effective agent recruitment, induction and maintenance. In recruiting, the minimum performance expectation (and the time to achieve it) should always be stated to avoid subsequent failure for both parties. Once operating, the agents should have a clear idea of what is expected of them (and conversely what the principal will do for the agent). Developing performance standards (see Question 12.51) for personnel over whom there is little control other than terminating the agency requires tact, advocacy and a lively awareness of conditions in the agent's territory and indeed within the agency itself.

Questions 12.70–12.74 deal with the thorny problem of getting the agents to report on their activities – something that can be demanded from an employed salesforce. The fact that agents often resent what they see as bureaucracy or interference in their business is because they do not know how the information is used. If firms demand agents' reports they are at the very least obligated to show how they will be used for the principal's and agent's benefit.

Question 12.75 requires financial analysis of the cost of maintaining agents and calls for a compilation of all the cost items involved. This list will be longer than the items previously referred to in this introduction and must include the cost of recruitment. Only if this figure is added will it become apparent, first, whether an agency system is viable and, second, how important it is to retain agencies and not to allow the system to atrophy.

Question 12.80 is an interesting one. Too many firms treat direct orders from an agent's territory or large orders as 'house accounts'. This may seem justified in financial terms, but the wider picture ought to be scrutinized before a decision of this sort is taken. Sharing a commission with the agent could produce a far more rewarding result than the commission saved. The same rule applies to hybrid orders, that is, where an order is placed in one territory for delivery in another, for example with central group purchasing of builders' supplies going into branches.

It is always well to remember that agents are freelance operators who are indeed in business for themselves. It is the job of the principal to make sure that the interest of both parties is aligned. This way the agency system can be profitable and relatively trouble-free. The care and feeding of agents is as crucial a marketing function as any other covered in these checklists.

The table in Appendix 12A – although compiled many years ago – illustrates in a succinct but comprehensive manner the types of marketing function that agents could conduct.

(The first questions apply only to companies not using agents. Later questions relate to businesses considering their use or already employing them.)

12.1 What were the reasons in the past for not using agents?
12.2 Are they still valid?
12.3 What circumstances would have to exist before we would consider appointing agents?
12.4 Is there any territory/industry/application, etc, uncovered or covered inadequately by our salesforce?
12.5 Would agents be able to fill the gap?
12.6 How does the proposed agency rate against qualification factors?
- commission/remuneration/expenses required
- organization soundly financed

- premises neat and orderly, and located conveniently for important customers
- (if stock carried) warehouse and equipment suitable, convenient access for freight carriers
- covers the market completely
- covers the required territory completely
- has a sufficiently large salesforce
- sales personnel suitably qualified
- belongs to appropriate trade associations
- consistent pattern of sales growth
- good reputation with customers
- non-competitive product range (see Question 12.12)

12.7 What would the agents have to provide in the way of facilities/coverage/services, etc, before the question of adopting an agency system would be considered?
- field sales
- sales promotion
- shipping
- complaint resolution
- invoicing
- brochures in local language
- local advertising and direct mail
- warehousing
- sales training
- market research
- sampling
- account collection
- technical advice

(See List 14, 'The distributive system', Question 14.12.)

12.8 Are our requirements rigid?
12.9 If we had/have agents, who in our company was, is, or would be responsible for them?
12.10 What proportion of that person's time was, is, or will be devoted to managing the agency structure?
12.11 What other products/manufacturers represented would be regarded as compatible/incompatible with our requirements? (See also answer to Question 12.79.)
12.12 How do our products/services rate in terms of importance and interest to the agency? (This question must inevitably include the realistic (as opposed to the negotiating) views on commission levels and reimbursable expenses.)

12.13 Are there any firms we would not be willing to share an agent with? (See also answer to question 12.79.)
12.14 What is the function of the agency system (eg all sales, support function for own salesforce, expediency, special circumstances)? (See also Appendix 12A.)
12.15 Do we have formal contracts with agents and agencies?
12.16 Is the relationship to be a sole one for the territory or partially restricted?
12.17 Is the territory clearly defined and agreed?
12.18 Is it logical in geographical and political terms?
12.19 Is it within the capability of the agency and the salesforce to service?
12.20 Are products/services within the agreement clearly specified?

- full or part range; if part, which part?
- situation concerning right of representation for new products/services

12.21 Does the agreement clearly specify the functions to be carried out? (See Question 12.7 and Appendix 12A.)
12.22 Is the position on commission for existing and future house accounts and direct orders set out and agreed?
12.23 What dates will the contract run from and to?
12.24 What are the conditions of termination and, if appropriate, compensation for either side?
12.25 Is the contract too restrictive to provide ongoing motivation and support?
12.26 Is there an arbitration provision?
12.27 What law and language is the contract written under and in?
12.28 If it is to be a dual language contract, is the prevailing text agreed?
12.29 Is the contract assignable?
12.30 Do we have a system for checking agreement compliance?
12.31 What actions are we prepared to take in any agreement breach?
12.32 Are agents aware of the role they play in our sales organization?
12.33 Do the agencies appointed fulfil the function we have designated to them? (See also Appendix 12A.)
12.34 If not, how can they be reorientated?
12.35 What is the target number of agencies and their geographical locations?
12.36 What has stopped us filling any vacancies? Identify constraints.
12.37 Are the constraints immutable, or can we adjust policy to resolve the problem?
12.38 Have we a screening system for agency recruitment? (See also List 5, 'Export marketing', Appendix 5A, Stage 5.)
12.39 What is the history of agent acquisition and loss?
12.40 Does it show a common pattern of losses?
12.41 Is this pattern a reflection of recruitment, induction, support methods, commission earned, or business conditions?
12.42 Do we have a formal induction system for new agents?

12.43 What are its components?
12.44 What evidence do we have that it is effective?
12.45 Do agents have formal training?
12.46 If so, with what frequency?
12.47 What techniques do we use to recruit agents (advertising, asking customers, professional or trade associations etc.)? (See List 5, 'Export marketing', Appendix 5A, Stage 7.)
12.48 Which are the most effective?
12.49 Would agency retention and performance improve with any change from/to any exclusive arrangements?
12.50 Is agency performance monitored?
12.51 What are the performance standards?
12.52 How were they arrived at?
12.53 Do the agents understand and accept them?
12.54 What happens with constant underperformance?
12.55 Are agents visited regularly by senior management in the company? (This question appears in different forms in other lists. See List 5, 'Export marketing', Questions 5.42–5.44; List 9, 'The salesforce and its management', Question 9.6; List 14, 'The distributive system', Question 14.72; and List 19, 'Key customer marketing', Question 19.21.)
12.56 What is the purpose of such visits?
12.57 Do agents approve or dislike them?
12.58 When was the last time each agency visited us?
12.59 What is the purpose of such visits?
12.60 What are the arrangements on reimbursing costs of visits?
12.61 Are the number of visits to us regarded as satisfactory by us and by the agents?
12.62 What support (sales aids, stocks, credit, joint advertising, order referral, etc) do our agents expect? (To expand on these prompts see List 13, 'Non-personal promotion: methods and media', Question 13.3.)
12.63 Are agents consulted concerning their support requirements?
12.64 What evidence is there that such support is fully utilized?
12.65 Are agents involved in the development of advertising material, brochures, work manuals and other print intended for local use?
12.66 What facilities do our agents provide? (Compare answer with Question 12.6 and Appendix 12A.)
12.67 How far do we meet their expectations and do they meet ours in regard to support?
12.68 What actions can and should be taken to bring expectations more into line?
12.69 What constraints prevent us from taking these actions?
12.70 Are agents expected to report on their activities (sales visits, enquiries, quotations, advertising, etc)? (See List 9, 'The salesforce and its management', Questions 9.118–9.121.)

12.71 Are these reports regarded by agents as onerous?
12.72 Is it feasible to check authenticity of reports?
12.73 How do we utilize the information?
12.74 Can the agents see any evidence of the use of their reports? (See Introduction, and also questions relating to the information role of the salesperson in List 9, 'The salesforce and its management', Question 9.45 and Appendix 9A.)
12.75 What are the elements of cost of agency support (samples, stocks, visits, entertainment, training, communication, etc.)? (See Introduction; List 9, 'The salesforce and its management', Question 9.67, might be helpful in identifying the components for consideration.)
12.76 How much does each agency cost us to support? (See Introduction.)
12.77 How profitable is each agency?
12.78 Assess the degree of interest the agency has in our products. (See also answer to Question 12.12.)
12.79 Who are the agency's most important principals? (See answer to Question 12.13.)
12.80 How are orders received directly from the agents' territory treated in regard to agents' commission? (This and the following question will have been dealt with relative to the sales team in List 9, 'The salesforce and its management', Questions 9.114 and 9.115.)
12.81 If direct orders are 'house accounts', would giving the agent part of the whole commission increase loyalty and interest, or alternatively not giving it lead to loss of agency interest and thus lost sales opportunities?
12.82 How vulnerable are our agents to our competitors' reaching an agreement with them? (See also List 20, 'Competitive intelligence', Question 20.47.)
12.83 What steps can we take to protect ourselves?

Appendix 12A
Marketing functions that agents could conduct

Type of Independent Sales Organization	Market Research	Field Sales	Sales Promotion	Sales Training	Application Engineering	Service	Warehousing	Shipping	Invoicing	Typical Industries Served
1 Manufacturer's agent selling on commission in exclusive territory – no field warehousing requirements	Not generally, but may assist manufacturer on specific request	Only function	Promotes own company in Yellow Pages by direct mail, trade shows	No – factory trains their salespeople	No	No	No	No	No	Stamping and forging screw machine parts, industrial ovens, vibratory feeders
2 Same as (1) except field warehousing required	Same as above	Yes, plus appoint and supervise type (6) distributors	Same as above	May be responsible for training distributor salespeople	No	No	These three functions performed by distributors agent appoints			Pumps, motors, belts, shop tools and supplies, bearings, valves and fittings
3 Agents who perform additional marketing activities (not including stock). For product types see last column	See last column In mass merchandise field agent may recommend packaging, select outlets, recommend pricing, etc	Yes	Same as above	Same as (2)	See last column for complex machinery, instruments or control systems	As required for this type of product (installation, maintenance, parts) Stock maintenance, detailing	No	No	No	Computers, optical instruments, machine tools, textile machines Garden tools, housewares, auto supplies, aerosols, novelties
4 Agents who carry stock on consignment basis	Same as (1)	Yes	Same as above	Same as (1)	Limited	Spare parts and replacement as product lines require	Carries limited stock	Yes	No. Billing for consigned goods by manufacturer	Instruments and controls, filters, recorders, analysers
5 Agents who act as speciality distributors	Same as (1)	Yes	Same as above	Same as (1)	Limited	Same as above	Carries a limited number of product lines in stock (contrast with type (6) distributor who stocks many lines)	Yes	Yes	Speciality valves, pumps, flowmeters, pressure gauges, thermocouples, fluid power equipment
6 Distributors and supply houses who stock a wide selection of products	Not as a rule	Sells standard product in local warehouse, fast delivery, generally no speciality sales, – works with type (2) agents or factory salespeople	Promotes products in stock – often prepares own catalogue – cooperates with agent or manufacturer on special promotions	Distributor salespeople are trained by type (1) agents or factory salesforce	No	Spare parts, consumable products and routine service	Primary functions			Industrial: motors, belting, grinding wheels, shop supplies Consumer: hardware appliances, auto supplies

Note: All independent sales organizations will not fall completely within these categories. Some will overlap from one to another. A few may perform services not listed.

List 13

Non-personal promotion: methods and media

INTRODUCTION

With the development of the Internet and electronic marketing and trading, marketing communications has widened astronomically. Although the World Wide Web is only one communication channel, its use is now almost universal and has the potential to become one of the major and perhaps the most important of all marketing methods. It must be said that in many instances the jury is still out as to the effectiveness of the way it is used at the present time. But it would be an unwise organization that was not prepared to seriously consider its adoption, to monitor its development and at least to have a contingency plan which will safeguard the company against any changes that occur which could impact on their operations.

However much the shape of marketing and its methods and media change, nothing alters the fundamentals. The marketing communication process is perhaps appropriately expressed at this stage. At its simplest, the task of marketing is to move the prospective purchaser from a condition of ignorance about the firm and its products/services, reputation, and customers, to a state of knowledge, then to achieve an understanding of the message which the marketer is conveying, leading to a belief in its accuracy. Only when these stages have been accomplished will buying action take place. It is illustrated in the model shown in Figure 13.1.

As with all aspects of marketing, unless objectives are clearly stated and understood there is no way of evaluating the success or otherwise of the marketing activity – most particularly the tools involved in non-personal promotion. The examples of objectives

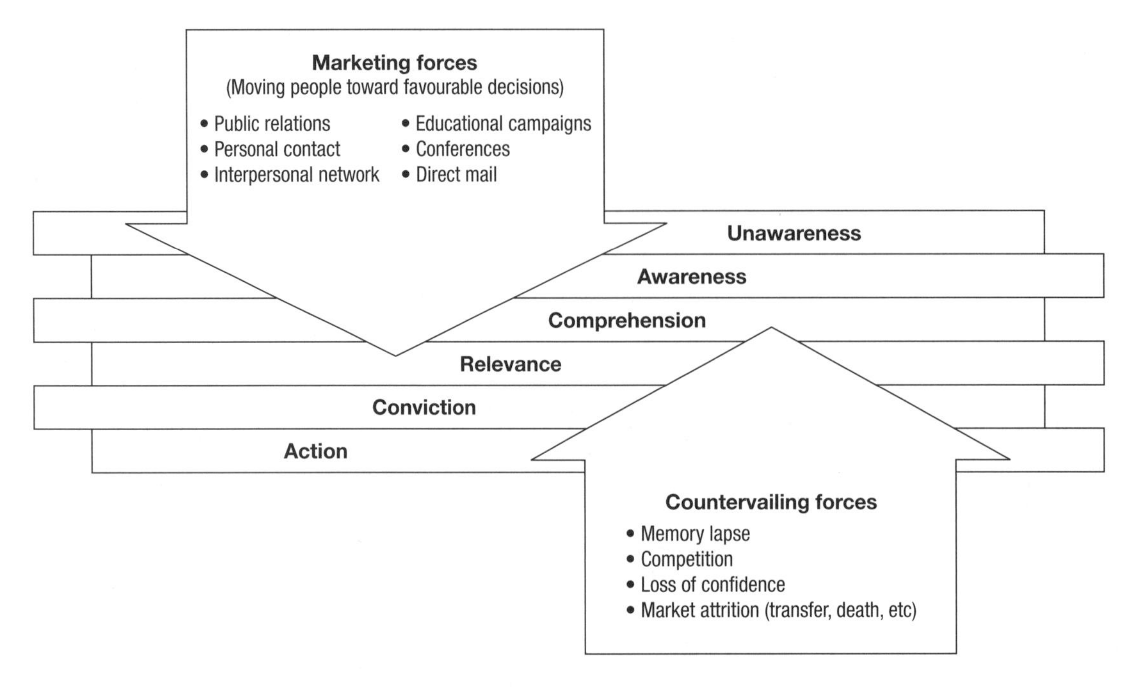

Figure 13.1 Marketing communication process

given in Question 13.1 are just that, examples. Each company will need to establish its own relevant goals.

A benchmark check on the level of awareness/unawareness can give an absolute answer which is of considerable value in measuring progress. As has already been stated in the Introduction to List 4, 'Company performance', it is an 'absolute' in marketing that if you are not known people cannot buy from you.

Question 13.3 lists some of the many tools and techniques available to the marketer; despite its length, it is not complete.[1] All auditors will be able to add other items if they choose. Because of the length of the compilation, it cuts across many questions in this and other lists. Not all of these are cross-referenced, since many of them will be obvious.

To achieve the purchasing actions set out in the sequence in List 15, 'The buying process', Introduction, and illustrated in Appendix 15A, the choice of marketing tools and media is bewilderingly wide, as can be seen, and, for business-to-business goods and services at least, largely unconsidered. Some valuable techniques are ignored in all types of marketing activity, however, because marketers consider many tools inappropriate for reasons ranging from cost to image. While there may be some validity in the reasons for rejection, all too rarely do firms reconsider the basis of their original objection and whether the conditions on which it was predicated have not changed, so as to permit the adoption of the promotional methods not attempted previously.

Another major reason for neglect is, of course, ignorance. Some of the promotional methods listed are unknown or improperly understood by marketers, most particularly by marketers of business-to-business goods and services and professional services. For example, many of them are unaware of the sponsored book, which is a highly effective, frequently self-liquidating method of promotion. Competitions are seen as strictly cornflake marketing, whereas they have been used with great success by both prestigious professional service companies and mundane office supplies firms.

Thus marketing auditors must resist the temptation to ignore any tools or methods that are not known or understood from their title. They should seek more information, which is easily obtainable from a large range of excellent books on marketing. Only with a knowledge of any particular technique is it possible to decide on its cost-effectiveness within the current or planned activities of the firm.

While Question 13.5 calls for details of appropriations, of equal importance is the method of arriving at the appropriation. This is a problem that exercises all marketing managers. Just how much resource should be devoted to any particular tool? All systems of arriving at marketing budgets are inadequate when the effect of individual promotional tools is not traceable. The marketer must select the least inadequate alternative, which stems from three requirements – least market waste, least risk to firm, best estimate of result. Appendix 13A explains some of the principal methods of setting budgets.

In List 4, 'Company performance', Introduction, it was suggested that the only accurate way of finding out which promotions (and, indeed, which salespeople and agents) are effective is to trace the source of enquiries and the conversion rate of business. Question 13.13 now puts a new element in the 'mix' in that a comparison is called for of expenditure between media, industry, applications, and other factors to see if there is a relationship between these and business obtained.[2] In other words, is time and talent being expended in, say, a specific industry campaign while business in fact emanates from another industry or from another promotion technique? If the promotional results are taken in a blanket form, a number of incorrect – dangerously and expensively incorrect – assumptions may be made. Just as much as marketing strategy calls for segmentation, so does promotion. Question 1.24 in List 1, 'Marketing strategy and planning', anticipated the point that has now been reached. An alignment between market segmentations and promotional activity is vital for success and economy.

Taking the analysis to its logical conclusion, answering Question 13.21 will display the strengths and weaknesses of all marketing activity. It will also reveal the quality of sales calls and provide information on the audience for different methods of non-personal promotion. Given that an objective is to obtain sales, raising a high number of unconverted enquiries would indicate a medium or method weaknesses. This is not, of course, to ignore any 'visibility' improvement and its long-term implications. In a sense this is the same situation as the low-selling product's marketing (as opposed to revenue) contribution, referred to in List 2, 'Product/service range', Introduction.

The suggestion that the most practical way of assessing marketing effectiveness is to attempt to relate enquiries and ultimately orders to any given marketing activity is nevertheless a very simplistic approach in that the various marketing methods interface, sometimes inextricably; not all customers can recall with accuracy their original sources of information, and competitors' marketing activities can impact favourably and unfavourably on the firm's marketing result. It may be crude but some form of evaluation is not only desirable, but necessary.

Question 13.22 is perhaps the most difficult, but also one of the most critical, in the entire checklist. Without some guidelines as to what in the marketing mix is working, there is no point in attempting to guide and control the marketing methods.

Measuring or evaluating the extent to which the message is understood is difficult and essentially qualitative, as indeed is the study of 'conviction'. Nevertheless, for all the problems of evaluation of non-personal selling methods, the attempt should be made on an ongoing basis. Questions 13.24–13.27 examine these points.

Questions 13.47 and 13.48 dealing with the use of exhibitions identify what for many firms can be a source of considerable wastage. The auditor is strongly recommended to study checklists that are specific to evaluating exhibitions, in terms of whether to exhibit, post-exhibition results analysis, and visiting exhibitions.[3]

Question 13.50 calls for salesforce views of the advertising and other promotional expenditure. Sales personnel do tend to regard all non-personal selling promotion as substantially wasteful and frequently irrelevant. Nothing could be further from the truth. Media advertising, to take just one tool, is complementary to personal selling but with a different function. If the salesforce cannot see how this assists them in their task, then sales management has failed miserably with its communications and with training. It is worth pausing to consider that differences between selling and advertising are not just semantic.

Features of selling	**Features of advertising**	
	Operational	*General*
• Flexibility: the message can be tailored precisely to the prospect's needs • Comprehensiveness: the most complex sales messages can be communicated and explained • Attention-getting: personal selling obtains and maintains a high level of attention	• Impersonal • Easily accessible • General interest only • One-way communication • Persuasive	• Creates awareness • Gives knowledge • Produces some level of attitude change or formation

The same problem does not arise with intermediaries (Question 13.52) who like to see a heavy volume of advertising addressed to their customers (rather than to themselves), because they appreciate the role a promotion can play in making it easier for them to sell. If this acceptance can be achieved among intermediaries, it must be asked why salesforces have been so slow to view non-personal selling as a sales aid. This is an area in which marketing management can achieve a great deal to obtain better mileage from promotional expenditure. It has been said with considerable truth that marketing's greatest failure is its inability to sell marketing to the salesforce. Here is an area where synergy can be introduced to everyone's benefit.

Many business people have become somewhat cynical about directories, since they have been the subject of the most persistent of confidence tricks over the years. Any business person who falls into this trap, which is so easy to avoid, deserves sympathy and nothing else. However, in the attempt to avoid fake directories, many valuable genuine ones can be omitted. Question 13.56 implies a full review periodically of all relevant directories, yearbooks and buyers' guides, and the decision on entry should be taken for each new edition, not automatically. A study of 500 businesses' sources of information for products and services revealed the classified telephone directories as the single most important medium. They are cost-effective, and all research shows they are heavily consulted, particularly by small companies.

Question 13.62, brief as it is, has valuable implications for most companies and usually reveals opportunities unexploited. Most guarantees are historical rather than realistic, as will be shown by a simple analysis of the cost of fulfilling guarantee claims (such as will be sought in List 28, 'Product/service financial information'). The answer to Question 28.52 will very clearly indicate how far a guarantee can be extended without the situation leading to losses.

A manufacturer of garment finishing equipment gave the conventional 12-month guarantee on the equipment. Guarantee claims in the first 36 months were negligible and would in any event have been met without a guarantee. He was thus able to offer a five-year guarantee at a budget cost which previously applied to 12 months and consequently had a very considerable 'plus' to promote. A long and unequivocal guarantee is a public affirmation of faith in the product, and as such it is a valuable marketing tool usually grossly neglected. 'Lifetime' guarantees on blank videotapes is an example of the use of guarantees as a powerful marketing tool.

Question 13.63 on direct response refers to database marketing. Database relationship marketing has the ability to identify and communicate more precisely with different market segments and incorporate the response back into the database. Information is gathered from many sources, much of which is already in most companies. The ability to store and analyse this was very limited until computer systems became ubiquitous by being cheaper and user friendly. Once the response information becomes part of the file it can be used for segmentation purposes in creating the next direct marketing programme. The advances in the data processing industry have made the storing of large amounts of information about prospects and customers much more affordable. The real benefit is in the analysis of the data and their application to a particular marketing problem.

This list ends with important questions concerning the Internet and electronic trading. Question 13.78 once again forces the consideration of objectives. It must be asked what the Web site is expected to achieve both in relation to the overall marketing strategy and at a tactical level. The question contains some eight specimen objectives to consider but, of course, each organization will need to add to and adjust those which are specific to their needs and markets. This question, among other issues, emphasizes the importance of having knowledge of customer preferences, needs and wants. It links closely to List 18, 'User Industry'.

Questions 13.84–13.86 seek to draw attention to the fact, often overlooked, that not everyone and every market has up-to-date computer facilities nor, despite its dominance, is English always the most appropriate language to communicate in. These are both issues that require attention.

It is obviously of critical importance that once a Web site is developed it should be easily accessible. However, the main checklist is not perhaps the most appropriate place for dealing with this issue. Appendix 13B poses some essential issues to be considered.

Questions 13.77 to the end and Appendix 13B have been compiled by Dr Carol O'Connor, based on her outstanding practical expertise in this area.

Again it is emphasized that the whole of this checklist should be viewed against what the objectives, the various methods, media, and expenditures of time and money are expected to achieve. Within an organization it is commonplace for a wide range of views to exist as to what a marketing campaign or a marketing tool is supposed to accomplish. A media advertising campaign may well be seen by the chief executive as having as its purpose greater visibility for the company; the sales manager expects it to help in reducing inventory; the works manager seeks a better spread of demand over machine and labour capacity; the personnel director hopes it will attract the best graduates to the firm. If it succeeds in only one of these it will be said to have failed in the others. If this type of disappointment and resultant criticism are to be avoided, objectives must always be specific and practical and clearly understood by all who are involved.

13.1 Have we clearly defined, understood and agreed promotional objectives? For example, to increase the proportion of the target audience which associates the product with us. (The answer should be aligned with those given for Questions 13.7, 13.34, 13.78 and compared with List 1, 'Marketing strategy and planning', Question 1.8. It will also be needed for List 24, 'Images and perceptions', Questions 24.33 and 24.34; and List 26, 'Non-differentiated products and commodities', Question 26.31.)

13.2 Do we have all the necessary information to make effective decisions in the choice of non-personal promotional tools? (See List 6, 'Marketing information: systems and use'.)

13.3 Which of the following non-personal methods have been/are being used, or have been considered and rejected?

	Used	**Used in the past**	**Considered and rejected**	**Not considered**
Affinity marketing				
Audio-visual				
Backing services				
Brochures and catalogues (including catalogue distribution and information services)				
Client training				
Company visits				
Competitions				
Cooperative promotion				
Couponing				
Database marketing				
Demonstrations and reference plant				
Design				
Directories/yearbooks				
Direct response (including E-mail)				
Distribution				
Educational campaigns				
Entertaining				
Exhibitions				
Financial incentives and aids				
Franchise dealings				
Free, self-liquidating and premium offers				
Full-range buying schemes				
Gifts				
Guarantee manipulation				
Incentive schemes				
Interactive marketing				
Interpersonal network (Referrals)				
Lead time				
Loan equipment				
Lotteries				

continued overleaf

13.3 *continued*

	Used	Used in the past	Considered and rejected	Not considered
Loyalty schemes				
Marketing research				
Media advertising (including Web sites and radio/TV)				
Merchandising techniques				
Newsletters				
Off-premises displays				
Posters				
Pricing strategies				
Product/packaging				
Public/press relations				
Range strategies				
Reciprocal trading				
Reuse container premiums				
Sampling				
Secondments				
Signage				
Sponsorships (events, charities, books, academic)				
Tele-sales				
Trade-in allowances				
Vehicle livery				

(This tabulation is referred to in many sections and its use is sufficiently obvious not to cross-reference it to each individual mention.)

13.4 What methods are adopted for setting budgets? (See Introduction and Appendix 13A for summary of methods, advantages and disadvantages.)

13.5 Give current appropriation (state period) for each tool used. (The answer to this question will be called for again in more detail in List 28, 'Product/service financial information', Questions 28.47–28.50.)

13.6 In what way and why does it vary from previous year(s)?

13.7 Are the targets and objectives qualitative and quantitative for each of the methods used, clearly set out, and known within the company? (See List 24, 'Images and perceptions', Questions 24.1 and 24.30.)

13.8 Relate the decision-making unit (DMU) target for each method used and justify in terms of effectiveness and numbers. (See List 15, 'The buying process', Questions 15.4–15.8; and List 16, 'Analysing lost business', Question 16.7.)

13.9 Are the reasons for discontinuing any previously used tools still valid?

13.10 What criteria were used in deciding to reject any particular marketing method not previously tried?
13.11 Are the criteria still valid?
13.12 What knowledge do we have of methods not used and not considered? (See Introduction.)
13.13 What is the marketing expenditure broken down by?

	Year	Amount
Method		
Season		
Geographical area		
Industry		
Application		
Product/service		

(Relate answers to those given in List 1, 'Marketing strategy and planning', Question 1.24, concerning segment priorities, and Introduction to List 4, 'Company performance'; the question will receive attention again in List 28, 'Product/service financial information', Questions 28.50 and 28.51.)

13.14 How does this compare with previous years?
13.15 What is the reason for any variation?
13.16 How does the expenditure compare with sources of business obtained using the same breakdowns? (This information will be called for again in List 28, 'Product/service financial information', Question 28.51.)
13.17 Does it show an imbalance?
13.18 Could this be rectified by an adjustment in the appropriation or the appropriation allocation?
13.19 How does the expenditure relate to the quality rather than the volume of business obtained?
13.20 What is the non-profit value of business obtained? (See List 19, 'Key customer marketing', Question 19.2, for a list of beyond profit factors.)
13.21 What is the cost of marketing (other than personal selling)?

- per enquiry
- per quotation
- per order
- by media
- by method

(See Introduction; this information will also be required to answer List 28, 'Product/service financial information', Question 28.51.)

13.22 Relate value of enquiries/orders received to any traceable medium or method. (Cross-relate answer to Questions 13.3 and 13.5; List 4, 'Company performance', Question 4.24; and List 28, 'Product/service financial information', Questions 28.50 and 28.51.)
13.23 What methods of evaluation of effectiveness of total marketing and of individual tools are used? (This information is referred to again in List 28, 'Product/service financial information', Question 28.51.)
13.24 Do we know the past and current level of 'visibility'? (See Introduction and also Introduction to List 4, 'Company performance'.)
13.25 Can we evaluate to what extent the messages we convey are understood?
13.26 Can we evaluate the level of conviction that our message carries?
13.27 How often is an evaluation of effectiveness made?
13.28 How does the firm's marketing history and performance compare with competitors? (See List 20, 'Competitive intelligence', Question 20.50 and Appendix 20A.)
13.29 Are any differences justified by comparative performances?
13.30 What are the principal media used by competitors?
13.31 What is the justification for these?
13.32 Are the facts on which the justification was based still valid (changes in product/services, markets, economy, publication circulation in numbers, audience and quality of readership, growth of competitive media)?
13.33 What is the copy strategy used for the firm's products/services during the last five years (ie to obtain visibility, unaided recall, image development, sell products/services, etc)? (See Introduction and Figure 13.1; align answer with those given for Question 13.1 and List 2, 'Product/service range', Questions 2.27 and 2.28.)
13.34 What are the major changes and causes of change in copy strategy that have occurred in the last five years?
13.35 To what type of advertising and media are users and potential users most exposed? (See List 18, 'User industries', Questions 18.65 and 18.66.)
13.36 How does this analysis compare with our media schedule?
13.37 When was advertising policy, expenditure, schedules and strategy last reviewed?
13.38 Does advertising and other promotional material emphasize benefits and features? (See Introduction to List 2, 'Product/service range', Questions 2.27 and 2.28; and List 4, 'Company performance', Question 4.2.)
13.39 Does our promotion identify any unique selling proposition or differentiated advantage? (See Introduction to List 2, 'Product/service range', and Question 2.42.)
13.40 Do we pre-test advertisements?
13.41 Do we act on the results?
13.42 Do we conduct post-campaign research?
13.43 Do we carry out forward advertising planning, taking into account the post-test results?

13.44 Do competitors manage their own advertising or use agencies? (Align answer to that given in response to Question 13.53. It will also be needed for List 20, 'Competitive intelligence', Question 20.32, and has to be related to the answer to List 24, 'Images and perceptions', Question 24.35.)
13.45 How does this differ from our policy and how is it justified?
13.46 What is the audience (in numbers) for each specific method of promotion?
13.47 Which exhibitions have we and our competitors shown at in the last year? (See Introduction concerning more detailed exhibition checklists.)
13.48 Have we any analysis of total attendance, stand visits, enquiries received, business obtained?
13.49 Should we continue to show at all/any exhibition(s)?
13.50 What is the salesforce view on the effectiveness of advertising and other promotion methods? (See Introduction.)
13.51 Would they make any changes, and if so, in what way?
13.52 What are intermediaries' views on advertising and other promotional effectiveness? (See Introduction.)
13.53 Which of the methods listed and used in Question 13.3 have been undertaken by ourselves, agencies, consultants or other specialists? (This question will have been partly answered in 13.44. The answer should be compared to that given for List 20, 'Competitive intelligence', Question 20.32 and Appendix 13A.)
13.54 How successful were our efforts as compared with outside marketing services companies and contractors?
13.55 Does the result of this analysis call for a review of policy in relation to the use of external marketing service companies and contractors?
13.56 Which directories, yearbooks and buyers' guides do we appear in? Is the list complete/efficient? What are their 'shelf' lives? (See Introduction.)
13.57 Is our policy on the use of brands valid? (This question will occur again in List 14, 'The distributive system', Question 14.56.)
13.58 Does our brand, as compared with the company's name, have 'visibility' and a good image? (The answer should be compared with those given for Question 13.24; List 4, 'Company performance', Question 4.37; and later List 24, 'Images and perceptions', Questions 24.14 and 24.34.)
13.59 Would we benefit by increasing/decreasing brand promotion?
13.60 How long and how comprehensive are our guarantees? (This question cross-links with a number of others which will provide corroborating answers. Notably List 6, 'Marketing information: systems and use', Questions 6.44–6.46; List 23, 'Pricing', Questions 23.1 and 23.2 on costs; List 26, 'Non-differentiated products and commodities', Questions 26.20–26.24; and the analyses required for List 28, 'Product/service financial information', Questions 28.41 and 28.52.)

13.61 How do our guarantees compare with those of our competitors and general industry practice? (See List 20, 'Competitive intelligence', Question 20.51.)
13.62 What would it cost us to extend our guarantees in coverage and in time by, say, three months? six months? nine months? one year? (See List 28, 'Product/service financial information', Questions 28.41 and 28.52.)
13.63 Have we considered database relationship marketing? (See Introduction.)
13.64 Is (should) direct mailing (be) part of the marketing mix?
13.65 What is the origin of our mailing list?
13.66 Is the mailing list valid and up to date?
13.67 What is the method and frequency of checking and updating?
13.68 What is the frequency of use?
13.69 (for bought-in lists) Is a random selection available for testing?
13.70 Is post-code selection available?
13.71 Are bulk-mailing rebates available?
13.72 Is telephone selling appropriate for our product/service?
13.73 What contribution would telephone selling make to marketing?
- release sales team time
- increase sales
- improve frequency of customer contact
- eliminate out-of-stock situations at customer level
- enhance communication with customers on special offers, stocks, new products/services, prices etc
- open new accounts
- revive lapsed accounts
- achieve better use of merchandising material

13.74 Are staff trained for telephone selling?
13.75 What means do we have for establishing if telephone selling is approved or resented by customers?
13.76 Does the sales office proactively sell or is their role confined to order taking? (See List 9, 'The salesforce and its management', Question 9.128.)
13.77 Have we considered/are we using a Web site? What were the reasons for retention/acceptance and are they still valid? (This question should be answered in conjunction with Appendix 13B concerning search engine selection and the use of *meta tags*.)
13.78 Have we established clear objectives in terms of what results we expect from the site? (See also Question 13.1, but among objectives to be considered are):
- sell our products/services to new and existing customers
- provide technical information
- learn more about our customers' preferences by asking for their feedback (see Introduction to this section)

- build alliances with companies selling related products and services
- supply added value information
- enhance image with a well designed and maintained site
- provide secure links with our suppliers
- promote the products/services differential advantages

(There will be links between this answer and List 18, 'User industries', Questions 18.18–18.22 but particularly Questions 18.37 and 18.63.)

13.79 Do our competitors already have a Web site?
13.80 How frequently do we visit these and do we think they are effective marketing tools? For example, would we do business with this site if we were potential customers?
13.81 If the intention is to sell goods or services through the site, have we established a way to accept payment so that customers can clearly see that their transactions and credit details are kept 'secure' and confidential?
13.82 What evaluations have been made of the risks of selling to anonymous Internet contacts?
13.83 What indications do we have that our customers are ready/willing or able to use the Internet?
13.84 Do all of our market segments or export destinations have access to the Internet?
13.85 Can we provide more than one version of our site to accommodate those with less sophisticated equipment?
13.86 Into what languages should we translate our site?
13.87 What kind of investment will be involved in the costs of maintaining the site content, its technical aspects, ongoing promotion, order fulfilment?
13.88 Can our professional or trade bodies, or local advice bureaux, provide information on the costs of developing a Web site? (This question arises again in List 22, 'Industry contacts', Question 22.5.)
13.89 Will our compliance procedures ensure that we do not breach any data protection legislation?
13.90 What criteria will we use to determine if our site is a success?
13.91 How frequently will we review whether our Internet presence contributes to our overall marketing strategy?

Appendix 13A
Setting marketing budgets

Principal methods

Method	Advantages	Disadvantages
Percentage of previous year's turnover	Always affordable so long as earnings are constant	No provision for growth or exploiting opportunities No allowance for inflation of marketing costs No flexibility if competition increases marketing effort Assumes inertia in market
Percentage of expected sales	Allows for growth Encourages stability in marketing	Sales appear to cause marketing Can lead to over- or under-spending in growth or declining markets Treats marketing as a constant factor irrespective of product position on life cycle
Percentage of profit excess	Extra profits invested in marketing offset against tax, therefore subsidized	Profits appear to cause marketing Plan will be unstable and can vary widely from year to year Risk of marketing appropriations being cut can cause anticipatory spending
Matching competition	Stabilizes marketing wars Creates a sensitivity to competitive situations	Competition appears to cause marketing Comparable expenditures difficult to estimate Expenditure level and quality of marketing not correlated Time lag to respond
Objective and task method	Forces detailed consideration of marketing objectives	Problems in attributing results Difficulty in establishing weight and form of marketing to reach objective
Equivalency	Historic performance gives reasonable and realistic guide to input levels and cost	Changes in personnel's performance and in markets may make historic situation invalid

Appendix 13B
Creating visibility through search engines[4]

1. Is there an understanding that *meta tags* are key words used to describe the business and that they are hidden from general view within the heading section of the Web site?
2. Have we identified a maximum of 30 key words to be included as *meta tags* in this section?
3. Have we considered how our company name could be misspelt by potential customers and so included these misspellings as key words?
4. Have we written a 20-word description of our business, including our company name? (It is critical that this short description, also hidden in the site's heading section as a *meta description*, is included.)
5. If we already have a Web site, do we check on our current *meta tag* and *meta description* sections (go to 'view' on the menu bar, then click on 'source' when the pop-up menu appears)?
6. Have we identified which search engines we want to recognize our site and are we aware that each of the major search engines categorizes sites differently? (The information about the way they categorize is readily available either through Web page developers or by searching for this information on Web page development sites. Using a customer perspective, have we asked any of these engines to find sites offering the kinds of products/services we sell?)
7. Have we/can we establish how each search engine evaluates a site to determine if it matches the request from a searcher for information?
8. Have we analysed the Top 20 results to see if our competitors are included and also what other kinds of sites have come up?
9. Should we revise our *meta tags* and *meta description* to encourage our inclusion?
10. Have we considered/should we consider adding links from our site to others offering complementary or related products and services, such as financial services to professional and industry groups? (Some leading search engines evaluate sites in terms of how many links they have to related sites so that they include sites in the Top 20 which have the greatest number of links.)
11. Can we analyse each Top 10 to establish if our competitors are included and to identify other kinds of sites?
12. How will we bring our site to the attention of the search engines? (Sites are dropped from the search engine's listings on a regular basis so that there is need to make ongoing contact to maintain the listing.)
13. Should we consider using one of the Internet-based services which specialize in helping companies stay listed with search engines?

Notes

1 There is no shortage of excellent books and articles dealing with the different tools which the auditor should consult if he or she is unsure of the technique or application. For example, 'affinity marketing', the first item, is not well known but is very thoroughly explained in Gordon Wills (1992) Journey to Marketing Clubland, *Marketing Intelligence and Planning*, **10** (2), MCB University Press, Bradford.

2 The conversion ratios will have been provided by the auditor's answers to List 4, 'Company performance', Questions 4.24 and 4.25; and this same analysis relative to one marketing tool – personal selling – will have been given in List 9, 'The salesforce and its management', Questions 9.49–9.51.

3 Alfred Alles (1988) *Exhibitions: Key to Effective Marketing*, Cassell, London, is quite the best book on the topic.

4 Checklist compiled by Dr Carol O'Conner

List 14

The distributive system

INTRODUCTION

Attitudes towards the introduction and use of intermediaries between suppliers and their ultimate customers tend to be cyclical, swinging from one extreme of direct supply to layering the distributive system. While it is obvious that changed conditions will require an adjustment in policies, both a sudden and a frequent switch will result in the worst of both worlds. Any change from direct to indirect supply requires careful consideration of the issues involved and judgement as to the outcome.

The term 'distributor' is used generically in the checklist that follows and includes all types of intermediaries who buy and sell in their own right as opposed to agents operating on a commission basis. Thus the nomenclatures 'stockist', 'wholesaler', 'dealer', 'merchant', 'importer', 'broker', etc, are all embraced by the term 'distributor'.

The decision to trade direct or through resellers is a very basic one, and the correct decision must influence the performance of the company favourably. Distributors have been referred to as 'an off-balance sheet resource', which accurately sums up their value if they are correctly incorporated into the marketing structure. Mixed systems do work, although there is plenty of evidence of an antipathy by distributors towards suppliers who compete directly with them, and naturally there is reluctance to support such suppliers. Questions 14.1 and 14.3 are concerned with the basic decision.

The problem of distributors, as with agents, has been summed up as being that 'they carry so many lines they are not interested in any of them'. While, like most exaggerations, it contains some truth, rectification of such a situation is not beyond the skills of any supplier who understands the interests and problems of distributors. It is up to suppliers to obtain and retain distributor loyalty and interest, and this is not only a question of margins.

Marketing auditors may find that many of the questions in List 5, 'Export marketing', relating to representation, can also be used in the profiling of distributors, their selection and monitoring, in so far as there is any choice in the use of distributors and the decision is not pre-empted by lack of choice.

In a changing world, particularly with the rapid adoption of electronic trading, the role of the distributor in most trades is also changing. Where distributors are used there is an international trend, as already noted, for the most efficient suppliers to develop exclusive arrangements with the most efficient distributors, leaving the less successful suppliers with the second-line distributors – a toxic combination. All suppliers need to look with increasing frequency at the distributive methods and the logistics they use and be ready and able to make changes when the moment occurs. Indeed, distributors, or lack of them, may be a major vulnerability of many suppliers.

The strategic issues for consideration are whether to increase distributor density and/or distributor volume. Would fewer distributors increase the sales of individual outlets and therefore the interest of those who remain? Would a wider distribution generate more sales than fewer larger intermediaries? Figure 14.1 illustrates the options and Questions 14.4 and 14.5 are concerned with the strategic dimensions illustrated in the figure.

It is not of course necessary to view the distributive system as a single-level structure. It is perfectly possible, and indeed often sensible, to develop a tiered system of, for example,

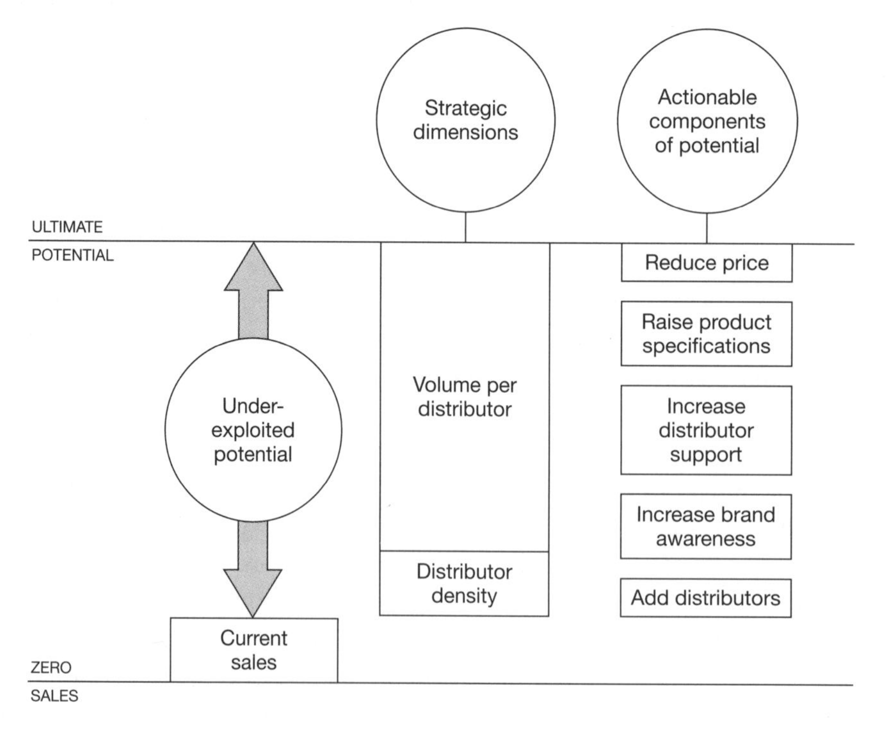

Figure 14.1 Market potential and its components

preferential distributors. Those selected on a preferential basis receive additional support in a number of ways and give an incentive to non-preferential distributors to develop their own operations to reach preferential status. A multi-tiered system has long been used in the automotive industry. A preferred distributor takes on the same importance as a key customer. Thus the auditor may well find much of the interrogation in List 19, 'Key customer marketing', also relevant.

Another form of preferential or exclusive trading is of course through franchise, licence or solus operations, which are all well worth considering. Franchising and solus trading are now very big business indeed, but for a franchise or solus deal to operate successfully, the supplier must have something very specific to offer if the franchisee or solus trader is to accept the constraints imposed by each system. To obtain some idea of the mutual commitments of franchiser and franchisee, it is only necessary to look at successful consumer goods and service operations. The subject is too vast, and its ramifications too complex, to be encompassed in this checklist, but market auditors are recommended to investigate the advantages of the systems if they themselves meet the criteria for the franchiser, and the prospective franchisees or solus traders exist or can be created. Question 14.21 seeks an examination of the gains and losses of a franchise or other form of exclusive trading system.

Needless to say, distributors' major interest will be the margins they can achieve, but they are not insensitive to the costs that will be involved in handling, installing, servicing or exchanging products. Ideally, the distributor would like a non-return valve in the distributive pipeline, so that when a product is sold all further responsibility ends. This of course cannot be, but clearly the distributors' loyalty and interest will be with the suppliers whose products cause the least problems and aggravation, whatever the source of these may be.

There is a dichotomy in distributors' thinking on price. While a high price with usually the same percentage margin means a higher return on the product, it does become more difficult to sell. A lower price with higher aggregate sales may give a better result in total. Either possibility can be promoted effectively, but suppliers' practice is often to impose a price without discussion or consideration of the distributors' needs and requirements.

Questions 14.42–14.49 on distributor stocks deal with a possible conflict between providing a service to the ultimate buyer by ensuring no out-of-stock situation occurs and discouraging the distributor from holding stocks either through stringent credit policies or the use of online terminals to show stock levels at the supplier's premises. If distributors are to hold what is considered a 'safe' stock level then other policies have to be adjusted to encourage this.

Just as agencies cost the company money to maintain, so do distributors. The queries posed in Questions 14.58–14.61 seek to identify when it is more profitable not to sell through distributors than it is to incorporate them in the marketing system. At the same time, it is always important not to allow a high sales potential distributor to be dropped because of perhaps current depressed sales. It is wrong to adopt a mechanistic approach, and every underperforming distributor needs to be looked at as an individual case before any decision is taken.

Sales support and other promotional material, referred to in Question 14.69, can be as important to the distributor as it is to the sales personnel, but frequently this is not appreciated. As with sales personnel, distributors have to be educated and motivated to use aids, often expensively produced. The bulk of sales aids, most particularly point-of-sale display items, are often not utilized, used incorrectly, or adopted and discarded too quickly, long before the end of their useful life. There should be a constant check of sales aid requirements and use.

Finally, there is a generally held view that services cannot be distributed since they cannot be stocked. This is a piece of pure academic nonsense designed to fit the conventional theory that services are always totally intangible, that they are consumed at the moment of production, and that the buyer of services must take part in their production. (See List 27, 'Service businesses'.) Services can indeed be distributed. Nothing could better illustrate this than the distributive system for financial services shown in Figure 14.2. Examples of other services that lean heavily on a distributive system are contract cleaning, pest control, copy shops, tyre and exhaust replacement, and security.

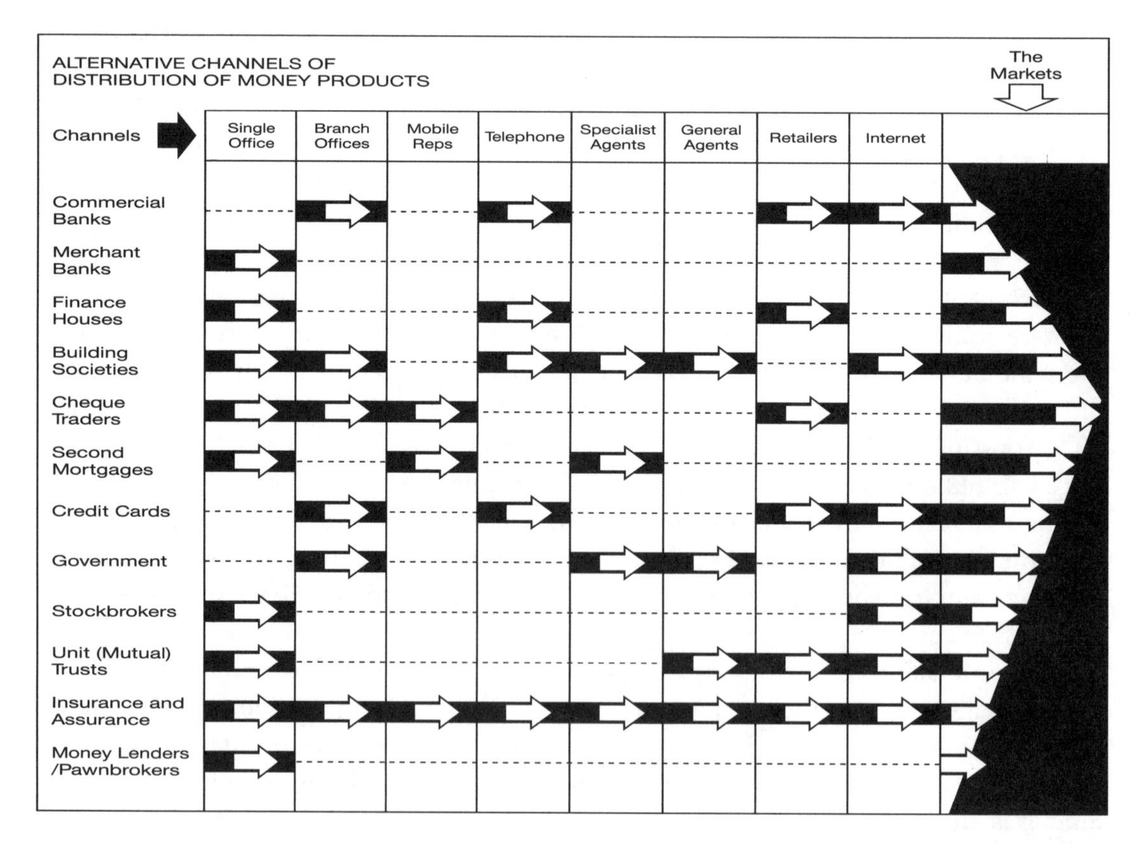

Figure 14.2 Alternative channels of distribution for money products (This diagram has been updated from Edwin Ornstein's (1972) *The Marketing of Money*, Gower, Aldershot. Although now a very old book, it remains a seminal work on the topic.)

14.1 Is the basis upon which the present distribution structure was devised, logical and still valid in terms of our corporate objectives?

14.2 What criteria are/were applied to decide whether distributors shall be used?

14.3 Are the criteria still valid?

14.4 If distributors are used, how many, when, where, and what volume of business is transacted through them? (This question was asked previously in List 4, 'Company performance', Question 4.30; but see Figure 14.1 also.)

14.5 Can we develop logistical alliances? (This topic is raised again in List 26, 'Non-differentiated products and commodities', Question 26.27.)

14.6 What should the terms of such alliances be?

14.7 Who will be responsible for devising, introducing and monitoring the alliance policy?

14.8 What types of distributors are used?

14.9 Are intermediaries selected, or are our recruitment efforts directed to all available outlets?

14.10 If selectivity is applied, what are the criteria for selection of intermediaries?

14.11 Would a multi-tiered system of preferential distributors improve sales? (See Introduction.)

14.12 What is the basis for selection or preferential treatment, eg turnover, stock levels held, quality of service, etc? (See Introduction and also the criteria for selecting agents in List 12, 'The agency system', Questions 12.6 and 12.7.)

14.13 What evidence is there that conditions are met?

14.14 Would sales prospects be improved by adopting/abandoning/liberalizing a selectivity policy?

14.15 Could we significantly increase our distribution coverage by changes in appointment conditions?

14.16 What is the policy on increasing/decreasing the type and use of distributors both domestically and internationally? (See Introduction and Figure 14.2 and compare answer to Question 14.73.)

14.17 What are/were the reasons for the policy?

14.18 Approximately how many distributors of the product are there in the market as a whole supplying our types of products/services?

14.19 What percentage of these do we supply and what limits the appointment of more distributors?

14.20 What percentage of the total market is supplied by distributors?

14.21 Would there be benefits in operating a franchise or solus arrangement? (See Introduction.)

14.22 If so, what would they be? Are they sufficient to warrant setting up franchise or solus distributors?

14.23 What benefits would we be able to offer a franchiser?

- know-how
- promotion of product/service

- local promotion of franchise
- financial assistance
- administrative procedures
- financial controls
- preferential purchasing deals
- training
- support stocks
- credit
- recruitment aid
- geographical exclusivity
- identification with franchise subject

14.24 What do we expect from a franchiser?

- no competitive trading
- agreed stock holding level
- right to purchase back franchise
- clear identification with us
- information on performance
- staffing – quality and numbers
- purchase of supplies from designated source
- minimum performance standards (sales, servicing)
- servicing
- maintenance of premises and/or equipment to agreed standards
- financial commitments
- display and merchandising
- consistent quality of customer
- service of agreed levels
- selling prices as set
- agreed sourcing of materials
- installation
- retro-fit
- commissioning

14.25 Do we possess the skills and resources to market a franchise system?

14.26 What other types of products/services do our distributors sell: directly competitive, indirectly competitive, non-competitive?

14.27 How do products/services of our type rate in terms of importance and interest to distributors?

14.28 Within this group, how do our own products/services rate in terms of importance and interest to the distributor?

14.29 What would make them more interesting to distributors? (Compare answer with Question 14.41.)

14.30 What policies could we adopt that would increase distributor interest and activity in and with our products/services?
14.31 What are our distributor sales by type of distributor, size of distributor, geographical location, industrial concentration, etc? (See List 4, 'Company performance', Question 4.30.)
14.32 How does this compare with our competitors? (List 20, 'Competitive intelligence', Question 20.41, will generate the same answer, and see Appendix 20A.)
14.33 Is any difference advantageous/disadvantageous to us?
14.34 Which competitors make the most and least use of distributors for the products under review? (See List 20, 'Competitive intelligence', Appendix A.)
14.35 How do we account for their policies?
14.36 How and why do they differ from our policy?
14.37 (if also selling direct) Do salespeople participate in distributor sales and do they service distributors?
14.38 Are sales personnel rewarded for distributor business whether obtained by them or received direct?
14.39 If not, would distributor sales and service be improved by changing salesforce remuneration to incorporate distributor sales?
14.40 How are direct sales in distributors' territory handled? (Compare with List 9, 'The salesforce and its management', Questions 9.26 and 9.114–9.115.)
14.41 Would a change of policy on direct sales improve/decrease distributor sales and interest? (Compare answers with Questions 14.29–14.30.)
14.42 What stocks are normally held by distributors? (See also answer in List 20, 'Competitive intelligence', Question 20.15.)
14.43 Are there seasonal variations?
14.44 What factors would induce distributors to even out stock holding?
14.45 What replenishment lead time is required by distributors? (Compare with the answer to List 4, 'Company performance', Question 4.23.)
14.46 How does this compare with direct account requirements? (See List 4, 'Company performance', Question 4.23.)
14.47 Have we considered a rack-jobbing tactic, and would it be acceptable to distributors?
14.48 What is the history of out-of-stock situations?
14.49 How far are 'out-of-stocks' our fault and how far the distributor's fault? (See answer to List 4, 'Company performance', Question 4.23.)
14.50 What is the size of discounts offered to distributors by the company and competitors? (In relation to this and the next three questions, see also List 20, 'Competitive intelligence', Questions 20.67 and 20.71–20.73; and List 23, 'Pricing', Question 23.14.)
14.51 What other financial and non-financial incentives do we and our competitors provide? (See List 20, 'Competitive intelligence', Question 20.42.)

14.52 How do credit terms compare with competitors?

14.53 How stringent are we on punctuality in payment? (See also List 20, 'Competitive intelligence', Introduction, and answer to Question 20.69.)

14.54 What types of customer/industry do distributors supply (eg across all industries, only to small companies)? (The answer to this question should align with List 18, 'User industries', Question 18.24.)

14.55 Are we satisfied with their customer spread?

14.56 Do distributors influence make/brand bought by customers?

14.57 Do they compete for customers with us? If so, to what degree? (Questions 14.37–14.41 relate to this situation.)

14.58 At what level of sales does a distributive outlet show us a profit? (This relates to customer value analysis (CVA), a brief explanation of which appears in List 18, 'User industries'. The answer to this question should be compared to those called for in Questions 18.77 and 18.78; List 19, 'Key customer marketing', Questions 19.9 and 19.11; and List 28, 'Product/service financial information', Introduction and Questions 28.1 and 28.2.)

14.59 Do we make this check at regular intervals?

14.60 If a distributive outlet is not profitable, is it relinquished?

14.61 What allowance is made for a distribution potential in deciding to relinquish a distributor?

14.62 What services do we offer to distributors? (See List 3, 'The service element in marketing', Appendix 3A, for a classification of services.)

14.63 What services do they not get but would like?

14.64 What constraints prevent us from providing them?

14.65 What would the benefits be in terms of increased sales and distributor interest and loyalty from the provision of services?

14.66 What services do distributors provide for their customers? (See Question 14.24 and List 3, 'The service element in marketing', Appendix 3A, for a classification of services.)

14.67 Would their sales increase if they in turn improved their services to their customers?

14.68 Are there any steps we can take to assist distributors to increase/improve services to their customers?

14.69 What sales and other promotional support do we provide for distributors? (See Introduction and also compare answer with List 13, 'Non-personal promotion', Question 13.3, and List 20, 'Competitive intelligence', Question 20.42.)

14.70 Are they used?

14.71 On what evidence is information on their use based? (eg observation, questioning, requests from distributors)?

14.72 How often are distributors visited and by whom? (This question will have been answered relative to exports in List 5, 'Export marketing', Questions 5.42–5.44; in List

9, 'The salesforce and its management', Question 9.6; List 12, 'The agency system', Question 12.55; and will occur again in List 19, 'Key customer marketing', Question 19.21.)

14.73 Is the role of the distributor increasing, decreasing or remaining constant in importance in the market under review? Why? (Compare with answer to Question 14.16.)

14.74 On what information is the reply based?

14.75 What changes are forecast that imply a requirement for a change in our policy?

14.76 What is our attitude and policy on 'own brand' trading? (See Question 14.56; List 4, 'Company performance', Questions 4.45 and 4.46; and List 13, 'Non-personal promotion: methods and media', Questions 13.57 and 13.58.)

14.77 To what extent are distributors verticalized or have formal or informal links with suppliers/customers?

List 15

The buying process

INTRODUCTION

The end purpose of all marketing is buying, although it would not be thought so judging by the way most marketing books and articles concentrate only on what the marketer should be doing, instead of aligning their activities with buying actions in their various sequences and classifications. Literature on the interface between buying and selling is still relatively rare.

If there is one audit list that defies use in isolation, it is this one. The link with selling and non-personal promotion is obvious, as will be the link with lost order analysis and pricing, which follow. Only the most important cross-references are given below. This section should be used with *all* other sections of the marketing audit.

Marketers not familiar with the work of the Marketing Science Institute in the USA in industrial purchasing may find strange some of the terms used. Briefly, the Marketing Science Institute publications recognize four aspects of significance in industrial purchasing: (1) *who buys* – the decision-making unit (DMU); (2a) *how they buy* – the buy phase – an eight-part progression from the recognition of a need to performance (of the supplier company) feedback; (2b) *how they buy* – the buy class – the classification of purchases into straight re-buys, modified re-buys, and new buys that have important strategic implications; (3) *why they buy* – the decision-forming factors.

Representatives tend to call on the person designated as 'buyer', although many others may be involved in a decision to purchase, particularly for a first-time order for a product/service or from a company. One study of buying practices showed that nearly 80 per cent of board members who were important in purchasing did not see salespersons. The early questions probe the communication targets and, where the DMU is not seen by the sales personnel, call for a consideration of the tools that can reach them. In particular, Questions 15.5 and 15.7 should be related to the answers given in List 13, 'Non-personal promotion: methods and media', since it is substantially non-personal techniques which can circumvent the buyer without destroying the relationship with the company's representative.

The buy class needs at least a crude explanation. Where a supplier is an 'outside' contender, because a straight re-buy and even a modified re-buy so strongly favours the 'in' supplier, the only strategy is to attempt to force a consideration of alternatives, of which the company's offering is one. To do this there has to be some innovation, not necessarily technical or patentable, but perhaps in service, guarantees, commercial terms, deliveries, etc. Questions 15.11 and 15.14 deal with this position. List 26, 'Non-differentiated products and commodities', offers a number of ways of forcing consideration of alternatives. Question 15.14 refers to the opposite strategy, which is for the 'in' supplier to do all possible to hold the purchase to a straight re-buy.

In the Introduction to List 4, 'Company performance', reference was made to the first two 'absolutes' in marketing. The third is that when all things are equal in a purchasing situation, the odds very heavily favour the existing supplier. It is very rare for purchasers to change suppliers for an 'all things equal' situation. This situation presents a strong case for protecting an 'inside' position and additional difficulty for the would-be supplier in attempting to wrest the business. Questions 15.11–15.14 identify the problem to which the answers should supply a solution.

It should also be noted that the buy class may have a pervasive effect on the composition of the DMU, which can change in accordance with the purchasing task. For example, the purchase of office consumables may well be left to an office manager or clerical staff but the decision to construct major plant will involve the board and the most senior management.

Decision-forming factors will vary depending upon the responsibilities of each member of the DMU. The production manager may be concerned with quality of output, the works manager with the physical dimensions of the equipment, the buyer with price and delivery. The message must be tailored for each person and must also be dynamic, in that the interests and responsibilities of an individual member of the DMU may change as the buying processes proceed. Question 15.16, although short, directs the auditor to this crucial subject.

Question 15.22 is an interesting one. It is not unusual for buying responsibilities and budgets to be limited by corporate policy. It may be advisable to adjust the offering so as to put the decision within the authority of a member of the DMU who favours the supplying firm. This can just as easily mean, for example, increasing price as decreasing it.

Questions 15.26–15.32, on 'short lists', 'approved suppliers', 'preferred suppliers', are frequently overlooked. The initial marketing task may well be to obtain entry to these lists rather than to sell products/services. But entry on such lists can also inhibit business. It is still commonplace in the capital equipment industries for a component supplier to be confined to a single component and not be considered for other products. Thus manufacturers of springs are only invited to tender for spring orders and do not have the opportunity of making other offerings from their ranges. While it is certainly better to be on an approved list for one item than not on at all, companies should be aware of the likelihood of such a list barring approval for a wider range of products or services.

It is increasingly common for large customers to operate vendor-rating systems. While some companies may receive approval, they may not always know why. It is important to be aware of the components of a rating system and the scoring method. This information is as valuable for maintaining a place on the approved list as for entering it in the first place. Questions 15.33 and 15.34 deal with that situation.

Question 15.36 is, in a sense, a warning that buyers tend to indicate a preference for selling methods that will be found on investigation not to reflect the real situation. Many buyers ask that there should be no sales calls and state they prefer to use catalogues or the Internet. Yet as several studies have shown, over 80 per cent of all significant business-to-business sales are closed by sales representatives.

The matrices that follow the checklist as Appendix 15A bring three of the four aspects of buying together. It is a model given as an example. Across the top are the individuals and departments that comprise the DMU; down the left-hand side are the eight stages of the buying process, and across the bottom the factors that are considered by the DMU. The figures represent the factors of concern to that member of the DMU at that stage of the buying process. The Appendix 15B matrix is blank. It can be used for deciding the approach to a specific firm or in a specific situation, or it can be adopted for a generalized approach to a particular customer industry. It could also highlight information which is missing in a specific sales situation. The marketing auditor may find it helpful in completing the matrix to take as an example a recent purchase and trace the DMU, the stages of their involvement and the decision-forming factors.

15.1 Which job functions comprise a typical decision-making unit (DMU) in our customer industries? (The answer will be required again in List 18, 'User industries', Question 18.13; List 19, 'Key customer marketing', Questions 19.13 and 19.14; and List 26, 'Non-differentiated products', Question 26.10.)

15.2 Which members of the DMU are outside the customer company (eg architects, consultants, accountants, advertising agencies, distributors, etc)? (See List 2, 'Product/service range', Introduction, and answer to Question 2.19; and List 18, 'User industries', Questions 18.39 and 18.54.)

15.3 How does the DMU vary between different purchases (eg size, frequency, cost, buy class, lead time, etc)?

15.4 Which member(s) of the decision-making unit receive sales visits? (List 19, 'Key customer marketing', Question 19.15.)

15.5 Do we have contact with others in the customer company who are not members of a DMU but who could influence it? (There is a link between this topic and List 13,

'Non-personal promotion: methods and media', Question 13.8; and List 16, 'Analysing lost business', Questions 16.6 and 16.7.)

15.6 How is this achieved?

15.7 Do our methods of communicating with others in the company create any antagonism with the buyer or buying department? (The answers to this and the two previous questions should be compared with those given in List 13, 'Non-personal promotion: methods and media', Question 13.8; and List 16, 'Analysing lost business', Question 16.7.)

15.8 What alternative methods for contacting other members of the DMU can we use without creating antagonisms?

15.9 At what point in the buying continuum is each member of the DMU involved? (See Introduction and Appendix 15A(i); List 16, 'Analysing lost business', Question 16.8; and List 18, 'User industries', Question 18.13.)

15.10 Which factors does each member of the DMU consider at each point of involvement in the purchasing process? (See List 2, 'Product/service range', Question 2.27; List 16, 'Analysing lost business', Question 16.10; and a compilation of some suggested factors in List 18, 'User industries', Question 18.18.)

15.11 Does the sales approach distinguish between new buy, modified re-buy and straight re-buy situations? (See Introduction and List 16, 'Analysing lost business', Question 16.9.)

15.12 How is information on the buy class gathered and used?

15.13 In the case of a potential customer in a straight re-buy situation, how can we adjust our offering to force a reconsideration of alternatives, of which ours will be one? List options. This is the development of unique selling propositions or packages. (See List 2, 'Product/service range', Introduction and Question 2.42. Some options for forcing a reconsideration will be found through List 26, 'Non-differentiated products and commodities'.)

15.14 Where we are the supplying company, what strategies do we adopt to hold the purchase as a straight re-buy? List options.

15.15 How does the DMU vary in each stage of the buying process? (See Introduction, relative to this and the next three questions.)

15.16 How do the stages of DMU involvement vary in each buy class?

15.17 What are the decision-forming factors in each buy class? (See Introduction to List 2, 'Product/service range', and List 18, 'User industries', Question 18.18 for a prompt list of examples of factors that might form part of the 'mix' in decision-making; and List 20, 'Competitive intelligence', answer to Question 20.10.)

15.18 Is this knowledge used in our marketing?

15.19 If so, in what way?

15.20 Have we linked benefits to the interests and responsibilities of different members of the DMU at different stages of the buying process and in different buy classes?

(Relate answers to Questions 15.10 and 15.17; List 2, 'Product/service range', Questions 2.27 and 2.28; and List 16, 'Analysing lost business', Question 16.11.)

15.21 Do we have any method for monitoring changes in customer and prospect companies?

15.22 Does purchasing responsibility divide at discrete points (ie size of purchases, unit price, value of contract etc)? (See Introduction.)

15.23 Where buying responsibility changes on value of contract, is there a tendency for a multiplicity of small orders to be given to circumvent the policy?

15.24 Does our knowledge of such a policy permit us to take advantage of the situation?

15.25 Is there any action we can take to move buying responsibility into the part of the DMU that may favour us?

15.26 Do customer firms usually have a short-list of potential or approved suppliers? (See answers in List 18, 'User industries', Questions 18.67–18.69; and List 20, 'Competitive intelligence', Question 20.23, relative to this and next six questions.)

15.27 Who is responsible for drawing up the list?

15.28 How frequently do we fail to obtain inclusion on any short-list?

15.29 To what reason can we attribute this failure?

15.30 Which competitors appear on most customer and prospective customer approved lists? (Check answer against List 20, 'Competitive intelligence', Question 20.23.)

15.31 How do we account for the frequency of their inclusion?

15.32 How can we obtain entry onto lists? (Compare answers to Questions 15.26–15.32 with List 16, 'Analysing lost business', Questions 16.16 and 16.17.)

15.33 Do customers operate a vendor-rating system?

15.34 Do we know the components of the rating system? (List 18, 'User industries', Question 18.18, almost certainly contains a number of components but it is important to research this for each customer.)

15.35 Do customers conduct purchase price cost analysis? (See List 23, 'Pricing', Figure 23.1.)

15.36 Do we have any knowledge of how members of the DMU prefer to be sold to, eg sales visit, catalogues, exhibitions, direct mail, demonstrations, Internet, reference plant? (See Introduction. The answer will be needed again for List 18, 'User industries', Question 18.63.)

15.37 Do our marketing and marketing 'mix' reflect this?

15.38 How far are expressed preferences a reflection of status rather than the reality? (See Introduction.)

15.39 Are specifications, when set, rigid?

15.40 When they are rigid, are the decision factors considered by the member of the DMU with whom the salesperson interfaces strictly only commercial?

15.41 To what extent can members of the DMU be persuaded to seek or press for a new or modified specification that favours us?

15.42 What information do we have on customers' product/service evaluation techniques? (The question is repeated in a number of lists and is also presented from different perspectives. The auditor should consult and compare answers with List 2, 'Product/service range', Question 2.45; List 16, 'Analysing lost business', Questions 16.14 and 16.15; List 18, 'User industries', Questions 18.50 and 18.51; List 20, 'Competitive intelligence', Question 20.61; List 23, 'Pricing', Question 23.22; and List 27, 'Service businesses', Question 27.38.)

15.43 As part of our promotion, can we persuade customers to use evaluation methods that favour us? (The answer should align with similar and related questions on evaluation and life expectancies. List 2, 'Product/service range', Question 2.45; List 16, 'Analysing lost business', Questions 16.14 and 16.15; List 18, 'User industries', Questions 18.50 and 18.51; List 20, 'Competitive intelligence', Question 20.61; and List 23, 'Pricing', Question 23.22.)

15.44 Is there a pattern in an analysis of business obtained (eg same type of DMU, customer purchasing practices, identical benefits sought, etc)? (But see some suggested factors in List 18, 'User industries', Questions 18.9, 18.12 and 18.13.)

15.45 Can this pattern be applied to prospective customers or used to identify high potential prospects? (See Introduction to List 9, 'The salesforce and its management', the answer to Question 9.100 and Appendix 9C, all concerning profiling.)

Appendix 15A
Completed model of the buying/selling interface

HOW TO USE THE MATRIX

Below are several decision-forming factors that will be considered by different managers at various stages of the buying process. Others can be added. To use the matrix, indicate under each management function, and at each stage of the buying process at which they are likely to be involved, those factors they will take into account in arriving at a decision. Check that the managers concerned have the appropriate information on your product/service and that the method of communicating this information to the managers is effective.

Example. Purchase of a standby generator. The Board is not involved but an Interdepartmental Committee is. The General Manager, other Interdepartmental Directors, (finance and production) and a consulting engineer are also involved. Thus at the 'evaluation of tender' stage (6) the General Manager will take into consideration price, delivery and payment terms. Also at this stage the Buyer will be involved and will be considering price, delivery, payment terms, credit and discounts. Outside the company the consultant will be considering the equipment's claimed performance, physical dimensions, energy consumption, back-up services and the reputation of the supplying firm.

FACTORS FOR CONSIDERATION

1 = Price
2 = Performance characteristics
3 = Physical dimensions
4 = Delivery
5 = Backup services
6 = Reliability
7 = Other user experience
8 = Guarantees and warranties
9 = Payment terms

Appendix 15A

	Collective decisions decision factors considered		Individual (non-departmental) decision factors considered				Departmental decisions decision factors considered						External
Stage of buying process	Board	Interdepartmental Management Committee	Managing Director	Other individual directors	General Manager	Company Secretary	Design Engineering	Production	Research and Development	Finance/ Accounts	Sales/ Marketing	Buying	Others outside company
1. Anticipation or recognition of a need or problem and a general solution		2			2		2	2					
		4			4		4						
2. Determination of characteristics of needed item			2				2	2	2	8			
							3	3		9			
							6	4					
3. Description of characteristics and quantity of needed item		2	2				7						2
		3											3
		6											4
4. Search for and qualification of potential sources of supply								7					2
													3
													4
5. Acquisition of tenders or proposals and analysis				7		6						1 9	
				8								4	
				9		8						6	
												7	
6. Evaluation of tenders and proposals and selection of supplier			1	1	1			2				6	2
			2	5	4			3				7	3
			4	9	9			4					6
			9					5					5
7. Selection of an order routine												9	
8. Performance feedback and evaluation													

Appendix 15B
Blank model of the buying/selling interface

	Collective decisions decision factors considered		Individual (non-departmental) decision factors considered				Departmental decisions decision factors considered						External
1. Anticipation or recognition of a need or problem and a general solution													
2. Determination of characteristics of needed item													
3. Description of characteristics and quantity of needed item													
4. Search for and qualification of potential sources of supply													
5. Acquisition of tenders or proposals and analysis													
6. Evaluation of tenders and proposals and selection of supplier													
7. Selection of an order routine													
8. Performance feedback and evaluation													

List 16

Analysing lost business

INTRODUCTION

Obviously, unless the reasons why business is lost are known, it will be difficult if not impossible to correct a fault that may be fundamental to the product/service or to the chemistry between the organization, its personnel and the customer. In many instances, a careful and ongoing analysis will enable companies to rectify the cause of the loss.

A distinction is needed to precede the use of the list. A customer may be lost or may have no current or foreseeable demand. In many product and service categories demand is sporadic and perhaps widely spread. New telecommunications systems are not purchased frequently or regularly like consumables or car fleets. It is commonplace for companies not to know if an account has been lost or is inactive. This is particularly true of professional services.

If a customer's business is worth having then it is worth monitoring to ensure that when a purchase is contemplated the supplier is 'visible' and favourably perceived. Moreover, the opportunity to introduce new products/services is often overlooked with customers who are not contacted frequently.

Having said this, 'lost business' falls into two categories: business lost for products/services that have been quoted for, and business lost because the enquiry or the request to quote was not received in the first place. Not to be considered for an enquiry can stem from lack of visibility or lack of credibility. It was stated earlier that one of the few absolutes in marketing is that, if prospects do not know you exist, they will not buy from you. The first task in marketing is always to obtain visibility and preferably absolutely unaided recall. (See List 13, 'Non-personal promotion: methods and media', Figure 13.1.)

Although the use of a company name or brand as a generic for the product group can be a two-edged weapon, overall it tends to favour the supplier. There are companies in the earth-moving equipment business who would be happy to have the product name association of JCB or Caterpillar, or in the small power tool business of Black & Decker. This generic use of a company or brand name for a product type will have been seen among the promotional objectives in List 13, 'Non-personal promotion: methods and media', Question 13.1.

To have received an initial enquiry but not be invited to go to the next stage of sampling, quoting (or tendering), or demonstration, if appropriate, cannot stem from lack of visibility. Here it must mean the vendor is not acceptable for some reason. At this point there may well be an image problem if the perception of the firm and its offering is that of a less credible or more expensive supplier than the others selected. Once again, with an understanding of this situation it is possible to rectify the position. (See Introduction to List 24, 'Images and perceptions'.)

These aspects of lost enquiries/business should emerge if Question 16.1 is answered objectively, but if needs be it should be researched.

The lost-customer analyses are difficult to achieve because everyone is defensive and even objective observers may be reluctant to comment critically on their superiors, peers or subordinates. One thing is certain: sales representatives are the world's worst reporters on lost business. They tend to blame 'price', as this is the one reason that excuses everyone – the buyer, the seller, production, warehousing, credit control. Yet, as will have been seen in List 2, 'Product/service range', Question 2.23, and later in List 23, 'Pricing', Figure 23.1, while price is not unimportant, it is by no means always the dominant issue in a buying decision. Customers buy more than price, as the introduction to List 26, 'Non-differentiated products and commodities', clearly shows. They also buy reliability, professionalism, stock, service, problem solving, image. In using this checklist, the marketing auditor must ask after each question: How valid is the answer? Where did the information come from? Has the informant any reason to be defensive? Some judgement of reliability has to be placed on every reply before it becomes usable.

Question 16.3, aligning reasons given with choice made, is often a good test of reliability. Where a lost order is reported as having been given to a higher-specification product, which on investigation is found to be similar, it is obvious that other factors led to the negative decision.

Questions 16.7 and 16.8, on communication methods, frequently produce conditioned replies. Here, as much as anywhere, proof is needed that the messages are getting through to the targeted people at the right time, and that they are understood and believed. Failure anywhere along this communication continuum will inevitably lead to lost business.

The matrix in List 15, 'The buying process', Appendix 15A, will have demonstrated both the complexity of the buying process and the multiplicity of messages needed for different members of the DMU at different times. Thus it is not a *single* message whose visibility, comprehensibility, relevance and conviction need to be traced, but *multiple* messages to multiple recipients.

Many firms' response to lost business is 'we wuz robbed'. This may indeed be true if the evaluation techniques used by customers fail to take into account all the features and benefits of the product, support services, and commercial terms. Too few sellers ask buyers about the evaluation techniques, and thus never attempt to influence them. Questions 16.14 and 16.15 centre on this point.

Question 16.27, on inducements, is a very difficult one to obtain a truthful answer to, at least in the more sophisticated markets of the world. It is even more difficult to decide policy for those countries and circumstances where the answer is positive. As was commented in List 5, 'Export marketing', Introduction, a checklist must necessarily be amoral. Each firm has to decide for itself how far it will comply with customary (or even not so customary) methods of doing business. In the Middle East and many parts of Central and South America it is a recognized way of negotiating contracts, so there will not be too much heart-burning. In other countries the issue is not so easily decided. Just when a gift becomes a bribe no one has actually designated. Question 13.3 in List 13, 'Non-personal promotion: methods and media', includes 'gifts' as a legitimate marketing tool but relates to such trivialities as diaries, calendars, pens, etc, and the token gift to the Japanese visitor, not to the £1 million 'fee' to the nephew of the ruler of a Middle East kingdom.

Analyses of guarantee and warranty claims and the reasons for issuing credit notes or refunds might well show a pattern of customer complaints or attitudes that can be anticipated and resolved. Questions 16.32 to 16.38 are concerned with this topic. However, Question 16.38 can reveal that the value inherent in guarantees and complaint resolution as marketing tools is easily lost unless these matters are dealt with sympathetically and expeditiously. Reluctant honouring of commitments or grudging acceptance of complaints – usually by blaming the customer – does not bring customers back.

The list, as it is given, assumes a total pattern of lost business. The pattern, however, may not be obvious unless there are some cross-analyses. For example, business might be lost continually in the private as opposed to public hospital sector; in one geographical area as compared to another; when a particular material is being used with customers' equipment, in benign as opposed to aggressive atmospheres, and so on. Because there is no total or obvious pattern of lost business, it must not be assumed that one could not be uncovered by analysing the material in a segmented as opposed to homogeneous manner.

A useful guide to possible causes of lost business might well be found by analysing customer complaints, warranty and guarantee claims, and credits issued. It is important to remember that not all customers do complain – they just do not come back. A customer-orientated approach will not eschew seeking out customer problems instead of just waiting for them to surface. Question 16.39 deals with this very fundamental issue. Without the analysis, the investigation of lost business becomes an interesting but not a useful exercise.

16.1 Do we have a mechanism for identifying lost business as opposed to customers with no immediate or foreseeable requirements?

16.2 What reasons are given for the loss of customer orders or enquiries? (Compare answer with List 9, 'The salesforce and its management', Question 9.122; and List 25, 'Quality in marketing', Question 25.12.)

16.3 Do those reasons align with the choice eventually made of product/service or suppliers?

16.4 What advantages did the competitors have?

16.5 How did they express them?

16.6 Did we contact the real decision-makers? (See List 15, 'The buying process', Questions 15.4, 15.5 and 15.46.)

16.7 Does the sales force consider that the techniques we are using to get our message to members of the DMU are effective? (Check against List 13, 'Non-personal promotion: methods and media'; and List 15, 'The buying process', Questions 15.7, 15.8 and 15.46.)

16.8 Do they intercept the buy phase of the moment of each member of the DMU's involvement in the purchase? (See List 15, 'The buying process', Question 15.9.)

16.9 Does our strategy take advantage of buy class knowledge? (See List 15, 'The buying process', Question 15.11.)

16.10 Do our marketing messages contain the information that the individual members of the DMU require, and is the information expressed as benefits? (This important topic is restated in other lists and the answers should be compared. See List 2, 'Product/service range', Question 2.23; List 20, 'Competitive intelligence', Question 20.58; List 23, 'Pricing', Question 23.29; and List 26, 'Non-differentiated products and commodities', Questions 26.33–26.35.)

16.11 Were our offers the correct ones for the prospective customer and for the DMU members involved? (See List 15, 'The buying process', Question 15.20, the answer to which should align with the response to this question.)

16.12 What proof do we have of the validity of the answer?

16.13 If the offer was not correct, in what way was it inappropriate?

16.14 What evaluation techniques did the customer use? (See List 6, 'Marketing information: systems and use', Question 6.44; and List 15, 'The buying process', Question 15.43; and the cross-references which follow both questions; List 23, 'Pricing', Question 23.22.)

16.15 How do our products/services measure up against the evaluation techniques and against our claims for the products/services? (The question is repeated in a number of lists from different perspectives. The auditor should consult and compare answers with List 2, 'Product/service range', Question 2.45; List 15, 'The buying process', Questions 15.42 and 15.43; List 18, 'User industries', Questions 18.50 and 18.52; List

20, 'Competitive intelligence', Question 20.61; List 23 'Pricing', Question 23.22; and List 27, 'Service businesses', Question 27.38.)

16.16 Which firms were invited to quote? (See List 15, 'The buying process', Questions 15.26 and 15.30–15.32.)

16.17 Are they comparable with us in terms of offerings?

16.18 What were the buying motives? (Compare answer with Questions 16.9 and 16.10 above.)

16.19 What were the buying resistances?

16.20 Did the benefits we offered meet the objections?

16.21 What proof did we offer that the benefits sought/offered would be delivered? (See Figure 2.1 in List 2, 'Product/service range'.)

16.22 Was the proof incontrovertible?

16.23 If not, how were our assurances expressed?

16.24 Were appropriate sales promotional materials used? (See List 13, 'Non-personal promotion: methods and media', Question 13.1.)

16.25 If not, would they have helped?

16.26 If so, were they relevant to the presentation?

16.27 Is there any evidence of inducements being offered to purchase? (See Introduction.)

16.28 Should we emulate these or report them?

16.29 Is it possible to discern a general or a segmented pattern of lost business? (See Introduction.)

16.30 How far could support staff have been responsible for customer losses? (See Introduction and List 9, 'The salesforce and its management', Question 9.112. Compare answers to that given for List 10, 'Customer care and support staff's role in marketing', Question 10.7.)

16.31 What steps can be taken to impress on support staff their importance in customer retention? (See List 10, 'Customer care and support staff's role in marketing', Questions 10.7 and 10.8.)

16.32 Are warranty and guarantee claims recorded and credit notes analysed? (Align answer to this and the next four questions to the answers given in List 25, 'Quality in marketing', Question 25.12.)

16.33 Is there a defined policy for handling claims?

16.34 Who is responsible for adjudicating on them?

16.35 How are complaints routed?

16.36 Are they analysed on a regular basis? (See List 10, 'Customer care and support staff's role in marketing', Question 10.13.)

16.37 What procedures do we adopt for resolving complaints? (See List 18, 'User industries' and the Introduction to this list.)

16.38 How liberal/strict are our interpretations and settlements of customer complaints?

16.39 Will our system of monitoring customer satisfaction enable us to identify unreported complaints? (See List 3, 'The service element in marketing', Question 3.33; List 13, 'Non-personal promotion: methods and media', Question 13.60; List 23, 'Pricing', Questions 23.1 and 23.2, which relate to the cost of complaint rectification; List 28, 'Product/service financial information', Question 28.52 on the cost of meeting guarantees.)

16.40 Were the quotation/proposal/tender documents delivered punctually?

16.41 Did they conform to the specification? (This question arises in a number of different contexts. The auditor should consult and compare answers given in List 4, 'Company performance', Questions 4.22–4.42; List 9, 'The salesforce and its management', Question 9.117; List 24, 'Images and perceptions', Questions 24.26 and 24.28; and List 25, 'Quality in marketing', Question 25.36. Some of the components for consideration will be found in Appendix 25A.)

List 17

Introducing new products/services

INTRODUCTION

The lifeblood of all organizations must be new products or services. Indeed, the genesis of most companies derived from an original (but not necessarily innovative) idea of its founders. However, there is among some managers a reluctance to accept that a once-new product or idea is becoming geriatric, or that any later development is an improvement over the old ways and materials.

New product/service search in many companies appears to be sporadic, undisciplined, without direction or focus, and undertaken by executives often highly unsuitable for the task, lacking personal and corporate imagination. This, however, is not the position in well-organized and motivated firms with a strong track record of successful new product introductions. Nevertheless, failure rates are high. For every DVD system, 3M 'Post-it' notes and Sony 'Walkman' there are 10 Laservisions, telepoints, 3D cameras and quadraphonic sound systems. The well-documented and now historic fiascos of the Ford Edsel, the Sinclair C5, Du Pont's Corfam and the tobacco substitute, and a million other unpublicized disasters, were as frequently the outcome of lack of market knowledge or sensitivity as of technical failure.

The search for new products/services should be a constant activity, ranking equal in importance with all other marketing functions, with the search area and evaluation methods subject to precise methodologies and criteria, as well as with the strictest disciplines.

This is not to say that a reactive or speculative approach will not also pay off. The methodical search for new products/services does not rule out entrepreneurial flair and opportunistic response or the exploitation of an idea that has emerged from outside the established search system. However, in developing new offers, it is important that the company should always work from inherent or acquirable strengths.

The list that follows is substantially in two parts. The first deals with the need for new products/services and the generating of new product/service ideas; the second with the markets that the new products/services may command.

There are four product options that can be considered in the context of the matrix in Figure 17.1; 'new' does not necessarily mean 'innovative', but new to the company.

Squares 1 and 2 fall outside this list, which concentrates on 3 and 4.

Square 3 is particularly interesting because, in looking for new product ideas, the question can be asked, 'What do our customers buy that they do not buy from us but that we could supply?', a question already raised in the Introduction to List 11, 'Cross-selling and internal marketing'. Because they are already customers, this represents a market resource or a strength that can be exploited. Question 17.10 could be the key to open the door to a whole range of suitable new products/services without the considerable investment in time and money usually necessary to acquire profitable additional offerings. List 11, 'Cross-selling and internal marketing', deals with this type of targeting in depth.

	Existing products	New products
Old markets	1	3
New markets	2	4

Figure 17.1 Product matrix

An existing customer has already expressed a preference for the supplier, whether it be positive – a liking for the company, a high regard for its products/services or some rub-off prestige – or negative – 'the best of a bad bunch'. The differential advantage referred to in the Introduction to List 4, 'Company performance', and Question 4.41, has thus been demonstrated to exist. It places the company seeking to supply a wider range of products/services to an established customer in a strong position to identify what the customer buys that the vendor could supply. The resultant extended product range may then very well have an application for other customers and prospects.

A schematic showing the preliminary steps required before actually beginning the search process and necessary to confine the search to manageable proportions is shown in Figure 17.2.

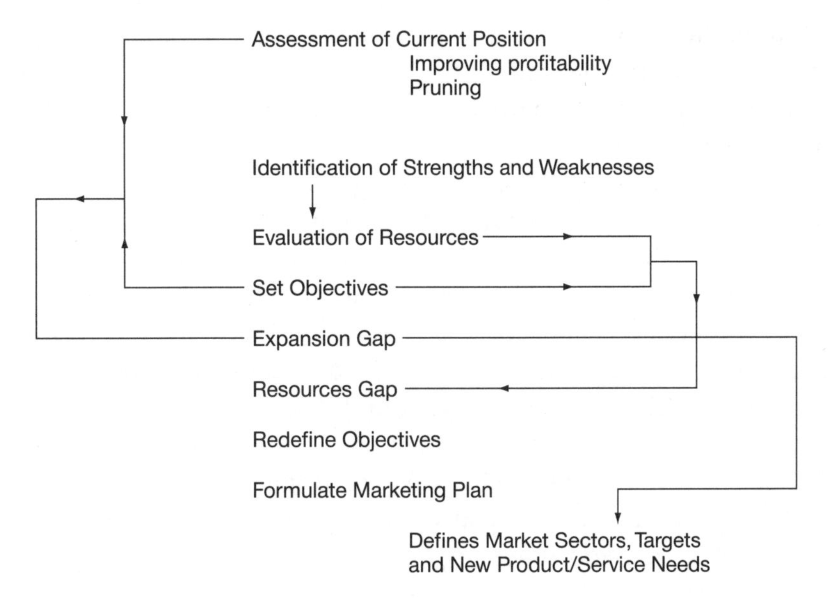

Figure 17.2 Setting the search boundaries (see also List 1, 'Marketing strategy and planning', Figure 1.2)

Questions 17.5–17.12 should lead to a consideration of the present position and opportunities before turning to the new product/service decision. In particular, Question 17.12, which is a Square 4 approach, requires consideration as to whether a proposed development is not from the weakest position, ie trying to market a new, unknown product (to the supplier) to new, unknown customers as compared with, say, attempting to market new products/services to existing customers or existing products/services to new customers. Square 4 products are not based on any resource – market, technical, procurement – and moreover they usually draw finance away from what might be better opportunities. Square 4 is a perfectly legitimate position to occupy for companies that must have 'lead' products, but most others would be well advised to look harder at the alternative options open to them.

The condition where sales reach the peak of the life cycle is known as 'top-out'. Auditors should try to identify recognizable symptoms that would indicate a 'top-out' position (Questions 17.13 and 17.14). The list suggests that life cycles are not necessarily immutable and under some circumstances can be extended (Question 17.15).

One problem bedevilling new product search is that companies do not always designate the parameters of the product/service, most particularly how much volume/revenue it is supposed to generate. A simple 'gap analysis' (Questions 17.20–17.22) will show at once, if the business continues along its present path and growth rate, how close to the target figure it will be in a given period of time. (Gap analysis was included in the first checklist: see Introduction to List 1, 'Marketing strategy and planning', Questions 1.10–1.13 and Figure 1.2.) It must then be asked, if existing products/services cannot fill the revenue profit gap, what volume the new product/service must be capable of achieving. Thus if £20 million must be found from a new offering with a total market of, say, £10 million, it cannot on its own close the gap. Gap analysis at least gives the size of the problem and one important parameter in choice.

Questions 17.31 and 17.34 will assist in setting yet another criterion for new product search – the commercial parameters, which must in turn line up with the gap analysis. The auditor will need to establish which items are irrelevant, which marginal and which vital, as well as to add others which may be crucial to the company.

Given that new products are needed, it is the source of ideas and the methods of evaluation that become key. The extremes of rejecting ideas because they are new, or of pursuing every idea, are wasteful in time, demoralizing and dangerous. Discipline in search, discipline in evaluation, discipline in development and, finally, discipline in exploitation are required. The inventors of the thermal imaging gun originally dismissed it as a toy, only to find later that it had been widely and successfully exploited in a huge world market by defence forces, police, fire and other organizations dealing with crime, accidents and disasters.

Once more, a checklist spawns another checklist. There are many useful guides in checklist form for new product idea generation and evaluation, and there are also systems for developing numerical criteria to achieve choice. The Qualitative Screening Process and the Product/Market Package are two such approaches.[1] For firms seriously engaged in the search for profitable new products and activities for the first time, these should be consulted.

Question 17.39 seeks to anticipate barriers to successful market entry and this is illustrated in a cascade diagram in Appendix 17A. 'Ease of market entry' is not a subject that has attracted much marketing comment and the auditor may find of some value one particular technique using a screening approach not dissimilar to that in Appendix 5A on export markets.[2]

The final questions, 17.53–17.60, draw attention to what can be a useful source for new product/service introductions, frequently at low cost and with low risk. This is inward licensing. In a sense, the questions are the mirror opposite to those formulated in List 5, 'Export marketing', where outward licensing was considered. Before a licence search is undertaken, if an inordinate amount of time is not to be lost, it is important to be quite clear about the role of any licensed product in the product 'mix', the parameters it must fit, and the conditions of licence that will be acceptable. It is all too easy to fall into the trap of a quickly available glamorous product, only to find at a later date that the licence contains many constraints or conditions which have been overlooked in the rush to get into production. Questions 17.53–17.58 seek to alert the auditor to the advantages and risks of inward licensing.

Appendix 17B contains some idea-spurring questions that the auditor can apply to existing products to add attributes which create new and possibly innovative offerings.

17.1 How many new products/services have been introduced in the last five years?

17.2 How many of them would be categorized as:
- highly successful?
- successful?
- fair?
- qualified failure?
- total failure?

17.3 What were the reasons for the performance noted?

17.4 What is the role of the new products?
- fills gap in existing range
- takes up spare production capacity
- increases competitiveness of existing product range
- exploits capacity of salesforce
- offers higher margins
- broadens product base
- opens up new market
- increases potential for additional sales to existing customers
- anti-cyclical demand

(See also answer required for Questions 17.31 and 17.56.)

17.5 What proportion of our present range of products/services are our own developments, licensed, traded, franchised, subcontracted? (Compare answers with List 2, 'Product/service range', Question 2.4; List 4, 'Company performance', Question 4.16.)

17.6 Do we need new products/services and when will we need them?

17.7 What types of businesses will use the new product/service?

17.8 Have we completely exploited the existing markets for our current range (Square 1 in Figure 17.1)?

17.9 How far have we attempted, and with what success, to sell our existing range to new customers (Square 2 in Figure 17.1)? (Cross-check answers to this and the two questions above with List 4, 'Company performance', Question 4.11.)

17.10 What do our customers buy that they do not buy from us but which we could supply (Square 3 in Figure 17.1)? (See Introduction and List 11, 'Cross-selling and internal marketing', Questions 11.9 and 11.10.)
17.11 Why do we not make and supply these products/services?
17.12 How far is our new product/service search directed to new products for new markets (Square 4 in Figure 17.1)?
17.13 Can we anticipate the conditions that will indicate when a product is approaching, or is in, a 'top-out' position? (See List 4, 'Company performance', Introduction, and List 23, 'Pricing', Questions 23.33 and 23.34, in relation to this and Questions 17.14–17.16.)
17.14 Do we have a monitoring system for reporting 'top-out' conditions?
17.15 What plans exist for extending product life cycles? (Compare answer with that given in List 7, 'Market size and structure', Questions 7.35 and 7.36; and List 23, 'Pricing', Questions 23.32 and 23.34.)
17.16 What plans exist for replacing products/services with declining demand?
17.17 Are there strong internal loyalties to existing products that might inhibit objective decision-taking on withdrawal?
17.18 Are there product 'champions' for new products/services?
17.19 Have we set out and agreed the point at which, or circumstances when, we will eliminate a product or service (ie sales, profit, stock levels, sporadic nature or demand, etc)? (List 2, 'Product/service range', Introduction, identifies a danger in product elimination based on sales.)
17.20 On a straight-line projection, what level of business will be achieved five years from now? (See List 1, 'Marketing strategy and planning', Figure 1.2.)
17.21 How does this compare with the target set for five years from now?
17.22 If there is a gap, with what product/service do we propose to fill it? (The Introduction and Figure 1.2 in List 1, 'Marketing strategy and planning', will give guidance on the last three questions, and Question 1.10 the answer concerning the gap.)
17.23 What are the qualitative objectives for closing the gap (eg on aggregation of small orders, large business, combination of both, multiple products/services, full-line operations)?
17.24 Is our new product search formal?
17.25 Are the programme steps clearly defined, tasks allocated by name and dates for completion agreed?

1. Initiate new product/service concept
2. Collect ideas centrally
3. Screen new product ideas
4. Approve for pre-development evaluation
5. Examine market feasibility
6. Examine financial feasibility
7. Examine technical feasibility

8 Request project approval
9 Approve
10 Set timetable and budget
11 Detailed study of the market
12 Design and engineering
13 Request approval for prototype
14 Approve
15 Obtain product for test
16 Obtain and evaluate manufacturing cost data from test
17 Prepare detailed plan for marketing and manufacture
18 Prepare and submit request
19 Supervise facility construction and start-up
20 Assume marketing and manufacturing responsibility

17.26 Who is responsible for the programme?

17.27 What are the limits of their authority and to whom do they report?

17.28 Can we test market the product/service?

17.29 How frequently is the programme reviewed and success/failure appraised? (See answer to Question 17.2.)

17.30 What is the consequence of success/failure to those involved in new products/services search?

17.31 What are the market performance and corporate parameters for the new product/service? (See Introduction.)

- volume of sales
- ROI
- anti-cyclical demand
- sales to existing customers
- marketing costs
- inventory costs
- value of sales
- industries served
- climate of competition
- servicing requirements
- procurement economies
- retrofit market
- credit costs
- potential profit
- compatibility with corporate plans and aspirations
- market potential
- range spread
- consumable/spares sales

- evening out production
- handling costs
- exit costs

17.32 Historically, where have successful/new product/service ideas come from? (Relate answers to those in 17.2 above; List 2, 'Product/service range', Question 2.4; and List 4, 'Company performance', Questions 4.16 and 4.17.)

17.33 Can previous sources be relied on in future and, if not, what system do we have for the searching (ie surveillance, material research, R&D, licensing, patent search, company or personnel acquisition)?

17.34 Does the new product/service offer any important competitive advantages in a developed field? What are they?

17.35 What information do we possess on the market for identified new products/services, particularly in relation to their location, segmentation and user attitudes?

17.36 What is the source and validity of our information? (See List 6, 'Marketing information, systems and use'; List 18, 'User industries'.)

17.37 Are we monitoring future market changes for new product/service opportunities? (See List 8, 'Future market', Questions 8.19–8.22.)

17.38 Do we have a market entry plan for any new product/service adopted?

17.39 Do any of the following inhibiting factors make market entry for a new product hazardous? (See Introduction and Appendix 17A.)

- lack of financial resource to support launch
- insufficient production capacity
- shortage of raw materials
- limitation of demand
- climate of competition
- deficiency in marketing skills
- failure of management skills
- product incompatibility with market needs or resources
- missing supplier credibility or track record
- availability of an effective distributive/servicing network
- need for approval from OMs or accreditation bodies
- operation of restrictive practices or cartels
- trade or political barriers
- need for a substantial asset base
- long pay-back period
- political factors
- exit costs

17.40 What resources will be allocated to it?

17.41 Is there a resource gap? (See Introduction and Figure 17.2 as well as Introduction to List 1, 'Marketing strategy and planning', Figure 1.2 and Question 1.10.)

17.42 How is it proposed to fill such a gap?
17.43 How well are the sales personnel inducted on new products/services?
17.44 Is the sales and product training manual effective?
17.45 Who is responsible for ensuring that the manual is followed?
17.46 What will the reaction of the competition be to the introduction of a new product/service?
17.47 Why should our customers buy the new product/service (benefits, patents, supply, shortage, multiple sourcing)?
17.48 Have we conducted a trade-off analysis? (See List 23, 'Pricing', Introduction.)
17.49 How acceptable will new products/services be to any intermediaries involved?
17.50 Will new products improve our procurement position?
17.51 Will they meet a demand in current or potential export markets?
17.52 How will they rate in terms of stability of demand, growth, marketability, lead-time to launch, life cycle, etc?
17.53 Would taking on overseas licence or cross-licensing provide new product(s)? (See List 5, 'Export marketing', Questions 5.60–5.71.)
17.54 What level of revenue must a licensed product produce to make it viable?
17.55 Would a licence release resources – marketing and production – that could be redeployed more profitably elsewhere?
17.56 What role in the product strategy would the licensed product/service fill? (Compare answer with that given for 17.4.)
17.57 What are the product/service parameters a licensed product must meet?
- will fill spare production capacity
- will round out range
- can be sold at lower price than competition
- can yield higher margins
- will release resources required for other product/services or activities
- will compensate for lack of R & D facilities
- will facilitate cross-licensing decisions
- will provide low-risk diversification
- will associate use with a reputable, highly regarded manufacturer or brand

17.58 What conditions must be met and how far are we prepared to accept them? For example:
- territorial limitation
- method of marketing
- minimum sales or royalties
- time limits
- non-competition with the licensor
- financial strength of licensor
- licensor known in our markets

- exclusivity
- access to onward development
- no claw-back arrangements
- no minimum or down payments
- willingness to have our names linked to the licensor's

17.59 What conditions do we require for a licence to be taken?

17.60 Given that licensing is a method for new product development, have we a properly developed system for licence search, and have the actions been allocated and scheduled and arrangements made for monitoring progress?

17.61 How will the new full line compare with those of competitors? (Compare the answer to that given to List 20, 'Competitive intelligence', Question 20.11.)

17.62 How deep-seated are existing loyalties and how receptive are buyers to new products/services?

17.63 Would an external benchmarking study be useful?

Appendix 17A
Market entry checklist

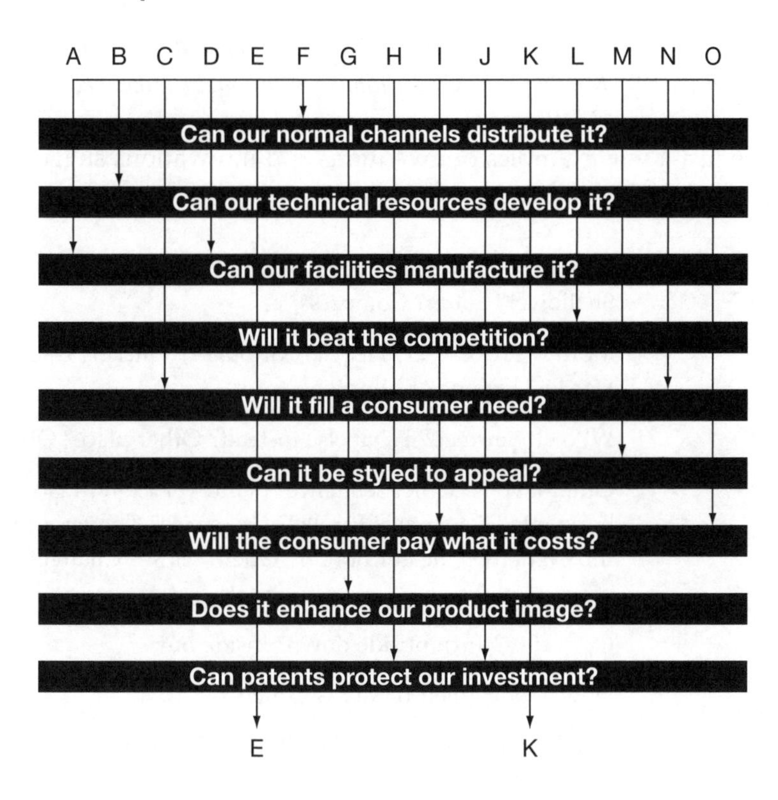

Appendix 17B
Some idea-spurring questions

Some options for developing benefits customers want and are prepared to pay for can be derived from a checklist compiled by SRI Menlo Park, California, in a privately published report, 'Structured Approaches to Creativity' by J McPherson.

Following are just a few examples of inventions and innovations suggested by specific questions of the idea-spurring type:

Minify	Fewer? Subtract? Eliminate? Smaller? Lighter? Shorter? Thinner? Shallower? Softer? Compress?
Magnify	More? Add? Larger? Heavier? Stronger? Thicker? Deeper? Harder? Expand? Multiply?
Substitute?	Who else instead? What else instead? Other place? Other time?
Rearrange?	Other layout? Other sequence? Stand vertically? Place horizontally? Slanted? Parallel? Crosswise? Converge? Diverge? Intervene? Delineate? Border? Open? Close? Change proportions?
Reverse	Opposites? Turn upside down? Inside out?
Combine?	How about a blend? An assortment?
Separate?	Combine purposes? Combine ideas? Fractionate? Assemble? Dissemble? Preform? Encapsulate?
Put to other uses?	New ways to use as is? Other uses if modified?
Adopt?	What else is like this? What other ideas does this suggest?
Modify?	Change meaning, colour, motion, sound, odour, taste, form, shape, temperature? Solidify? Liquefy? Vaporize? Pulverize? Make disposable? Abrade? Lubricate? Insulate? Wetter? Drier? Effervesce? Coagulate? Elasticize? Electrify?
Change time element	Faster? Slower? More frequently? Less frequently? Chronologize? Perpetuate? Synchronize? Anticipate? Renew? Recur? Alternate?

Following are just a few examples of inventions and innovations suggested by specific questions of the idea-spurring type:

Harden	cream (instead of liquid) shampoo
Preform	prefabricated houses
Disposable	clench type bottlecaps, disposable diapers, paper dresses and tissues
Incorporate	counting register on printing press
Parted	tractor tread, split-level highway
Solidify	soup and beverage mixes
Liquefy	plant food chemicals
Vaporize	nasal medication vaporizers
Pulverize	powdered eggs, leaf mulcher attachment to lawn mower, kitchen sink garbage disposal unit
Abrade	snow tyres, snow chains
Wetter	hydraulic brakes
Insulate	food pads, thermal containers
Compress	medicinal tablets
Effervesce	analgesic preparations
Coagulate	gelatin desserts
Elasticize	bubble gum, belts
Electrify	electric blankets
Heavier	can opener with weighted stand

As examples of variations on the idea-spurring question theme, in a course in Creative Design at Massachusetts Institute of Technology, Professor John Arnold advocated the use of questions such as the following for product improvement:

- Can we increase the function?
- Can we make the product do more things?
- Can we get a higher performance level?
- Make the product longer-lived?
- More reliable?
- More accurate?
- Safer?
- More convenient to use?

- Easier to repair and maintain?
- Can we lower the cost?
- Eliminate excess parts?
- Substitute cheaper materials?
- Design to reduce hand labour or for complete automation?
- Increase the saleability?
- Improve the appearance of the product?
- Improve the package?
- Improve its point of sale?

Notes

1 Aubrey Wilson (1991) A systematic approach to evaluating new markets, in *New Directions in Marketing*, Kogan Page, London.
2 Planning a Diversification Strategy, published privately by Industrial Market Research Ltd (n.d.).

List 18

User industries

INTRODUCTION

This list attempts first to encourage an open-minded reconsideration of firms' markets, and then to review customers' policies, practices, perceptions and problems as they might impact on the supplier.

All too often, markets are frozen into a pattern determined by the original product/service concept or the entrepreneur's or management's views as to the market configurations. Many opportunities are lost because of this rigidity in thinking. The spring balancers referred to in List 7, 'Market size and structure', Introduction, are largely associated with the small machine tool and lighting industries but were found to have wide application in abattoirs, paint spraying and tanneries, areas far outside the market conceptualization of the makers of the equipment.

In the final analysis, the accuracy and efficiency of the segmentations adopted and referred to frequently in earlier lists can be judged by only one criterion: not the ease in selling into the segment; not the penetration achieved; not the image obtained; but profitability. That is what it is all about. Thus it is as well, early in this list, to compare the segments with the profit they generate.

Question 18.10 can be answered sensibly only if the auditor has already decided in what terms profitability will be measured and how. He or she will need to know the composition of the major cost factors such as discounts, promotional costs, inventory and product/service mix. The auditor should also ascertain whether the items are costed or estimated. A discrepancy here can well lead to an incorrect deduction from the analyses.

Question 18.11 draws attention to a frequently overlooked fact touched on in List 15, 'The buying process'. A firm's regular customers often have some common characteristic, either because of the original segmentation or because, in a sense, customers of this type select certain suppliers. If such a pattern exists it may provide very precise guidance as to which non-customers represent the best potential prospects. The profiling method is a technique successfully adopted by many British companies. (See Introduction to List 9, 'The salesforce and its management'.)

The profiling method referred to there can be taken further by breaking down the market beyond 'regular customers'. If, in addition, its composition is grouped into sporadic, one-off, and lost customers, and prospects who invite the firm to quote and those who do not, then the common characteristics of firms in each croup can be identified. This will provide accurate guidelines for prospective customers to avoid or to place on a low-priority basis and, as with the suggestion in the Introduction to List 16, 'Analysing lost business', and the response to Question 16.29, it will be found possible to decide what action to take, if any, to recoup the position. In the introductory section to this book, 'The marketing audit', this customer categorization is suggested as applicable to a number of situations being analysed.

A general, somewhat cynical, view is that the requirements of all customers are half the price, twice the quality, and delivery ex-stock. While it is not suggested that such desiderata would not be appreciated, buying and buyers are more sophisticated than this. It is wrong but nevertheless common to assume that all customer requirements are known. Research frequently shows requirements that have not been appreciated by suppliers and indeed often not enunciated by buyers themselves, since they too have blockages and can easily assume that a requirement cannot be met. Question 18.18 gives some objective and perceptual items which in various combinations lead to a favourable decision.

But in looking at choice it is as well to warn of a phenomenon that has probably caused more marketing disasters than any other single factor: namely, the idea that in expressing a preference for one supplier or product/service buyers are also expressing a satisfaction. They are not. Preference rarely equals satisfaction. The only statement buyers are making is that they favour a particular offering above all others at that particular point in time; like the majority of purchases, business-to-business and personal, an element of compromise usually exists. The gap between preference and satisfaction, if it can be ascertained, represents the best opportunity to wrest business from a competitor or to consolidate existing business. Anyone who can close the satisfaction gap must succeed.

Question 18.35 is frequently answered in good faith but nevertheless incorrectly. Too many firms take the dispatch date as the comparison with delivery promises. The customer will always take the receipt date, a difference that may be a critical number of days or even weeks. Telling the customer that the consignment has been dispatched might appear to exonerate the sender from responsibility for the delay: it does not. The question indirectly calls for a reconsideration of transport and delivery methods, which is dealt with in more detail in List 21, 'Physical distribution and packaging'.

Question 18.39 touches on reciprocal trading and other closed arrangements, overt and covert. Proof of cost benefit can often unsettle such arrangements, but by and large these represent 'hard' market targets and are better avoided in favour of 'softer' targets which may exist. It has been said that it is an absurd exercise to bang your head against a brick wall, but it is lunacy to build one specially for the purpose. Attacking a reciprocally trading market can absorb far too much of a firm's resources, particularly marketing resources, without either the hope or realization of success.

Question 18.57 relates to the positioning map in List 7, 'Market size and structure', Question 7.37. It was used to show the realities of a price situation in terms of market requirements and purchasing. Here it is used to indicate the positioning of the company's product/service as perceived by the market. First mark the position in the appropriate quartile where the firm considers itself to be. This might be done by the auditor, or by a consensus from within the firm. Then, so far as possible, compare this with the customers' perception of the position, if needs be by asking them directly through market research or (but not recommended) through the salesforce. Any discrepancy reveals an incorrect perception, which calls for an image correction or educational campaign.

This assessment may well reveal that the company is living in cloud cuckoo land with an unjustified complacency, or it could indicate a market with uninformed or incorrect perceptions. Either situation calls for immediate remedial action, but getting the market's and the company's view to line up does not ensure success. It is the optimum position (Question 18.61) that will produce the conditions of market leadership. List 24, 'Images and perceptions', also deals with this point.

Questions 18.67–18.69 turn to the issue of preferential or selected supplier lists, already mentioned in List 15, 'The buying process', and which will occur again in List 20, 'Competitive intelligence'. The need to know if such a list exists and the conditions for entry are so obviously important that it can only be wondered why many businesses persist in attempting to sell direct without first obtaining 'club' membership.

The five questions 18.70–18.74 could provide an explanation for something that sometimes mystifies firms. While the terms of payment may be identical in an industry, some companies enforce rigid payment on due date and ruthlessly refuse settlement discounts on late payment, while others, unofficially at least, ignore the late payment provided it does not become too onerous. Some organizations succeed in developing tactful and pleasant, but firm, methods of requesting payment while others are undiplomatic and rude. These different attitudes of two companies, both officially following the same policy, can well account for success and failure with any particular customer, who will obviously favour the less demanding company when all other things are equal. List 20, 'Competitive intelligence', Question 20.73, also covers this point.

Question 18.77 opens up considerable opportunities for both improving profitability and cutting marketing costs. Two customers each producing the same revenue do not necessarily provide the same profitability. Regularity in purchasing, size of individual 'drops', numbers of sales calls, numbers of complaints, speed in settlement of accounts are just a few of the factors which can enhance or reduce profitability of the individual customer. Customer value analysis will reveal ways of improving profitability, cutting costs by reducing support of unprofitable accounts and reallocating marketing resources.

The technique forms an important part of the output of product/service financial information, which comprises List 28, 'Product/service financial information'.

18.1 Which are the main and subsidiary user industries? (This information will have been compiled in response to List 4, 'Company performance', Questions 4.4 and 4.10; and List 7, 'Market size and structure', Questions 7.1 and 7.10.)

18.2 What research/application engineering has been done to prove the accuracy of the list?

18.3 What are the main constraints on demand?

18.4 What are the main stimulants of demand?

18.5 Are there any actions we can take to remove or distance the constraints?

18.6 Would new applications be opened up with product/service modifications, or changes in our commercial policies, including price? (A useful comparison could be made with List 4, 'Company performance', Questions 4.9 and 4.11; and List 7, 'Market size and structure', Question 7.25.)

18.7 What is the total number of organizations or installations that could feasibly use the product? (The answer to this question will have been given in List 7, 'Market size and structure', Question 7.7.)

18.8 What proportion of these represents a practical market target for us? (Compare this answer with List 4, 'Company performance', Questions 4.4, 4.10 and 4.11.)

18.9 How does demand vary among the various segments of the market? (Compare answer with List 1, 'Marketing strategy and planning', Question 1.21; and List 2, 'Product/service range', Question 2.2.)

- geographical
- process of application
- frequency of purchase
- benefit received
- form of customer organization
- demographic factors
- buyer's job function
- guarantee claims
- cost per sale
- industry or trade
- size of customer company
- size of order
- psychographic factors
- full-line or limited-range purchase

- seasonal
- lead time required
- order source (eg OEM distributor)
- servicing requirements
- value added
- credit requirements

(Many of these are a repeat of the suggested segmentation criteria given in List 2, 'Product/service range', Question 2.2. See also answers to List 4, 'Company performance', Questions 4.4 and 4.5. The answer will also help with profiling referred to in List 9, 'The salesforce and its management', Question 9.100.)

18.10 How does profitability vary between these and other segments? (See Introduction and the answers required for Questions 18.77–18.79.)

18.11 What characteristics identify our largest/smallest customers? (See Introduction, List 9, 'The salesforce and its management', Question 9.100 and Appendix 9B; and answers to List 15, 'The buying process', Questions 15.44 and 15.45; List 19, 'Key customer marketing', Questions 19.1 and 19.2.)

18.12 Can these profiles be used to direct the salesforce to and from similar potential customers? (See List 9, 'The salesforce and its management', Questions 9.100 and 9.101; and List 15, 'The buying process', Questions 15.44 and 15.45.)

18.13 What job functions are responsible for (a) initiating a purchase, (b) deciding the product/service type, (c) specifying, (d) selection of the suppliers? (See List 15, 'The buying process', Questions 15.1–15.9.)

Possible answers to the next four questions may be found in List 17, 'Introducing new products/services', Appendix 17B.)

18.14 Why do customers carry out the function the product/service is intended for in a particular way?

18.15 Would they prefer to do it in some other way or using some other type of product or service?

18.16 Would they like to omit the operations or activities the product/service carried out?

18.17 What improvement in the outcome of the use of the product or service would they like? (See List 17, 'Introducing new products/services', Appendix 17B.)

18.18 What are the major decision-forming factors – subjective and objective – in relation to suppliers?

- quality of product or service
- size of operation
- administrative efficiency
- guarantee – length and coverage

- delivery speed
- price, credit, discounts
- problem-solving
- quality of marketing
- geographic location
- links with industry
- full-line operation
- geographical coverage
- stock holding
- consignment selling policy
- specialization
- frequency of contact
- quality of salesforce
- servicing capability
- support services
- production facilities
- technical advice
- asset base
- joint research
- image, reputation and track record
- quality of management
- packaging and transport methods
- climate of industrial relations
- R & D
- 'approvals'

(The question arises in a number of different forms in different lists and answers should be compared and aligned. See especially List 3, 'The service element in marketing', Question 3.6; List 15, 'The buying process', Questions 15.10, 15.17–15.20; List 19, 'Key customer marketing', Question 19.29; and List 20, 'Competitive intelligence', Questions 20.10 and 20.20. Comparisons should be made with the self-image arising from List 24, 'Images and perceptions', Questions 24.8, 24.18 and 24.21.)

18.19 Is the portion of the target audience that is aware of the product/service sufficiently large?

18.20 Is the percentage of the target audience that prefers the product/service over the competition large enough to support sales and market share forecasts?

18.21 Is the target audience sufficiently aware of the offer's main advantage over the competition, and does the audience consider that advantage important? (The answer to this and the next question should be compared with List 2, 'Product/service range', Questions 2.23 and 2.27; and List 20, 'Competitive intelligence', Questions 2.60–2.66.)

18.22 Is the target audience fully aware of the offer's features, benefits, advantages and applications, and how important does the audience consider them?
18.23 Is it possible to assess how far purchasing decisions are a compromise and how far choices fall short of the desired true requirements? (See Introduction.)
18.24 Do user industries buy direct or through other channels (eg distributors, contractors)? (The answer to this question should align with List 14, 'The distributive system', Question 14.54.)
18.25 What are the reasons behind their policy to purchase through one route or another?
18.26 Should we incorporate the alternative supply channels into our marketing systems?
18.27 Can we adjust our product/service or commercial terms to win business from the alternative distributive channels?
18.28 Is purchasing cyclical or seasonal?
18.29 Are there any actions we can take to reduce peaks or troughs?
18.30 How are orders placed (ie bulk with call-off, ad hoc, etc.)?
18.31 What method favours us?
18.32 What adjustments must we make to meet ordering requirements of customers or to persuade them to order in a way that favours us?
18.33 What are users' lead-time requirements?
18.34 How does this compare with our lead-time quotations?
18.35 How reliable are our delivery quotations? (See Introduction and List 21, 'Physical distribution and packaging', Question 21.7.)
18.36 Are any actions required to improve our delivery performance, and if so, what are they? (Use List 21, 'Physical distribution and packaging', in conjunction with this question.)
18.37 Are there any known customer requirements not being met? (See Introduction and the items in Question 18.18; and List 17, 'Introducing new products/services', Appendix 17B.) What prevents us from meeting them?
18.38 Would relationship marketing assist us in meeting customer requirements? (See also List 1, 'Marketing strategy and planning', Question 1.33; List 13, 'Non-personal promotion', Question 13.63.)
18.39 Are there technical or commercial links between our competitors and customers that influence the market for the specified products/services, including reciprocal trading? (See Introduction as well as Introduction to List 7, 'Market size and structure', and consult answer to Question 7.2; List 20, 'Competitive intelligence', Appendix 20A.)
18.40 Is there any way we can counter these?
18.41 What proportion of our sales to user industries are through OEMs reselling to end users? (The answer in List 4, 'Company performance', Question 4.4, will give total sales *to* OEMs but not *through* OEMs. The difference may indicate a substantial profitable direct market.)
18.42 Should we seek this business direct?
18.43 What would be the gains and losses of adopting this approach?

18.44 What developments are occurring in the user industries that are likely to inhibit or stimulate a demand? (See List 1, 'Marketing strategy and planning', reference to vulnerability analysis.)
18.45 What actions are we taking to avert or exploit the situation?
18.46 What services are required? (See whole of List 3, 'The service element in marketing'.)
18.47 What knowledge do the user industries have of directly and indirectly competitive products/services?
18.48 What is the extent of misuse of the product/service?
18.49 Can we correct this misuse by training, educational campaigns or improved operating or maintenance manuals?
18.50 How does the user judge the end of the useful life of the product? (The question is repeated in a number of lists and is also presented from different perspectives. For this question and the following the auditor should consult and compare List 15, 'The buying process', Question 15.42; List 16, 'Analysing lost business', Questions 16.14 and 16.15; List 20, 'Competitive intelligence', Question 20.61; and List 23, 'Pricing', Question 23.22.)
18.51 Do the criteria for judging the end of useful life of our product differ by industry, application or other factors?
18.52 Are the criteria for judging the end of the useful life or our product the same as those applied to competitors' products? (Apart from the cross-references in Question 18.50 above, at this point it would be as well to ensure that the answers given in List 16, 'Analysing lost business', Question 16.15, and List 20, 'Competitive intelligence', Questions 20.60 and 20.61, also correspond.)
18.53 If not, why not?
18.54 Is purchasing or specification influenced or decided by individuals or companies not part of the management team? Who are they? (See List 15, 'The buying process', Questions 15.2, 15.5, 15.6.)
18.55 How stable would demand be in time of depression?
18.56 Is there a requirement for hire or lease facilities, and if so, can we provide it?
18.57 Complete the diagram showing our views of the company's position and of its products/services and the view of the market. (See Introduction; and use the answer in conjunction with List 7, 'Market size and structure', Questions 7.37; and List 23, 'Pricing', Question 23.5.)

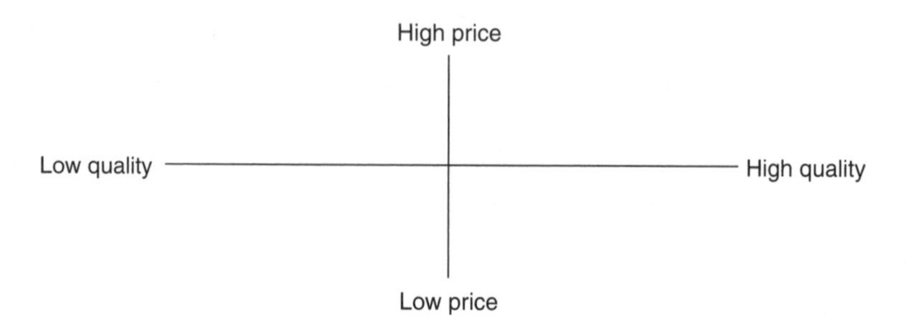

18.58 On what information is the above answer based?

18.59 Is there a gap between our position and the market's view of our position? (See List 24, 'Images and perceptions', Question 24.25.)

18.60 What action can we take to close it? (This question relates to List 24, 'Images and perceptions', Question 24.25.)

18.61 Does either the customers' perception of us or our own self-perception represent the optimum situation for us?

18.62 Should we try to move the market towards our perceived position or ourselves towards the market's view? (See Introduction to List 24, 'Images and perceptions', and Questions 24.18 and 24.28.)

18.63 What marketing methods are preferred by customers? How do they compare with those used by the company? (See List 15, 'The buying process', Question 15.36.)

18.64 If they differ, why do we not attempt to meet expressed customer preferences?

18.65 What are the usual media read/seen?

18.66 Are these reflected in our PR and advertising activities? (See List 13, 'Non-personal promotion: methods and media', Question 13.35.)

18.67 Do we know which customers or prospective customers have short-lists or approved supplier lists? (See List 20, 'Competitive intelligence', Question 20.23.)

18.68 Do we know the conditions for obtaining entry to the lists?

18.69 Can we meet them? (See Introduction; the answer to the last three questions should also be compared with List 15, 'The buying process', Questions 15.26, 15.30 and 15.32.)

18.70 What are the customary discount and credit terms? (The answer will be called for again in List 20, 'Competitive intelligence', Questions 20.68, 20.70 and 20.73.)

18.71 How stringent in terms of punctuality in payment do users regard our business terms? (See Introduction; and compare answer with List 20, 'Competitive intelligence', Questions 20.69 and 20.73.)

18.72 Do competitors apply similar policies?

18.73 Would an unofficial easing of stringency assist business?

18.74 What would such a policy cost the firm?

18.75 What are the user requirements for shipment and/or packaging requirements?

18.76 How closely do our shipment/packaging methods conform to user requirements? (See List 21, 'Physical distribution and packaging'.)

18.77 Have we conducted a customer value analysis (CVA)? (See Introduction; answers should be compared with those given in List 14, 'The distributive system', Question 14.58; List 19, 'Key customer marketing', Questions 19.9 and 19.11; List 28, 'Product/service financial information', Introduction and Questions 28.1 and 28.2.)

18.78 What factors were considered in such an analysis?

- size of order
- lead-time requirements
- order content

- use of services
- discounts given
- ratio of sales calls to enquiries
- ratio of quotations to orders
- level of guarantee and warranty claims
- level of other customer complaints
- packaging shipment requirements
- frequency of order
- location of deliveries
- size of drop
- prices obtained
- credit given and taken
- extent of returns and credits
- exit costs
- full range purchasing

18.79 Does the analysis take into account 'beyond profit' factors?

- growth of potential customer
- technological leadership of customer
- reputation of customer
- high share of customer requirements
- continuity
- opportunity to sell or develop new product/service
- opens new market sector

18.80 How postponable is purchasing?

18.81 What is the level of demand for own branding? Should we supply?

List 19

Key customer marketing

INTRODUCTION

Most organizations have a small number of customers who make a disproportionate contribution to the prosperity of the company or its prospects, yet few organizations have developed a coherent and consistent marketing policy which reflects this favourable inequality.

Even the largest company cannot claim to have unlimited resources for marketing, although it is worth quoting an ex-chairman of IBM: 'My marketing department has unlimited resources and it exceeds them every year.' Since finance, skills and time available for marketing are highly constrained, particularly for the small and medium-sized company, it must make business sense to stratify customers in terms of the extent to which they are to be nurtured.

A key customer might be described as one whose loss or gain would have a significant impact on the supplier's performance. This does not necessarily relate to turnover or profit generated. A customer could be 'key' because of the merits of the business obtained; that is, knowledge and experience which would be gained in obtaining entry into a new market sector; the customer organization is a high-profile prestigious company; it has the potential for generating greatly increased orders; or it opens up possibilities of developing new products.

Thus the first step is for companies to examine their customer base and potential customers and to create classifications to decide which of these should command disproportionate resources. Question 19.2 will assist in this process. The classification should divide customers as follows:

1. those which are to be the target for major marketing activities by the supplier because circumstances and requirements favour both the customers and the supplier;

2. those which could be considered for a major marketing effort because circumstances favour the customer but not necessarily the supplier, thus calling for some change in the latter's activities and their 'offer';
3. those which are easy and low-cost to supply but have only a low or irregular need;
4. those which can never achieve key customer status because of the type, quality, timing of their requirements, nil or low-growth prospects and competition.

Obviously the most interesting customers and potential customers are in group (1); that is, an organization with a high growth and profit potential where circumstances also favour the suppliers, so that competition is more easily countered and held off.

Group (2) represents a more difficult and longer-term situation but, nevertheless, is a category which has to be considered carefully. Here perhaps the customers' activities and growth prospects make them highly suitable targets, but it is a situation in which the competition usually has some unique facility, resource, product or skill which makes them the favoured supplier. The task must be to identify the competitive advantage and to evaluate both the possibilities of matching and surpassing it and the profitability of so doing.

Group (3) customers should command only the minimum amount of effort required to maintain the *status quo*. Their potential compared to key customers is small and the cost of meeting this must be kept low. Thus, although volume or value may not be great, profits may well be in the higher quartile.

Group (4) customers have no growth potential for the company, competition is keen and, in fact, the mirror opposite situation to group (1) exists. While such customers should never be arbitrarily dropped, certainly they must not command or dilute limited marketing resources.

The next stage is to examine the character of customer relationship within the designated key customer company; that is, who within the customer organization is known and by whom in the supplier company and the quality of that relationship. Questions 19.13–19.17 cover this, but a simple exercise, perhaps using the format shown in Figure 19.1, is extremely valuable. The horizontal column shows those in the company who interface with the customer; the vertical column gives the names of those with whom they have contact. The letters indicate in a semantic code the quality of the link.

Looking at the specimen form, it can be seen at once that there are two vulnerabilities. First, only one person in the supply firm knows the production director, who can be an important decision-maker, depending on the purchase. If this director leaves the company, the excellent relationship at that level is lost. If the production manager is promoted, the supplier now has only two relatively poor quality contacts. Second, 'DMG' has eight contacts within the customer firm. Should DMG's position change, there is only one quality link left at service manager level and none at works manager.

A chart such as this shows quickly and efficiently just who within the customer company must be the target for key customer marketing and possibly the form those activities could take.

Name and title	Our contacts DMG	GBA	GP	DJ	Others
Production director: M.J. Harrap	A				
Production manager: T.C. Addison	C		D		
Works manager: P.V. Longman	A	B		D	
Chief buyer: W. Chambers	B	A	B	A	(J.B.)
Maintenance engineer: D.M. Evans	A	D	A		
Design department manager: R.P. Cass	D	A		D	
Service department manager: A.C. Turnbull	C			B	(A.K.)
Works manager: R Butler	A				

A Close relationship, partly personal
B Good relationship but formal
C Occasional contact
D Has met but not worked with

Figure 19.1 Relationship with decision-makers

What is now required is, for example, for the senior managers to set themselves both an inward and outward visit schedule so that contact with the decision-makers and influencers can be widened and made regularly and the perception of the supplier as committed to and concerned with the development of that customer clearly demonstrated.

It is particularly important to note that there must be an equivalency between the answers to Questions 19.13–19.14 and 19.21, in terms of matching status between buyer (or buying influence) and seller.

An intensive customer and contact programme must be developed, most particularly in the form of a regular check on the quality of the products/services delivered; in addition, frequent *relevant* communications which might take the form of newsletters, reprints of articles and press releases, proactive marketing by identifying with the customer interests, and anticipating needs and problems should all be an important part of the activity 'mix'. Accessibility to members of the supplier company has to be of high order, and punctuality and a quick response maintained even if it is at the expense of non-key customers.

Question 19.24 raises a matter that is frequently treated in a cavalier fashion. In seeking to persuade customers to visit the office or plant, there has to be a trade-off benefit for customers' investment of time. What will they learn or gain by making such a visit? The answer should be clear before any invitation is made. The logistics of any visit must be carefully planned to make it easy and economic for the customer; provision of travel tickets or facilities, hotel accommodation and schedules. Equally, internal preparation for the visitor's reception and contacts, meetings and plant inspections requires organizing. Taking a visitor round a plant or office while the staff are taking a meal break does not create an impression of busy efficiency.

Key customers are usually aware of their status. Thus they have a favourable negotiating position which demands that the supplier must also have exceptional skills in negotiation. Questions 19.47–19.55 focus on this important topic.

But key customers are not just the concern of marketing personnel. Everyone without exception down to the lowliest members of the company must know who are the key customers. These are the ones who are not kept waiting on the telephone or in reception, are not subject to peremptory demands for payment; they do not receive non-personalized correspondence, and are not asked to adjust their schedules and timing to fit in with the suppliers' needs or convenience; and knowledge of their organization and of their own personal position and likings is never superficial or non-existent.

In this respect Questions 19.58–19.61 are of importance. It has been said with considerable truth that the odds are weighted heavily against any selling organization: the arithmetic clearly demonstrates that few people can obtain customers but anyone in the organization can lose them.

Again, because of their leverage, key customers may well require special backup services which it would not be profitable to deliver to all customers. (See List 3, 'The service element in marketing', Appendix 3A). Only a total customer value analysis (CVA) will enable the supplier to decide if it is appropriate to supply them.

The last question, 19.69, on just-in-time (JIT) delivery, of course opens up a totally new area and one in which marketing has taken too small a part. JIT can be as important a marketing tool as any other technique once it is appreciated that its value goes far beyond its original conception as a production supply technique. The implications throughout the company of adopting a JIT system are considerable and it cannot be viewed in isolation, but this does not mean it ought not to be considered as a valid, profitable and sustainable marketing advantage.

Key account marketing does not differ fundamentally from any other marketing except in its frequency, intensity and type and level of contact. However, more than a change of emphasis is needed if it is to be successful. What is also required is a change of attitude towards actual and potential key customers and towards the marketing itself.

These principal points should be noted:

- Closer working relationships must be developed.
- Negotiating skills are needed.
- Improved internal coordination is vital.
- More and better back-up services have to be available.
- Optimum follow-up is necessary.
- Better intelligence means fewer missed opportunities.

19.1 Which customers and *potential* customers meet the key customer profile requirement (by name)?

19.2 What are the reasons for allocating them this status? (This question will have been partly answered in List 18, 'User industries', Question 18.11.)

- volume of business

- potential business
- method of purchasing
- anti-cyclical purchasing
- opportunity for new product introductions
- size of order drop
- generates demand for complementary products
- quality of business
- purchasing frequency
- regularity of purchasing and timing
- customer's prestige
- procurement advantages
- opens new market segment
- opportunity for reciprocal trading
- others

19.3 On a comparison of profit as against turnover, is the categorization of 'key' customer valid?

19.4 What share of customer's total demand do we command?

19.5 What trends will reduce or increase demand for both actual and potential key customers?

19.6 What do the major accounts require now that they did not five years ago?

19.7 What changes have there been in the relative importance of distribution channels over the last five years, either as key accounts themselves or as intermediaries supplying key customers?

19.8 How has the average size of key customers varied over the last five years?

19.9 How has profitability varied over the last five years (CVA). (Answers should be compared with those given and called for in List 14, 'The distributive system', Question 14.58; List 18, 'User industries', Question 18.77; and List 28, 'Product/service financial information', Introduction and Questions 28.1 and 28.2.)

19.10 What future trends are likely?

19.11 Have we conducted, or can we conduct a CVA to confirm key customer status? (See List 18, 'User industries', Introduction and Questions 18.77 and 18.78; and List 28, 'Product/service financial information', Questions 28.1 and 28.2.)

19.12 How much information do we have on each designated key and potential key customer?

- turnover by product/service type
- size by numbers employed
- organizational structure
- major competitors
- form of ownership
- subsidiary/parent company

- links with competitors
- share of their own markets
- growth/decline trends
- quality management
- full potential for our product/service

(See also List 6, 'Marketing information: systems and use'.)

19.13 Who are our contacts within the customer company? (See Introduction and Figure 19.1; and List 15, 'The buying process', for decision-making unit information.)
19.14 Who are the powerful decision-makers and influences within the key customer company? (See List 15, 'The buying process', Questions 15.1–15.5.)
19.15 Who in our company has contact with the important decision-makers and influencers? (See Figure 19.1; also List 15, 'The buying process', Question 15.4.)
19.16 What formal and informal relationships exist with major customers?
19.17 What is the quality of our contact with the DMU? (See Introduction and Figure 19.1.)
19.18 How are informal relationships monitored?
19.19 Can we make better use of the informal relationships?
19.20 What methods will achieve this?
19.21 What should be the managerial level of personnel in contact with the customer? (The question occurs again in different contexts elsewhere: Question 19.15; List 5, 'Export marketing', Questions 5.42–5.44; List 9, 'The salesforce and its management', Question 9.6; List 12, 'The agency system', Question 12.55; and List 14, 'The distributive system', Question 14.72.)
19.22 What knowledge exists, and how valid and recent is it, of customer policies, needs, aspirations, problems? (See List 18, 'User industries'.)
19.23 Does the present contact cycle reflect the importance of the customer?
19.24 What is the programme for inward visits (plant, office site, etc.)? (See Introduction.)
19.25 What benefit will members of the customer's DMU perceive in visiting our premises? (See Introduction.)
19.26 What actions are we proposing to establish and implement frequency of visits?
19.27 How entrenched is our position with customers?
19.28 What are our main vulnerabilities with each key customer?
19.29 What is the nature of the specific competition for each key client's business? (The question arises in a number of different forms in different lists. See specifically List 3, 'The service element in marketing', Question 3.6; List 18, 'User industries', Question 18.18; List 20, 'Competitive intelligence', Question 20.20. A comparison should be made with the self-image arising from List 24, 'Images and perceptions', Question 24.8.)
19.30 Is there a special surveillance of competitive actions to penetrate key client accounts? (See List 20, 'Competitive intelligence', Appendix 20A.)

19.31 How are sales to major customers currently forecast and how should this be improved?
19.32 Have we a clearly defined key customer strategy and action plan to ensure customer retention and expansion of business?
19.33 Are our personnel with customer contact involved in creating the strategy and with its implementation?
19.34 What training is required to ensure that the necessary staff:
- understand the plans?
- can forecast realistically?
- can develop strategy?
- can implement tactics effectively?

19.35 Do we have the necessary resources to conduct the nurturing tactics, most particularly human resources?
19.36 What steps can be taken to fill any gaps?
19.37 In what way will the reallocation of resources impact on non-key customers?
19.38 Is this impact acceptable?
19.39 Will our present marketing/sales system require adjustment to accommodate a key customer strategy?
19.40 If so, in what way?
19.41 How will we ensure coordination of effort?
19.42 Do we have a monitoring system to identify changes in customer-purchasing patterns, circumstance and markets?
19.43 Does the action plan require regular discussions on our personnel with client contacts on progress, changes in status and opportunities?
19.44 Is there a clearly defined system for promotion to or removal from key customer status?
19.45 Do visit reports provide usable information on customers? (See List 9, 'The salesforce and its management', Questions 9.94–9.100 and 9.118.)
19.46 Is such information used and in what way?
19.47 Are our negotiating skills sufficient to ensure profitable sales? (Compare answer with that in List 9, 'The salesforce and its management', Question 9.47; and later with List 23, 'Pricing', Questions 23.37 and 23.38.)
19.48 What countervailing negotiating skills do we command?
19.49 If none, what actions should be taken to acquire them?
19.50 Are negotiations planned?
19.51 If so, in what way?
19.52 What existing concessions should be renegotiated in a more favourable form?
19.53 What preparation occurs for team negotiation?
19.54 What post-negotiation analysis occurs?

19.55 What negotiation training is given to:
- sales staff?
- sales support staff?

19.56 Is this sufficient?

19.57 How will a key customer designation impact on prices obtained? (See List 9, 'The salesforce and its management', Question 9.47; and List 23, 'Pricing'.)

19.58 Are all staff, most particularly sales office staff, aware of key customer status? (The whole of List 10, 'Customer care and support staff's role in marketing', should be studied relative to this topic.)

19.59 What additional training/motivation do they require to ensure appropriate treatment of key customers?

19.60 Does everyone in the company interfacing with the customer know by name the personnel who are in contact with us?

19.61 Can non-sales personnel who have customer contact, both direct and indirect, identify key customer personnel by name?

19.62 Will a key customer strategy require more and/or better service backing?

19.63 What service backing is needed? (See List 3, 'The service element in marketing', Appendix 3A.)

19.64 Can we provide this service backing?

19.65 Is it possible to use key customers as 'demonstration plant'?

19.66 What mechanisms exist within the company to enable effective coordination of all the necessary key customer activities to occur?

19.67 What weaknesses exist in these mechanisms and how should they be remedied?

19.68 Who in the company will be responsible for implementing and monitoring key customer strategy and activities?

19.69 Could we consolidate our position with key customers by developing and offering a just-in-time (JIT) delivery service? (Compare the answer to that given in List 20, 'Competitive intelligence', Question 20.17; and see Introduction to List 21, 'Physical distribution and packaging', and Questions 21.16–21.19.)

List 20

Competitive intelligence

INTRODUCTION

It is a rare industry or activity where competition can be ignored. The very largest as well as the very smallest of firms are all affected. Unfortunately, looking into competitors' activities is particularly hazardous, in that it is difficult, if not impossible, to be totally objective. Many views on competition are based on multiple hearsay – hair-raising stories put out by sales and service staff, trade paper rumours and wishful thinking. If any section in this book requires the marketing auditor to stand back and be totally objective, it is this one. In every case the unwritten questions that follow each item are 'How do we know?' and 'How reliable is the information?' Also underlying each question is the evaluation of 'Why does our policy differ from competitors? Should it?'

Christopher West, a leading expert in competitive intelligence, correctly points out that in order to compete it is essential not only to identify the competition but also to understand their resources, their strategies, their strengths and weaknesses as perceived by customers, the threat they pose to other suppliers and their vulnerabilities to attack. Detailed knowledge of competitors has never been easy to acquire and marketing history is littered with examples of successful businesses that have been brought down by competition which was either unknown or known but undervalued. There are also countless examples of opportunities missed through failures to capitalize on competitors' weaknesses.

Keeping abreast of competition is becoming increasingly difficult as the pace of change in markets accelerates. Competitive tension is being heightened by powerful forces which are driving existing competitors to be more aggressive and at the same time attracting new competitors. Deregulation, reductions in trade barriers, radical political realignments and the increasing globalization of supply all create new opportunities but at the same time threaten those who fail to appreciate that the competitive environment is changing and that previous competitive boundaries have been blurred. The auditor should look closely at the carefully compiled (and field tested for practicality) list created by Christopher West for his own book.[1] It is reproduced as Appendix 20A with his permission.

The questions in this list can also be augmented by reference to the sections on competitors in List 6, 'Marketing information: systems and use'. Competitor data are much more easily available than many firms imagine, from both direct and indirect enquiries. Interviewing competitors is not industrial espionage and need be neither feared nor shunned.

In examining competition it is important not to be too parochial. While direct competition – comparison of equivalent products and services – is obvious, there is also that part of the market where requirements are met by totally different approaches. For example, a competitor of air filters and their components is the vacuum collection of dust and swarf from machines. Some medical procedures can be carried out using electronics or pharmaceuticals; and, in this same field, disposables of all types compete with sterilizers and laundries. Thus, the need is to see how the total requirement is met, not just the part that is satisfied by directly competitive offerings. Questions 20.1 and 20.2 cover this point.

Question 20.11, on rating particular aspects of the offering and performance with either a major competitor or with competitors generally, can be refined by using a numerical rating and indeed by weighting the various issues in relative importance to each other. The same technique was suggested for selecting an export market. (List 5, 'Export marketing', Appendix 5A, explains the method.)

Suppliers rarely give much thought to how deep their 'visibility' may be in firms – both customers and prospects. The fact they are known by buyers does not necessarily imply that other members of the DMU will know them and prefer them. Marketing must penetrate further than the buying office. Marketing auditors should look at the answer to List 15, 'The buying process', Question 15.1, and ask if all the key members of the DMU are as likely to know them as well as they do their competitors. Question 20.22 focuses on this aspect of marketing. If the format in List 19, 'Key customers', Figure 19.1, is completed the situation will become clear.

'Break cost', referred to in Question 20.28, can be a profitable strategy. This comprises making the cost of switching suppliers sufficiently high to lock in the customers. Any uniquely modular system does this as the customer has to continue to buy the module to maintain compatibility. The more they buy, the more expensive it may become to switch. Thus the concomitant strategy may be low capital cost and high consumable, spare, or add-on cost.

The distribution of competitors' sales will frequently correlate with the offices of salespeople or agents, or the location of distributors. It is useful to plot these from competitors' literature – a quick and simple method of gaining some insight into the geographical distribution of business. Question 20.41 can often be answered in this way. In any event, an often overlooked but valuable activity is to collect and collate competitors' promotional material, including of course Web sites. (See Appendix 20A.)

Estimating a competitor's marketing appropriations, as is called for in Question 20.50, may seem an impossible task. There is no doubt it can be very difficult, but some aspects of promotion are capable of at least rough estimation. There are published statistics of some media advertising expenditure, and this is also calculable by the onerous but moderately accurate method of measuring or timing advertisements, noting their composition (colour, black and white, bleed, etc) and frequency, and aggregating the expenditure by reference to that medium's rate-card multiplied by the number of insertions or exposures on radio/TV.

Sales representatives' costs can sometimes be gauged from formal published surveys, vacancies advertised, trade associations and from 'head hunters' and employment agencies. 'Add-ons' such as the quality of vehicles supplied, health insurance schemes, bonuses and other elements in the total package are not so easy to estimate accurately. Exhibitions are calculable on the same basis as advertisements, using stand size and position and organizers' charges, but a notional figure may have to go in for stand construction and fitting costs and manning. A number of commercial services provide online surveillance of media comment on named competitors, so it is possible to obtain at very least a 'feel' for how much press exposure is being achieved and thus the extent and success of their PR activities.

Questions 20.67–20.77 again seek to distinguish what customers pay for a product as opposed to what it actually costs them. It is doubly important in relation to competitors. Any differences that can be accounted for will negate an apparent price advantage. However, differences can be real but difficult to determine. The price of zinc and copper process printing plate in Holland was found to be directly comparable to, or even marginally higher than, British products until the enhanced price offered for used plate was investigated. This gave a clear advantage to the Dutch product. Question 20.71 asks the auditor to look much more widely than apparent similarities and differences justify. In this respect, List 23, 'Pricing', Figure 23.1, will provide some items for comparison to arrive at the true price.

In any event, in looking at price it is always as well to remember that pressure for lower prices by comparison with an apparently lower competitive price frequently comes not from the buyer but from the salesperson, where the method of remuneration may favour such pressure. The Introduction to List 9, 'The salesforce', shows the arithmetic of such a situation. Thus, all questions on competitive prices need doubly careful scrutiny as to source and indeed motive.

To be effective, competitive strategy must not just be defensive. There must also be an attacking element through which consistent and determined marketing efforts can wrest business from the competition. Question 20.83 suggests where vulnerabilities might exist. It should be noted, however, that there are other possible weak areas which are beyond the range of marketing activities to attack, for example the supply of materials, key personnel, equipment, purchased services and possibly even finance.

20.1 Which companies make directly competitive products (type and range spread) or provide directly competitive services? (Detailed examination of competitors' brochures and catalogues makes the plotting of this information simple if sometimes onerous.)

20.2 Which firms make indirectly competitive products or provide indirect competitive services? (See Introduction; some additional guidance in completing the question might be obtained from the answers to List 7, 'Market size and structure', Questions 7.5 and 7.7.)

Additional information which might be required for Questions 20.1 and 20.2 includes:

- location
- headquarters
- production
- marketing
- warehousing
- key financial data
- production capacity
- main suppliers
- extent of outsourcing of marketing activities
- physical distribution methods
- number of employees

20.3 What are their market shares? (This information will have been provided in the answer to List 7, 'Market size and structure', Question 7.14.)

20.4 How deeply entrenched are they in the market?

20.5 Which are our fastest-growing competitors?

20.6 How do we account for their success? (This point may have been answered in part in List 7, 'Market size and structure', Question 7.16.)

20.7 Which competitors (by name) are likely to leave the market in the next 3–5 years? (This answer was required for List 8, 'Future market', Question 8.27.)

20.8 What is the basis for their customers' loyalty? (This information will have been provided in the answer to List 7, 'Market size and structure', Question 7.16; List 10, 'Customer care and support staff's role in marketing', Question 10.7, may possibly also provide some answers; and further probing will occur in List 25, 'Quality in marketing', Question 25.29.)

20.9 Where in their operations are they vulnerable? (See Introduction and Question 20.83.)

Resources they use	*Resources they generate*
material	products
personnel	customer loyalty
machines	goodwill
finance	brand awareness and visibility

20.10 What competitive advantages do (a) we and (b) the market consider that our main and indirect competitors have or claim? (See Question 20.20 and Appendix 20A, but the topic arises in a number of different forms in different lists. See specifically List 3, 'The service element in marketing', Question 3.6; List 15, 'The buying process', Question 15.17; List 18, 'User industries', Question 18.18. A comparison should be made with the self-image arising from List 24, 'Images and perceptions', Question 24.8, and List 25, 'Quality in marketing', Question 25.37.)

- administrative efficiency
- backup services
- commercial terms
- delivery
- financial strength
- full-line operation
- guarantees
- licences – inward and outward
- marketing skills
- packaging and shipment methods
- problem-solving ability
- production facilities
- protection – official and unofficial
- quality of management
- servicing capability
- technical advice/joint research
- track record and image
- approvals
- climate of industrial relations
- distribution network
- franchises
- geographical location
- joint research
- links with customer industries
- ownership of brands
- patents
- procurement strength
- product/service quality
- quality of marketing and coverage
- reputation
- size of operation
- technical support
- unique selling proposition

20.11 How far do competitors' products/services compare with our own on the following issues? (See Introduction; also List 17, 'Introducing new products/services, Question 17.61; List 25, 'Quality in marketing', Question 25.7 and Appendix 25A.)

Better/Worse	*Better/Worse*
technical leadership	life expectancy
quality	energy/consumable costs
performance	maintenance costs
reliability	including down time
finish	upgrade capability
design	physical dimensions
adaptability	ease of installation
trade-in value	reliability
range-width and depth	upgrade and retro-fit
size of operation	capability

20.12 Which of the following are key factors in purchasing decisions and how are we and our competitors rated on each one?

OURSELVES **COMPETITORS A B C**

price
technical leadership
other physical characteristics
delivery reliability and service
packaging or packing method
supporting services provided
company's reputation and guarantees
brand or product reputation
reciprocal trade agreements
company affiliations
personal relationships
approvals
add others

20.13 Rate the quality of competitors' management and management systems. (Relate Questions 20.18–20.20 to the answer.)
20.14 What stocks do competitors normally hold?
20.15 What stocks of competitors' products do distributors hold? (See List 14, 'The distributive system', Question 14.42.)
20.16 What are competitors' distributor and user policies relative to stock-holding?
20.17 Are any of the competitors providing a JIT service to their customers? (See List 19, 'Key customer marketing', Introduction and Question 19.69; and List 21, 'Physical distribution and packaging', Questions 21.16–21.19.)

20.18 Have competitors' performances (profit, sales, exports, etc) paralleled our own and the fluctuations in the economy over the last few years? (Compare with answer to Questions 20.12 and 20.13 and see Appendix 20A.)
20.19 If not, how have they varied, and how can we account for any disparity with our own performance?
20.20 What is each competitor's claimed major strength and weakness and reputation among users? How far is the claim justified? (See Appendix 20A and cross-check with the answer to Question 20.10 and compare our own views and the market perceptions with competitors' claims. Additionally, use answers derived from List 3, 'The service element in marketing', Question 3.6; and List 19, 'Key customer marketing', Question 19.29.)
20.21 Are there any steps we can take to exploit their weaknesses or counteract their strengths? (See Introduction.)
20.22 How far beyond the purchasing department in customer firms are competitive products/services known, and how far are they associated with competitors by name? (See Introduction, List 15, 'The buying process', Question 15.26; and List 19, 'Key customer marketing', Figure 19.1.)
20.23 Is there any evidence that our competitors obtain entry to short-lists or approved supplier lists more frequently than we do? (Compare answers with List 15, 'The buying process', Questions 15.30 and 15.31; and List 18, 'User industries', Question 18.67.)
20.24 Estimate extent of competitors' direct and indirect exports and list main export territories.
20.25 Are the major competitors known to do marketing research? (See Appendix 20A.)
20.26 Is this conducted by internal departments or agencies?
20.27 What image do we have of the main competitors and how does it compare with the image their customers and non-customers have of them? (See answers to List 24, 'Images and perceptions', Questions 24.8, 24.11 and 24.12.)
20.28 Is there any break-cost element in competitors' marketing or product strategy? (See Introduction.)
20.29 Are our competitors known by name or brand?
20.30 Is there a brand that is a generic for the product/service (eg Hoover – vacuum cleaner; JCB – earth mover)?
20.31 Do our competitors manufacture for companies with private brands?
20.32 Do our competitors manage their own advertising or use agencies? (This question will have been answered in List 13, 'Non-personal promotion: methods and media', Question 13.44.)
20.33 What services do our competitors offer? (For classifications see List 3, 'The service element in marketing', Appendix 3A.)
20.34 Is any part of our industry or activities likely to be the subject of official inquiry (eg Office of Fair Trading, Monopolies Commission, EU)? (See answer to Question 20.79.)

20.35 If so, is our firm likely to be part of the inquiry?
20.36 Would we benefit by an inquiry into trade practices?
20.37 To what extent is competition from foreign sources judged unfair?
20.38 What individual, or joint, action (trade association) can we take to rectify or modify the position? (See List 22, 'Industry contacts', Questions 22.6–22.8.)
20.39 Does membership of a trade association, professional body or other organization limit our competitiveness? (See List 22, 'Industry contacts', Question 22.10, which will also require this information, and List 27, 'Service businesses', Introduction and Question 27.8.)
20.40 What would be the advantages/disadvantages of terminating membership? (See List 22, 'Industry contacts', Question 22.17.)
20.41 What methods of distribution do our major competitors use? (Compare answer with List 14, 'The distributive system', Questions 14.32–14.36 and List 21, 'Physical distribution packaging', Question 21.52.)
20.42 What aids do our competitors give distributors? (Compare with answer in List 14, 'The distributive system', Question 14.51.)
20.43 Is a franchise system operated? (See Introduction to List 14, 'The distributive system'.)
20.44 How many salespeople and/or agents do our competitors employ? (See Introduction.)
20.45 What is their geographical spread? (See Introduction.)
20.46 What type and quality of salespeople or agents are employed – technical, semi-technical, non-technical – in our application/industry? (See answers in List 9, 'The salesforce and its management', Questions 9.11–9.13; and List 26, 'Non-differentiated products and commodities', Questions 26.25 and 26.26.)
20.47 What is the competitor policy on the use of agents? (See List 12, 'The agency system', Question 12.82, which might indicate a vulnerability.)
20.48 Can we identify their agents?
20.49 Shall we attempt to recruit them?

(The answers to questions on agents should be compared with List 12, 'The agency system', Questions 12.79 and 12.82, but it would also be useful to complete List 12 as far as possible in relation to competitors' policies and activities.)

20.50 What are the competitors' promotion messages, media and methods, and appropriations? (See Introduction and Appendix 20A; List 13, 'Non-personal promotion: methods and media', Questions 13.28 and 13.29.)
20.51 What are our competitors' policies on guarantees and warranties? (This question has been asked in List 13, 'Non-personal promotion: methods and media', Question 13.61; but also compare answer with List 26, 'Non-differentiated products and commodities', Questions 26.20–26.24.)

20.52 How stringently or liberally are guarantee and warranty policies applied?

20.53 What are our competitors' packaging and shipment methods and how do they compare to our own? (See Appendix 20A. This answer will also be required in List 21, 'Physical distribution and packaging', Question 21.5.)

20.54 Do competitors make additional charges for packaging/delivery/returns, etc.?

20.55 Should we follow their policy or exploit it?

20.56 What competitor technical or commercial policies are developing or planned which will impact on the demand for our product or service? (At least part of the answer will have been provided in response to List 8, 'Future market', Questions 8.16, 8.27 and 8.32.)

20.57 Overall, does any difference in our policies account for any performance differences?

20.58 How far do competitors' products accord with an idealized 'profile' of the product/service? (This important topic is restated in other lists and the answers should be compared. See List 2, 'Product/service range', Question 2.43; List 16, 'Analysing lost business', Question 16.10; List 23, 'Pricing', Question 23.29; and List 26, 'Non-differentiated products and commodities', Questions 26.33–26.35.)

20.59 Are the purchasing decision factors applied to competitors' products/services the same as our own? (See answer to List 15, 'The buying process', Questions 15.10 and 15.17; and List 18, 'User industries', Questions 18.50 and 18.51.)

20.60 Are our competitors' products used in a different way to that for which they are promoted? (See List 16, 'Analysing lost business', Questions 16.14–16.17.)

20.61 Is the end of the useful life of competitors' products judged by the same criteria as our own? (The question is repeated in a number of lists and is also presented from different perspectives. The auditor should consult and compare answers with List 2, 'Product/service range', Question 2.45; List 15, 'The buying process', Questions 15.42 and 15.43; List 16, 'Analysing lost business', Questions 16.14 and 16.15; List 18, 'User industries', Questions 18.50 and 18.51; and List 23, 'Pricing', Question 23.22.)

20.62 What changes have competitors made in their products/services since they were introduced?

20.63 What reasons can these changes be attributed to?

20.64 How closely do competitors' products conform to official and unofficial standards?

20.65 What is the extent of competitors' product/service research and development?

20.66 What is their history of new product introductions? Rate their successes and failures and give reasons for them.

20.67 How do gross and nett prices compare with similar products or services? (See Introduction; List 14, 'The distributive system', Question 14.50; and List 23, 'Pricing', Question 23.29, where this reply is again required; but also compare answer with List 2, 'Product/service range', Question 2.23; and List 28, 'Product/service financial information', Question 28.13.)

20.68 How do gross and nett prices compare with substitute products or services? (See List 23, 'Pricing', Questions 23.4 and 23.14.)

20.69 What are the competitors' usual credit and discount terms? (See List 14, 'The distributive system', Question 14.50; List 18, 'User industries', Questions 18.71 and 18.72 for a comparison; and answers in List 23, 'Pricing', Question 23.14.)

20.70 Is there any evidence of hidden discounts?

20.71 Are there any other offsetting factors to take into account (eg trade-in values, low-cost consumables, free service, free training, long guarantees, etc)? (See Introduction; and List 14, 'The distributive system', Question 14.51. Additionally, some offsetting factors will be found in List 23, 'Pricing', Figure 23.1 and the accompanying explanation.)

20.72 What is the price history of the most popular/least popular unit of sale?

20.73 How do competitors' margins and credit terms to distributors and other intermediaries compare with our own? (See answers in List 14, 'The distributive system', to Questions 14.50–14.53 for comparison purposes; Introduction to List 18, 'User industries', Questions 18.70–18.74; and List 23, 'Pricing', Question 23.14.)

20.74 What incentives – financial and non-financial – do our competitors provide for their distributors?

20.75 Where did the information to make this comparison come from and how reliable is it?

20.76 What reasons can we ascribe for fluctuations in price?

20.77 Is price consciously used as part of competitors' marketing strategy? (See List 23, 'Pricing', and Appendix 23A.)

20.78 How do charges (if any) for different support services compare with our own?

20.79 Is there any evidence of price-fixing – overt or covert? (Compare with answer to Question 20.34.)

20.80 Have we made any 'cost-in-use' comparisons between our own and competitors' products? (See List 23, 'Pricing', Figure 23.1.)

20.81 Have we identified the attributes of the product/service most/least valued by customers? (See the Introduction to List 23, which gives a brief explanation of attribute research.)

20.82 Do our competitors hold any accreditations (eg ISO 9000, Baldrige, OEM etc)?

20.83 What is our strategy for attacking any competitive vulnerabilities in terms of product or service weaknesses, customer loyalty, goodwill, brand awareness or visibility, distributive network, cooperative arrangements with other business or organizations?

Appendix 20A
The competitive intelligence checklist[2]

The coverage of any competitive intelligence exercise will vary according to business area, the companies to be included and the purposes for which the results will be used. The checklist that follows lists the generic topics that can be researched.

Who are the competitors?

- Current direct competitors
- Current indirect competitors
- Potential future competitors

Profiles of current and potential competitors

Company details

- Headquarters
- Company structure
- Production locations
- Sales offices (domestic and foreign)
- Key executives (background, previous employment, track record)
- Total number of employees (administration, production and sales and marketing)
- Ownership
- Subsidiaries
- Affiliates

Organization

- Organizational structure
- Key operating divisions
- Resourcing of each division
- Activities of each division

Financial performance

- Consolidated key financial performance data
- Divisional financial performance

Products

- Products/services supplied
- Specifications of products/services
- Claimed technical/specification advantages
- Major product applications

Physical distribution

- Distribution channels used
- Key distributors
- Relative importance of each distribution channel
- Distribution methods (own transport resources, subcontracted logistics services)
- Size and structure of transport fleet
- Use of vehicle livery for advertising

Marketing

- Target market segments
- Market shares in key segments
- Size and structure of the sales and marketing department
- Outline of marketing and promotion methods
- Brochures and catalogues
  - format
  - coverage
  - content
- Newsletters
- Advertising
  - advertising objectives
  - advertising expenditure
  - media used (TV, radio, national press, trade, technical and professional press, cinema, posters and non-conventional media)
  - advertising messages
  - advertising agencies used
- Direct marketing
  - direct mail programmes
  - telesales
  - role of the telesales department
  - balance between inbound and outbound activity
  - locations of call centres
  - number of telesales agents
  - sources of databases
- PR (programmes and resources)
  - agencies used
  - news items issued
  - volume of coverage obtained
- Sales promotion
  - programmes
  - incentives
  - resources

- exhibitions attended
- sponsorship
  - events sponsored
  - value of sponsorships
- corporate hospitality
  - events used
- merchandising
- customer/distributor service programmes
- market research
  - commitment to research
  - size of research department
  - types of research carried out

Web site

- role of the Web site within the e-business strategy (see below)
- format (text, graphics)
- coverage and content
- extent to which the Web site is transactional and types of transactions available
- hyperlinks to other sites
- number of visitors/hits to Web site

E-business

- existence of an e-business strategy
- role of e-business in the overall strategy
- e-business objectives
- e-business initiatives
  - electronic information exchanges with suppliers and customers
  - e-procurement
  - transactional services (ordering, inventory data, order status, payment information, payments)
- proportion of sales made through e-business channels
- use of Internet trading sites
- use of extranets and Web portals

Prices and discounts

- price of ranges per product line
- price positioning
- discount structure

Relationships/partnerships
- licences
- joint ventures
- distribution agreements
- marketing partnerships
- length of time relationships/partnerships have been running
- affiliations/membership of trade bodies

Export activity
- export sales
- importance of exports in total revenues
- export methods (through overseas subsidiaries, agents, distributors)
- countries in which export sales are made and local resources in each country
- export marketing activity

Overseas subsidiaries
- countries
- locations
- activities (representation, local production, sales and marketing)
- products sold
- contribution to consolidated revenues

INTERPRETATION

The data collected on each company can be analysed and interpreted in order to deduce those aspects of their activities on which direct information is unlikely to be collected. These will include:

- apparent overall strategic intent
- strategic directions
- methods of implementing the strategy
  - apparent market positioning
  - products
  - technology
  - target markets (customer segments, geographical)
  - apparent distribution strategy
  - apparent pricing strategy
  - promotion and communications strategy

- extent and nature of competitive threat
- resources and resource limitations on the business
- potential retaliation to competitive action (intensity and direction)

COUNTER-INTELLIGENCE

On the assumption that all companies seeking competitive intelligence are also likely to be the subject of competitive intelligence-gathering exercises by their competitors, equal consideration should be given to the task of minimizing information outflows. A key task is to balance essential information outflows (for marketing, procurement and other purposes) with the need to restrict information flows to competitors or those acting on their behalf. The relevant questions to be asked are:

- Who is likely to be seeking information about our activities?
- What information needs to be protected?
- Who has access to the information?
  - within the organization
  - externally
- Are we vulnerable to information outflows from distributors?
- Are we vulnerable to information outflows from customers?
- Are we vulnerable to information outflows from advisors and consultants?
- Have those with access to the information signed confidentiality agreements?
- What physical measures are in place to prevent/control information outflows?
  - from full time employed staff
  - from part time staff
  - from the staff of distributors and associates
  - by observation
- Who screens all documents passing out of the company for their information content?
  - brochures and catalogues
  - newsletters
  - annual reports
  - other official filings

Notes

1 Christopher West (2001) *Competitive Intelligence*, Palgrave, Basingstoke.
2 ibid

List 21

Physical distribution and packaging[1]

INTRODUCTION

Physical distribution and packaging frequently offer opportunities, and not just for considerable cost savings. They can be designed to meet customer requirements rather than supplier convenience and give a valuable market 'plus'.

Industry goes to extreme lengths to shade superfluous cost and design features out of a product or material and to use the most sophisticated value analysis techniques. Yet the savings achieved are often thrown away in the physical distribution methods or packaging. An electro-submersible pump that had been value analysed and redesigned to a lower, highly competitive but still profitable price was packed using a material and in a manner that absorbed all the savings achieved in procurement and manufacture.

In contra-distinction, if the total pack material and design and handling costs are considered, it might be found that an increase in material costs will lead to a greater reduction in handling costs or in the costs of complaint rectification. Packaging, packing and shipment have to be seen as a totality.

Whether a company has its own transport fleet, outsources its requirements, uses public services or adopts cooperative schemes with other organizations, all the options require careful consideration. All are identified as possible methods for consideration. The first questions are concerned with this aspect of operations.

Question 21.4 has important implications for goods moved over long distances, particularly internationally, and which are not time-sensitive. It is often possible, by trans-shipment and utilizing mixed modes of transport, to achieve considerable savings in total cost. 'Least-cost' route analyses are not often attempted but are always worth examining.

It was pointed out in the Introduction to List 18, 'User industries', Question 18.35, that suppliers usually take dispatch date for conformance with delivery requirements whereas the customer takes receipt of goods as the effective date. This difference can be critical. There is no need for a supplier to be blamed for late delivery if it is the carrier at fault, but this will inevitably happen if customers are not informed of dispatch date and carrier. This is a simple action to take and in many cases defuses an explosive situation. Many carriers now offer a monitoring and tracing service for shipments and this, where available, should always be used. In any event, suppliers should monitor the performance of their carriers, and devise a system to keep the customer informed of the position. Questions 21.7–21.10 cover these points.

While customers rarely object to a supplier's examining their handling and storage methods with the aim of improving services to them, few suppliers would ever think of undertaking this study despite the obvious marketing advantages it would bring. Questions 21.11 and 21.12 draw attention to this point.

On transport methods, compatibility between the supplier's delivery methods and transport and the customer's facilities and handling methods must stand the vendor in good stead. From the simple situation of a fuel tanker too big to negotiate easily the customer's receiving area to the complexity of supplier–customer interactive computer systems, compatibility offers marketing advantages.

The question of delivery charges should also be considered in terms of the customer's perception of the final offer. Such a charge can easily be perceived as a partly hidden price premium. However, the opposite risk is that an all-in delivered price may appear uncompetitive against a product where delivery is in addition to the purchase price. The issue needs careful consideration in terms of how the charge is shown. Question 21.13 is concerned with this subject.

JIT (just-in-time) delivery systems, as the introduction to List 19, 'Key customer marketing', states, have become commonplace and they offer an invaluable marketing opportunity for companies. It is a technique that can lock suppliers and customers into long-term, mutually beneficial, stable and profitable relationships. While it is true that a JIT agreement can increase production, transport and inventory costs, it has the effect of reducing marketing costs and the nature of marketing. Under JIT the marketing task changes and the old adversarial buying situation is substituted by partnerships. Questions 21.16–21.19 introduce the subject.

If both packaging and packing are viewed as an entity, it is always possible that an improvement in material or design of either type of protection might remove the necessity for one or the other and thus reduce the total cost to the vendor and remove part of the disposal problem for the user. This double benefit is one that is frequently overlooked. Question 21.24 could well reveal an important answer in terms of reducing marketing costs and increasing customer satisfaction.

Suppliers frequently fail to consider how the pack is stored, used, and disposed of. All three elements are often capable of improvement to aid the customer's utilization, and anything that aids the customer must be of marketing value. Despite the sophisticated use of packaging as a marketing tool in the consumer goods industry, in business-to-business it still has far to go in the marketing 'convenience' as well as the product.

Good marketing always considers activities from the viewpoint of the customer, but marketers (or indeed anyone in the vendor company) rarely bother to investigate the problems caused by packaging. Not all firms have incinerators to dispose of inflammable waste, and those that do may be reluctant to put through plastic waste. Pallets, crates and containers awaiting collection can cause storage problems. Questions 21.27–21.29 will demand that marketing auditors consider these points, which are of considerable importance to the customer.

Another often overlooked aspect of packaging are the advantages inherent in enabling the customer to maintain better visual stock control by distant identification of pack and remaining contents (Questions 21.37 and 21.38).

A glance around any storeroom shows how frequently industrial goods and materials manufacturers fail to take advantage of the pack itself to convey an advertising message. It is useful to examine whether or not a promotional opportunity is being wasted, as might be the case. The answer to Question 21.39 will reveal if this is so.

All in all, both physical distribution and packaging offer splendid opportunities for improving relationships with customers and strengthening loyalties. Reliable delivery, it has been proved over and over again, is almost invariably more important than quick delivery. Indeed, the call for stock is often only a symptom of disbelief of suppliers' delivery promises. Similarly, easy handling of products within the plant and easy disposal of packaging are both factors that will enable suppliers to obtain premium prices.

21.1 What delivery methods are we currently using?

21.2 Have we considered the merits of alternative transport and shipment methods?

- own fleet
- public carriers
- contract distribution
- cooperative arrangements
- back haul
- groupage

21.3 What are comparative transport costs and times using alternative methods?

21.4 Have we attempted any 'least-cost' route analyses? (See Introduction.)

21.5 How do our transport and packaging methods compare with competitors on cost, speed, liability to damage and pilferage? (The answer to this point will have been given in List 20, 'Competitive intelligence', Questions 20.41 and 20.53.)

21.6 What are the reasons for rejection of alternative methods, and how do they relate to current conditions?

21.7 Are customers notified of dispatch on day of dispatch? (See Introduction and answer to List 18, 'User industries', Question 18.35.)

21.8 To what extent are late deliveries caused by delayed dispatches and to what extent by unpunctual transport methods and handling?
21.9 Do we know when delays are caused by carriers?
21.10 If not, is it possible to design a system whereby we can monitor delivery time after our products leave the plant?
21.11 How compatible are our transport method, delivery systems and hardware with clients' acceptance systems and hardware? (See Introduction; also List 26, 'Non-differentiated products and commodities', Question 26.18.)
21.12 Is there any way we can improve its acceptability?
21.13 Is delivery charged for as a separate item? (See Introduction; and List 23, 'Pricing', Introduction and Figure 23.1, concerning inclusion or exclusion of any price component.)
21.14 Could it or should it be incorporated into price?
21.15 What are our competitors' policies in this respect?
21.16 Should we seek JIT (just-in-time) agreements? (See Introduction; answers to List 19, 'Key customer marketing', Question 19.69; and List 20, 'Competitive intelligence', Question 20.17.)
21.17 Can our production, delivery and administration systems, as they are constituted, meet JIT requirements?
21.18 If not, what changes are needed?
21.19 Are we capable of introducing and implementing them?
21.20 Are orders delivered complete?
21.21 If not, what is the typical drop size and redeliveries?
21.22 Can we improve this?
21.23 Could stock levels be reduced by improved forecasting?
21.24 Have we carried out a value analysis of packaging costs? (See Introduction.)
21.25 Is the packaging material and design the most efficient to withstand damage in transit, handling and storage by impact, pilferage, tampering, moisture, infestation or temperature?
21.26 Would it be possible to standardize the shipment packaging to reduce transport costs?
21.27 Is the shipment packaging destroyed, returned or reused?
21.28 Would there be any advantages to us or the customer to change the shipment packaging to another type?
21.29 How are empties stored? Can we redesign the packaging to minimize storage space required by customers, or to make disposal easier?
21.30 How is the pack used (eg holds contents until emptied; fully unpacked on receipt)?
21.31 What is the average amount of contents taken on each occasion?
21.32 Would it be a 'plus' if the packing had a dispensing/measuring device?
21.33 Has the packing a second use? Could we redesign it to give such a function?

21.34 Does the packing material, size and configuration take into account customers' views and needs?
21.35 Does the packing contain clearly understandable instructions and warnings for handling?
21.36 How long, on average, is the packing held in stock?
21.37 Can the contents be easily identified from the packing, including numbers/volume/value remaining?
21.38 Over what distance must the packing be identifiable? (See Introduction.)
21.39 Do the contents and shipment pack contain an advertising message? (See Introduction.)
21.40 What reporting system do we have, and what analyses have we undertaken, of customer complaints relative to delivery performance, shortages, damages, etc.? (This topic will be probed in greater depth in List 25, 'Quality in marketing'.)
21.41 Do we have a formal system for resolving complaints? Is responsibility for this allocated and monitored?

Notes

1 The term 'packaging' is used to refer to all wrappings, covers and containers in which products are held prior to use: 'packing' is the protective material for shipment. 'Packaging' often has a merchandising rather than a protective function.

List 22

Industry contacts

INTRODUCTION

No business can operate in isolation and for many the contacts industry can provide are a vital input to their information systems and sales opportunities. Industry in this context is the whole complex of customers, competitors, distributors, influence formers, associations and government.

A company's image within its own industry will often be a powerful incentive or disincentive for customers to purchase from it. Regular, creative industry contacts can materially assist a firm in many ways by providing 'visibility' and conveying credible messages concerning competence, expertise, reliability, quality, technical leadership, and so on.

The idea that all competitors are enemies is both anachronistic and absurd, and the exchange of information with competitors and contacts regularly can have a value far greater than the time involved might imply. Indeed the growth and success of Benchmarking is proof of the values to be obtained by cooperation with competitors. Meeting and, indeed, interviewing competitors is neither unethical nor difficult; and whether such meetings are formal and private or informal, the value remains the same. The Adam Smith dictum that the men of the same trade gathering together 'ends in a conspiracy against the public...' may well still have some justification but, by and large, associations of all types can and do accomplish an excellent job in promoting both their own industry and customer industry interest. They also provide internal industry information, market data, interpretation of government regulations, representation to government, and a host of other valuable inputs to a firm's marketing.

For services, particularly professional services, the interpersonal network (referrals) is the single most important business source, and thus there is a strong additional reason for close industry or professional contacts. Companies should consider the value of every industry group, as Questions 22.1, 22.4, 22.18, 22.19 and 22.21 suggest – whether this be horizontal, such as Chambers of Commerce, or vertical, such as for manufacturers in the same industry or a research association – and evaluate the cost and usefulness of each of them. Those who are highly critical of associations must realize that it is within the power of members to shape them to their needs in terms of services and information they provide.

For the senior professions, membership of their collegial body is compulsory; for everyone else there is a choice. Before a decision is made to join (or indeed to leave) there has to be a trade-off between the benefits and the disadvantages. A firm of consulting engineers was very active in its professional association, which had extremely strong and mandatory rules that virtually inhibited marketing. As a result of a marketing audit it was recommended that the benefits of membership should be forgone to allow aggressive marketing and thus to improve market share. The recommendation was rejected but some two years later legislation forced the association to repeal its rules. A two-year lead-time advantage had been lost. Questions 22.10 and 22.11 call for careful considerations of circumstances such as these.

Contacts not usually considered in this context, because they are seen as a training or educational facility, are conferences, seminars and other meetings. A training officer will evaluate these in terms of their training value. The marketing managers will or should see them as opportunities for useful industry links and sales opportunities. As such, details of these types of function (even those that have no direct relevance to marketing) should be circulated to marketing departments. Question 22.26 seeks to ensure that these important activities are not set aside as irrelevant.

Another often overlooked contact point is government and non-governmental organizations. For example, an ad hoc committee was formed to examine how the numerical analysis services of the National Physical Laboratory, which were freely available, could become a profit centre. At least two members of that committee were drawn from industry and obtained useful ongoing contacts for themselves and for the NPL.

List 13, 'Non-personal promotion: methods and media', Question 13.3, had an item 'secondments'. This can be a valuable marketing tool for promotional purposes and equally valuable for developing and cementing contacts. Secondments can be from the company to government or private organizations, and in reverse from government and other organizations into the company.

Finally, Question 22.32 suggests that it is possible to create a forum for contacts if one does not exist. At one time an association of business-to-business advertisers was created by a media owner, and a society of long-range planners by a management consultancy.

Having said all this, however, it is also necessary to add that an inordinate amount of time and money can be wasted on industry contacts that often deteriorate into little more than 'talk shops' and eating and drinking sessions. This is an obvious danger to be watched, and a comparison must be made of the value that comes from contacts with the value that might accrue from using the same investment of time and money in other marketing activities or other parts of the information-gathering system. Each firm should do an audit of its industry contacts and decide if they are adequate or capable of improvement and if they are being thoroughly exploited.

There is an obvious link between the list that follows and List 6, 'Marketing information: systems and use', and the two should be used in conjunction.

22.1 Which trade and/or professional associations do we belong to? (See List 6, 'Marketing information: systems and use', Questions 6.32 and 6.33.)
22.2 List the relevant trade/professional and other associations responsible for our products/services.
22.3 What informal industry and inter-industry groups exist?
22.4 Would it be advantageous to belong?
22.5 Are the subscriptions justified by the services we receive from them? (Review and evaluate services offered and see List 5, 'Export marketing', Question 5.7; List 6, 'Marketing information: systems and use', Question 6.32.)
22.6 Are there services available we do not use? (See List 6, 'Marketing information: systems and use', Question 6.32. Align answers with those of List 20, 'Competitive intelligence', Question 20.38.)
22.7 Why do we not use them?
22.8 What services would we like which the association could provide but does not? (See List 6, 'Marketing information: systems and use', Question 6.33.)
22.9 Does our membership give us any form of accreditation or acceptability?
22.10 Does membership inhibit our marketing in any way? (See Introduction, but this question will have been answered in List 20, 'Competitive intelligence', Question 20.39; and List 27, 'Service businesses', Question 27.8.)
22.11 What is the trade-off between imposed constraints and membership benefit?
22.12 Who represents the company at association or group meetings?
22.13 Do they hold any official positions?
22.14 Should they?
22.15 How frequently do they attend meetings?
22.16 Is the cost of the time input justified by the benefits the company receives? (The answer should be combined with Question 22.5.)
22.17 What disadvantages would we suffer if we terminated membership? (See also List 20, 'Competitive intelligence', Question 20.39.)
22.18 Which trade/professional associations do our customers belong to?
22.19 If it is possible, would it be beneficial to us to obtain membership?
22.20 Which general business associations do we, or a member of the company, belong to (eg Institutes of Management; Institutes of Marketing; Chambers of Commerce or trade groups)?

22.21 What marketing value does each one have?
22.22 Which research associations do we belong to?
22.23 Is the company represented on any government, non-governmental organizations or communal bodies?
22.24 Would it be advantageous to be part of such groups?
22.25 Where do members of the company meet competitors and government?
22.26 Are we fully informed of conferences, symposia, seminars and meetings for both our own and our customers' industries?
22.27 Who in our organization is responsible for gathering information on seminars, conferences and meetings relative to our own and customer industries?
22.28 Is the information disseminated in the company, and who receives it?
22.29 Who decides whether such meetings shall be attended, and who attends?
22.30 Would releasing staff on secondment to customers, or to government, trade or other associations, create valuable industry contacts?
22.31 Is there any aspect of our operations that customers may want to adopt and for which we could provide client staff training? (See List 3, 'The service element in marketing', Question 3.34 and Appendix 3A.)
22.32 If no industry contact vehicle exists, would it be useful for us to create a forum for the exchange of information and general liaison?
22.33 Would *pro Bono* work provide useful contacts?

List 23

Pricing

INTRODUCTION

Perhaps the marketing auditor's task comes closest to the financial auditor's work in consideration of pricing. Pricing clearly has critical profit implications, but it also has other equally important, if not so obvious, functions which in turn will reflect on profit. For example, the psychological implications of price in terms of the positioning of the product or service and the firm are vital in marketing terms; market share is unquestionably a function of price related to other objective and subjective factors; new product/service development and launches may well be totally dependent on the achieved price of existing products/services. Whatever price is adopted, it has to support the cost of the marketing 'mix'. Thus, getting the price right is clearly a critical combined financial and marketing task.

Although pricing is simply one more marketing tool and as such was just a single item in the long list of marketing tools presented in List 13, 'Non-personal promotion: methods and media', Question 13.3, its importance and complexity are such that it demands a separate checklist because pricing decisions have an all-pervasive effect on the company's performance.

However, good pricing depends first and foremost on good costing, so in looking at the whole area of price as a marketing tool it is necessary to step back and also look at costing methods. There are at least 16 different ways of arriving at price besides the ubiquitous 'cost plus' and the even more frequently used 'what the market will bear'. These are listed in Question 23.4 and are essentially marketing tools, not an accountancy formula. An explanation of the different techniques is given in Appendix 23A. List 28, 'Product/service financial information', goes further into this topic.

As a marketing tool, pricing has a great advantage over almost all the others in that it is easier and quicker to change a price than to change a product or service, appoint an advertising strategy, design an exhibit, or alter a brochure. Moreover, the effect of pricing decisions is immediate. Pricing does not, however – contrary to the much-loved folklore of industry – mean price-cutting. On the contrary, it can as easily mean price increases. It has already been suggested in List 15, 'The buying process', Question 15.22, that the responsibility for buying decisions may change at discrete price points, and it may be advantageous to move prices upward to move into the decision area of a DMU that may favour the firm.

In using the price as a marketing tool, the marketer cannot escape the immutable formula:

High price	=	high profits	=	low chance of success
Low price	=	low profits	=	high chance of success

Marketers must position themselves correctly along the continuum. To arrive at this positioning, considerable internal and external information is required and the marketing audit can make a great contribution to the final pricing decisions.

Question 23.9 – whether sales representatives should have price authority – is in many firms a very touchy question. On the benefit side, it gives them greater standing in their relationship with their customers and enables them to be flexible and move quickly in response to a developing situation. On the minus side, as was pointed out in the Introduction to List 9, 'The salesforce and its management', in these circumstances price tends to descend to the lowest permissible level. The case history of the company marketing electrical insulation material referred to in the Introduction to that List shows one approach to overcoming this problem.

Questions 23.26–23.28 bring in the 'price and the perception of performance' approach, which seeks, by the use of trade-off analysis, to place a monetary value on different attributes, the final price being based on the values that customers ascribe to the different attributes. It is never pure products that are purchased so much as a cluster of attributes surrounding the product. Isolating attributes for which buyers are prepared to pay has a considerable marketing spin-off. Research leading to attribute identification, although sophisticated and difficult to accomplish, repays the effort in many ways. It enables the marketing message to be fine-tuned; it identifies market segments where attributes are most valued and thus aids segmentation and targeting; it indicates which attributes might be dropped without reducing the selling price and which attributes customers are prepared to pay a premium price to retain; it looks at whether marketing ought to seek to change perceptions or values; it shows where customer perceptions are incorrect or unformed and makes numerous other contributions to product development or modification, marketing techniques and tools and marketing messages. Apart from the pricing implications of this approach, it also enables a number of other marketing decisions to be made with greater precision.[1]

Question 23.31 has been anticipated in at least eight or nine previous lists. Anything to do with benefits, price as a decision-forming factor, price flexibility, sales and promotional platforms, unique selling propositions and, of course, competition must impact on the way in which a price is perceived and evaluated. In stating price baldly, the real price of a product or service is frequently overlooked or disguised, and this real cost might well be more favourable than the quoted price. The elements of 'true' price could include such items as servicing charges, consumables, life expectancy, disturbance, downtime, energy costs, availability of loan equipment, retrofit capability, trade-in or scrap values. Each significant item should be costed and offset or added to the price to arrive at the 'true' cost to the buyer on purchase and over the life of the product. A different series of factors will of course be required for assessing the 'true' price of a service.

Presenting to a buyer what is really paid for a product is a powerful sales tool, particularly if an accurate comparison can be made with similar products or services. Indeed, if the components of the model are presented to buyers and they are allowed to make their own evaluation, including those factors that are necessarily based on judgement and unquantifiable, such as labour attitudes, but which will also make a contribution to a decision, the resultant bottom-line figure will have a credibility of considerable strength (see Figure 23.1.)

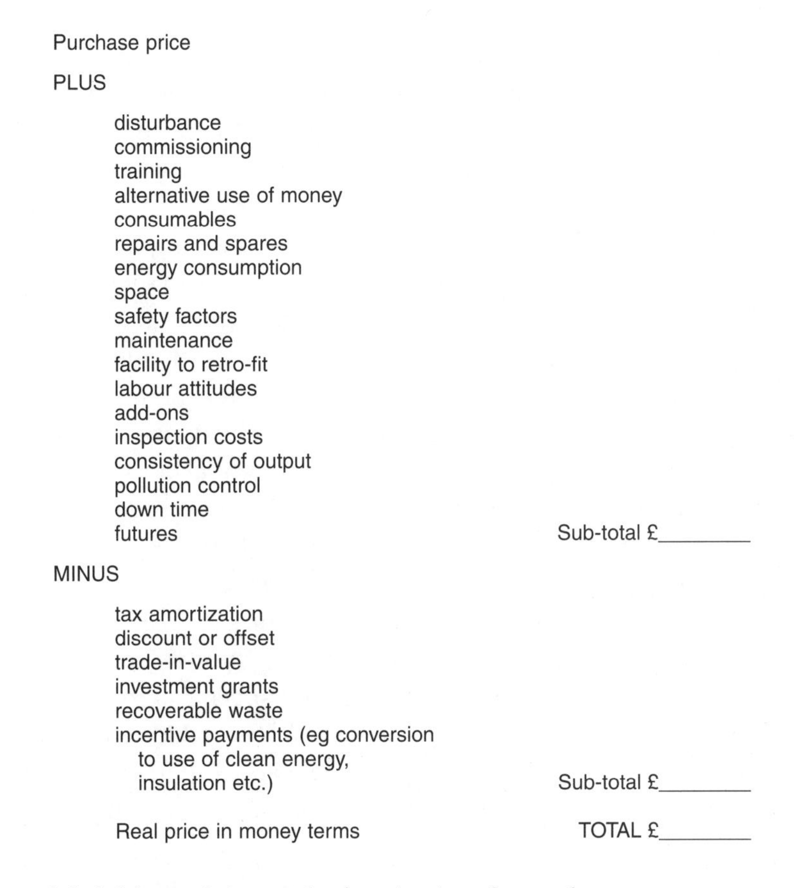

Figure 23.1 Model for arriving at the 'true' price of a product

It is rare that inflation can be considered advantageous, but in terms of price movements it does offer a very easily explainable justification for price changes and helps break through the rigid price ceilings that perhaps used to exist and were difficult to penetrate. Conversely, holding price in the teeth of inflation is also a substantial marketing 'plus' without the unfortunate concomitants of price-cutting. Questions 23.35 and 23.36 open up this possibility for consideration.

Negotiating ability is an essential element in achieving satisfactory prices and whether this task is left to sales representatives or others in the company, it is an area where a high skill level must be achieved and maintained. If price has to be reduced at the negotiating stage, tactically it is important the customer gives something in exchange. Examples are:

- paying sooner, or even partially 'up front';
- phasing the order to suit production schedules;
- increasing the order, or at least giving a firm indication that this will occur if the buyer is satisfied on the first few batches.

If it is known that a particular customer will expect a price reduction, it is as well to avoid giving away 'extras' that are normally granted to other customers, or, alternatively, the granting of such extras to this customer can be used to justify the price.

Questions 23.40–23.42 deal with the extraordinarily difficult question of bidding. The information a company should have in order to bid accurately is rarely available, but this is never any reason not to state the requirements as an ideal. Bidding is unquestionably as much an art as a science and, in assigning values to the variables involved in a bid, it is as well to check that such information as is available is used in arriving at the bid price.

Another pitfall of tendering is the use of referential bids, by which one tenderer says that the price is £x below the lowest of all the other prices. Often this is ruled out by the tendering terms but, if not, the tenderer should be aware of the danger of ridiculously low competitive prices being submitted. To overcome this, a referential bid should be expressed as 'the higher of £y and a sum that is £x below the lowest of all the other prices', in which £y is the lowest figure that is acceptable to the seller. Care needs to be taken in drafting a referential bid lest the customer argue, for example, that one price is £x below another referential tenderer's price, which is £q below the lowest firm price.

Finally, Question 23.43 deals with what is often a lost opportunity. Tenders are frequently drawn so tightly it is impossible to demonstrate a superior specification. It is always worth requesting the opportunity to submit non-compliant bids. That is, bids which do not necessarily fit the tender specifications but which would deliver a superior product/service to that which has been specified. This is one method to avoid competing on price.

23.1 Are our costing methods realistic? (See List 21, 'Physical distribution and packaging', Question 21.13; and List 28, 'Product/service financial information', Question 28.3.)

23.2 How were they arrived at?
23.3 Should they be reviewed?
23.4 What pricing tactics (or 'mix' of tactics) do we use? (See Introduction and explanation in Appendix 23A.)
- loss leading
- diversionary
- discount
- price lining
- skimming
- cost plus
- contingency pay pricing
- offset
- discrete
- guarantee
- conditional
- predatory
- referential
- value (what the market will bear)
- competitive pay pricing
- premium

23.5 Do our prices support our positioning policy and reflect market perceptions – actual and optimum? (Examine the positioning maps in List 7, 'Market size and structure', Question 7.37; and List 18, 'User industries', Question 18.57.)
23.6 Will our prices support the marketing 'mix' we have adopted or will adopt?
23.7 How is the quoted price for an order calculated (eg individually for every order, individually only for large orders, standard list prices and discounts)?
23.8 Do market conditions demand a greater flexibility?
23.9 Do the sales representatives have any pricing authority? (See Introduction; List 9, 'The salesforce and its management', Introduction and answer to Question 9.47; and List 28, 'Product/service financial information', Question 28.16.)
23.10 If so, are the rules and the policy for price adjustments clearly set out?
23.11 Who is responsible for monitoring price variances introduced by the salesforce? (Cross-check answer with List 28, 'Product/service financial information', Questions 28.18 and 28.19.)
23.12 Would it enhance the sales representatives' role if they were given some degree of price authority? (See List 9, 'The salesforce and its management', Introduction, and answer to Question 9.47.)
23.13 What pricing tactics are appropriate for achieving the marketing/profit objectives? (See Appendix 23A.)
23.14 What discount structure do we and our competitors operate? (Compare answer to that given in List 14, 'The distributive system', Question 14.50; List 20, 'Competitive

intelligence', Questions 20.68, 20.69 and 20.73 and Appendix 20A; eg bulk; seasonal; settlement; retrospective; type of customer, ie OEM, contractor, wholesaler, end user, other.)

23.15 What has been the annual average change in price of products/services over the last five years?

23.16 What were the reasons for these changes?

23.17 What percentage of the overall price change over the last five years has been due to product/service modifications?

23.18 Are the modifications and adjusted price as perceived by the buyers justified?

23.19 Would price-lining (holding price and reducing quantity or quality) be preferred to price increases?

23.20 When was the last price change?

23.21 Has it been justified to customers?

23.22 Over what period do users tend to write off the product or the equipment into which it is incorporated? How does it compare with competitors? (The question is repeated in a number of lists and is also presented with different perspectives. The auditor should consult and compare answers with List 2, 'Product/service range', Question 2.45; List 15, 'The buying process', Questions 15.42 and 15.43; List 16, 'Analysing lost business', Questions 16.14 and 16.15; List 18, 'User industries', Questions 18.50 and 18.51; and List 20, 'Competitive intelligence', Question 20.61.)

23.23 Is the amortized price comparable with competitors? (See Figure 23.1.)

23.24 Do any of the products/services under review act as 'loss leaders' to the total range? If so, which?

23.25 What evidence is there that loss leaders bring in additional business?

23.26 What knowledge do we have of the attributes of our products/services that customers most value and prefer and are willing to pay for? (See Introduction.)

23.27 What knowledge do we have of the attributes of our product/service that customers either do not value or rate as similar to competitors?

23.28 Would customers pay more/less to retain/drop any attributes? (See List 26, 'Non-differentiated products', Questions 26.32 and 26.33, relative to this.)

23.29 What cost-benefit analyses have been undertaken to demonstrate any superiority in purchase of use of the products/services? (This important topic is restated in other lists and the answers should be compared. See List 2, 'Product/service range', Question 2.23; List 16, 'Analysing lost business', Question 16.10; List 20, 'Competitive intelligence', Question 20.58; and List 26, 'Non-differentiated products and commodities', Questions 26.33–26.35.)

23.30 Have any 'true' product/service price analyses been conducted? (See Figure 23.1; also Introduction to List 2, 'Product/service range', and Question 2.23; and List 26, 'Non-differentiated products', Question 26.35.)

23.31 Do our selling and promotional platforms reflect any benefits inherent in the total cost analysis? (See cross-references in Question 23.29 above.)

23.32 Is it possible to evaluate our product/service position on the life cycle? (For this and the two following questions, see List 4, 'Company performance', Introduction; and List 17, 'Introducing new products/services', Questions 17.13–17.16.)

23.33 Should price strategy reflect the product/service position along the life cycle?

23.34 Would a change in price extend the life cycle? (The answer to this question could provide an input in answering List 17, 'Introducing new products/services', Questions 17.15 and 17.16.)

23.35 Do our prices move in line with/behind/ahead of inflation? (See Introduction and List 8, 'Future market', Question 8.26.)

23.36 Can we justify/exploit inflation-induced price changes?

23.37 Do our negotiating skills match those of our customers/competitors?

23.38 What steps can be taken to improve negotiating skills? (This and the preceding question will have been wholly or partly covered in List 9, 'The salesforce and its management', Question 9.47; and List 19, 'Key-customer marketing', Questions 19.47–19.56 will provide answers in depth to assessment of negotiating skills.)

23.39 In setting price, do we consider its impact on others (besides customers) who may influence our performance? (See List 24, 'Images and perceptions', Figure 24.1, for the various 'publics' that must be considered in setting price.)

23.40 What information is sought and used in bidding (eg estimate of direct costs, amount of past successful bids, average of all bids, identification of bidders, amount of individual bids, each bid as a percentage of own direct cost estimates, estimate of each bidder's workload)? (See Introduction.)

23.41 How common is referential bidding? (See Introduction.)

23.42 Do we have a policy for dealing with referential bids?

23.43 Can we offer a non-compliant bid?

Appendix 23A
Examples of pricing tactics

Name	Description	Effect
Loss leader	Deliberately deflated price to obtain 'first' business or to 'get in'	Successful with unsophisticated buyers, but tends to give a price ceiling which is difficult to penetrate later
Offset	Low basic price with recouping on extras	Psychologically favourable at the quotation stage, but can easily lead to difficulties on implementation. Advantages in some cases of customer being able to control extent of commitment
Divisionary	Low basic price on selected product to develop image of low-cost structure which 'rubs off' on total operation	Generally effective so long as no suggestion of 'switch selling' is allowed to develop
Discrete	Price pitched to bring a decision into an area of authority of a DMU favouring the company. A lower price may take decision to lower management; a high price to the board. This tactic necessarily requires an intimate knowledge of the prospect company	While the decision can be moved into the DMU responsibility area favouring the company or better able to appreciate the offer, price movements upwards or downwards have associated risks
Discount	Price quotation subject to discounts on a predetermined basis, eg time schedule, extent of commitment, magnitude of order	Positive encouragement to buyer to structure orders on mutually favourable basis
Guarantee	Price includes an undertaking to achieve certain qualities or performance – the guarantee out-guaranteeing competitors	Moves competition from price to value area and places high-quality products/services in most favourable position to compete with low-quality products/services

Name	Description	Effect
Conditional	Price is conditional on the purchase of other product(s)	Tied-in product has to be attractive in its own right otherwise basic product potential is reduced. Illegal in some countries
Predatory	Price set well below competition as a means to removing it	Requires accurate assessment of competitor's resources. Can be self-destructive and illegal
Skimming	Price set high when demand is inelastic or capacity short and gradually reduced as situation becomes competitive	Gives extra profitability and a hedge against later substandard profit. Enables a company to keep a competitive edge if the original high price has been maintained long enough
Referential (for tendering)	Ensures lowest price is quoted	No fail-safe mechanism unless limits are placed on lowest level. Depends on open tendering procedures
Price lining	Price kept constant but quality or quantity adjusted to reflect changes in cost	Removes price as a major negotiating point, substituting product, but note effect above for diversionary pricing
Contingency pay pricing	Price (or fee) based on results to be obtained or activities to be completed	Gives a guarantee of performance to the purchaser
Cost plus	Summation of all chargeable costs plus a desired profit	Guarantees a profit and easy to calculate but takes no account of competitive climate
Value	An assessment of what the market will bear	High possibility of sales but profit can be eroded or a loss incurred. Strong negotiation skills needed.
Premium	Extra charge for non-standard product/service or unusual circumstances	Unless presented carefully can be resented by customer. Total CVA required to use premium pricing creatively
Competitive pay pricing (service firms only)	Can be used when costing is on a time basis (ie hourly, daily) and is related to salary level of personnel involved	Allows for accuracy in costing and for competitive pricing where salary levels in the trade or profession are in line. Not always possible to know the skill or seniority level of personnel who will be working on the assignment

Notes

1 For a full description of the technique see Aubrey Wilson (1991) *New Directions in Marketing*, Chapter 2, Kogan Page, London.

List 24

Images and perceptions

INTRODUCTION

It has long been insufficient for an organization merely to survive in order to be credible in its chosen field of activity. Increasing sophistication in the buying/selling interface has led to a questioning of the approach to business that simply accepted that if an organization existed there must necessarily be an economic and profit justification. Today a company not only has the task of survival, it has to survive in a way that makes it credible to its customers, its employees, its shareholders and others. (Some of these 'others' are listed in Figure 24.1.) The perceptions that various 'publics' have of companies is summarized in the word 'image', but this embraces concepts far more complex than the definition suggests. The problem is that 'image' has been abused, vilified and raped until finally it has become a slightly pejorative term of abuse like 'slick'. It is always unfortunate when a useful term and a useful tool is debased and mishandled. Image sensitivity and image development are an important part of marketing; indeed, they are marketing itself.

Whereas few would argue about the usefulness of the image concept in consumer goods marketing, it was much later before it was appreciated that the perception a business-to-business customer may have of a supplier and its products, or clients of the professional practices they use, despite the latter's usual lack of obvious marketing activity, impacts on decisions. The notion that non-consumer and professional services buying is wholly rational and based entirely on technical, commercial and expertise consideration is still widely held, although there is a considerable volume of evidence to show that this is not so, as will be obvious from many of the questions in List 15, 'The buying process'.

Throughout the preceding checklists there have been direct and indirect references to the image aspects of marketing. For example, all references to customer benefits include not just those that are measurable, but also those that are perceptual. List 9, 'The salesforce and its management', Question 9.46, asks about the sales platform emphasis, which includes both tangible and intangible elements, while Question 9.64 refers to the company's reputation – a pure perceptual factor. List 13, 'Non-personal promotion: methods and media', Question 13.7, refers directly to image factors; and List 18, 'User industries', Question 18.18, is related strongly to the subject. The position map in List 18, 'User industries', Question 18.57, is a pure image evaluation. Thus it can be seen from these few examples how images and perceptions impact in many sectors of marketing activity.

In examining images, it is important not to overlook the *industry* image. Frequently this will rub off on the individual company, or can create a far more intractable problem if it is unfavourable. There is no need to look further than second-hand vehicles, double glazing and plumbing to see how a bad image impacts on companies and individuals working in those trades. While it is possible to separate the organization from the industry, it is not easily or cheaply accomplished (Questions 24.9 and 24.10). Figure 24.1 shows the interrelationship of industry and organization images and their publics.

It is difficult if not impossible for the individual organization, unless it dominates its sector, to change the industry image. This perhaps is a collective activity for members of the industry.

Two important aspects in interpreting image inquiries results are covered in Question 24.16, which draws attention to the need to understand just how knowledgeable the customer might be about the supplier. Responses from 'known only by name' are not going to be as insightful as 'direct experience'. This is not to say that the images held by potential customers are not an important factor in marketing.

Question 24.17 returns to the customer characterization referred to in 'How to use the Checklists' on pages 7 and 12. Obviously customers in different groupings will have different images of the supplier. A regular customer is unlikely to hold the same perceptions

	The industry's publics	**The organization's publics**
Users		•
Customer industries		•
Community	•	•
Staff		•
Shareholders		•
Suppliers		•
Government	•	•
Financial community		•
Media	•	•
Opinion formers	•	•
Special interest groups	•	•
Educational bodies	•	•
Unions		•
Internal referrers		•

Figure 24.1 Target publics

as a lost customer. Thus in examining images the responses must be related to the customer and not treated as a blanket response applicable to the whole market.

Images exist on different levels. There is the *current* image, an encapsulated version of how the market really sees the image subject; the *mirror* image, the way the image subject thinks it is seen; the *wish* image, the way the image subject would like to be seen; and finally, the *optimum* image, that is, the one that will help achieve the company's objectives.

A printing company specializing in financial documents believed their image to be one of a 'large company, old established, but using the latest printing technology and providing excellent service' (the *mirror* image). In addition they wanted to be seen as a 'caring company, responsive, specialized in City work' (the *wish* image). Research showed they were in fact seen as 'staid, monolithic, bureaucratic, not interested in small customers' (*current* image). What customers wanted, however, had nothing to do with these factors. They required 'speed, accuracy and confidentiality' (the *optimum* image). It can be seen from this example how images can clash and, as a result, blur. It is to these aspects that Questions 24.18 and 24.21 refer.

Any gap between the way the company or its products/services are seen and the reality is known as the 'image interval'. A major market objective must be to assess if such an interval exists, if so, its extent, and then to take actions to eliminate it, either by moving the market's perceptions closer to the reality or by changing the image subject to match up to the market's perceptions. List 18, 'User industries', Introduction, has already touched on this, but Questions 24.24 and 24.25 reopen the issue.

Images are formed on first impressions and these are difficult to change. Every organization should check, and check frequently, just what view is gained of the company on first contact. Question 24.26 lists some of the components to be monitored and calls for the auditor to ascertain if the company is perceived in a favourable way when first viewed through the customers' eyes. Because of the importance of first impressions, an additional checklist is provided in Appendix 24A.

However, a firm does not have a single image, since everything it is, does, and has creates its own image – the products/services, the premises, the staff, the vehicles, even the paper heading. This is just one dimension, and some examples, which are covered in Question 24.27. The other is that in image studies 'truth' in a sense is of no consequence. Whether perceptions are incorrect or not does not matter. It matters only how the image subject is seen and, if a sense of injustice results, then there is an image correction campaign to be undertaken, making sure that the true situation is communicated to the sector of the firm's public concerned.

An almost totally neglected image aspect is documentation, which inevitably creates perception of efficiency, professionalism, good organization and good communication – or the lack of them. All documentation the customer receives – proposals or tenders, confirmation of orders, invoicing, statements – should be scrutinized for its marketing impact. Question 24.28 identifies the principles of good practice in documentation.[1]

There is a very close link between images and perceptions and 'quality', which is itself an intangible and difficult-to-define attribute. The auditor should combine the answers in this list with those generated by List 25, 'Quality in marketing'.

A final and important warning: images that are not based on substance invariably end up placing their subject in an infinitely worse position. There should never be an attempt to promote an image that cannot stand up to reality. It is better to have no image than a bad image. It is cheaper, quicker and easier to build an image that it is to correct one.

24.1 Do we have a formal image objective and development policy? (The answer to this question should have been included with the response to List 13, 'Non-personal promotion: methods and media', Questions 13.1 and 13.7.)
24.2 What is it?
24.3 Is it relevant in the light of today's business conditions?
24.4 Assess the degree of image sensitivity throughout the company, particularly among those members of the organization and those aspects of the operation (eg premises, vehicles, paper heading, etc) that the customers experience or see.
24.5 Who in the company is responsible for image development?
24.6 How substantial a part of the job activity does this represent?
24.7 Should the time devoted to image development be increased/decreased?
24.8 What is the image of the company, its products/services and operations as perceived by the different publics in Figure 24.1? (This question links with List 11, 'Cross-selling and internal marketing', Questions 11.33–11.36; and List 23, 'Pricing', Question 23.39, but a comparison should also be made with the competition. This is dealt with in List 3, 'The service element in marketing', Questions 3.6 and 3.18; List 18, 'User industries', Question 18.18; List 19, 'Key customer marketing', Question 19.29; and List 20, 'Competitive intelligence', Questions 20.10, 20.20 and 20.27.)
24.9 What is the image of our industry? (See Introduction and Figure 24.1.)
24.10 Does it represent the industry's own view of how it is seen, or is it an independent assessment?
24.11 How far does the industry image impact on our own and on competitors' images favourably/unfavourably? (See Introduction.)
24.12 Does the industry image affect competitors differently from ourselves?
24.13 If so, why and in what way?
24.14 Are we as a company, or our products and brands, 'visible'? (See List 4, 'Company performance', Introduction, and the response to Question 4.37; and List 13, 'Non-personal promotion: methods and media', Introduction, particularly Figure 13.1 and Question 13.58.)
24.15 Would visibility be achieved with aided recall?
24.16 What part of the image perception is based on direct experience of company or reputation or name?

24.17 What evidence exists to support the answers to the previous six questions?

The next six questions should be applied to the following key market groups:

- regular customers;
- sporadic customers;
- one-off customers;
- potential customers where quotations have failed;
- potential customers where we have not been invited to quote.

(See introductory section, 'The marketing audit', page vii; and List 18, 'User industries', Introduction.)

24.18 How do we think we are perceived by the various publics listed in Figure 24.1 (*mirror image*)?
24.19 How are we actually perceived by the various publics (*current image*)?
24.20 How would we wish to be perceived by the various publics (*wish image*)?
24.21 What image is likely to assist most in achieving our objectives (*optimum image*)? (See also Introduction to List 18, 'User industries'.)
24.22 What reasons can be ascribed to any variation between the images?
24.23 What actions are required to achieve the optimum image?
24.24 How far does the reality of our operations match up with our image and the optimum image?
24.25 What actions must be taken to close any gap between the image and the reality? (See Introduction and correlate answer with List 18, 'User industries', Question 18.59.)
24.26 What are the first impressions of the company?
  - premises – clean, tidy, well maintained
  - vehicles – clean, quiet, efficient, vehicle livery
  - equipment – clean, up-to-date, efficient
  - documentation – appearance, content, finality, protection
  - people – clean, tidy, appropriately dressed, efficient, friendly, helpful, responsive, enthusiastic
  - print – clear, modern, comprehensive, memorable

(Components of this list reoccur in a number of different contexts. The auditor should consult and compare answers given in List 4, 'Company performance', Questions 4.42–4.44; List 9, 'The salesforce and its management', Question 9.117; List 16, 'Analysing lost business', Questions 16.39–16.41; List 18, 'User industries', Question 18.62; and List 25, 'Quality in marketing', Question 25.36.)

24.27 What is the image of the different aspects of the company's products/services and operations? (See also items in List 18, 'User industries', in Question 18.18.) For example:

- delivery capability
- price
- marketing techniques
- degree of independence
- production facilities
- control systems
- punctuality – meetings response, delivery
- influential associates or links
- training aids
- management and organization
- moral/legal issues
- labour relations record
- quality
- services
- technical capability
- performance history
- aid and advice
- print
- financial position
- attitude towards buyers
- bidding compliance
- communication process
- packaging capability
- geographic location
- presentations

24.28 Could our documentation be improved and in what way in terms of:

- appearance?
- content?
- finality?
- protection?

(This question may have been answered in List 4, 'Company performance', Questions 4.43 and 4.44; List 9, 'The salesforce and its management', Question 9.117; and List 16, 'Analysing lost business', Question 16.41; and arises again in List 25, 'Quality in marketing', Question 25.36.)

24.29 How do the total and individual perceptions vary among the different members of DMUs?

24.30 Are the marketing tools we are using compatible with the image we seek to create? (See answer to List 13, 'Non-personal promotion: methods and media', Questions 13.33 and 13.34.)
24.31 How frequently will image benchmark checks be made?
24.32 What variants will initiate action?
24.33 How far are our promotional and personal selling activities deliberately intended to enhance our image? (See the answers in List 13, 'Non-personal promotion: methods and media', Question 13.7.)
24.34 Should there be a change of policy to intensify image development aspects of our promotion and personal selling activity? (See List 13, 'Non-personal promotion: methods and media', Question 13.1.)
24.35 Would image development be enhanced by the use of specialist agencies? (See the answers to List 13, 'Non-personal promotion: methods and media', Questions 13.53–13.55.)

Appendix 24A
First impressions checklist

Phone calls

telephones are answered promptly
telephonist identifies herself/himself
telephonist 'smiles' over the phone
response is friendly, helpful, interested
other

Arrival

customer has clear directions to office/factory/site
parking is available
reception location is easily ascertained
outer door is clearly marked
other

Reception area

is clean, tidy, well maintained, orderly
has up-to-date decor
has comfortable furniture
has 'warm' lighting
has current publications, neatly stacked or displayed,
and company literature
has no signs
does not smell
has no barriers to receptionist
atmosphere is warm, friendly and helpful
other

Initial welcome

receptionist is on hand to greet customer
customer is made to feel welcome
customer is not loaded with paperwork
other

Punctuality

meeting and greeting on time
any delay fully explained
customers kept informed
appropriate apologies for any unpunctuality

Staff members

are clean and neat
are dressed professionally
are friendly and helpful
smile
other

You

are clean and neat
are dressed for success
are smiling, enthusiastic and friendly
appear unrushed
take time with customer
other

Notes

1 For a thorough coverage of this topic *New Directions in Marketing*, *op cit*, Chapter 9.

List 25

Quality in marketing

INTRODUCTION

The search for quality continues to be one of the most important trends in marketing and consumer demand. In the past, quality was perceived in fairly crude terms and as the subject of many clichés: 'Quality is getting it right first time, every time'; 'Quality is meeting client expectations'; 'Quality is how the customer defines it'. To complicate matters further, there has been and continues to be confusion between value and quality: Quality is an intrinsic measure and defines the product or service. It may contribute to value but is not itself value.

The whole issue of value and quality has been largely ignored yet the two are inseparable. It is important to recognize that value can be viewed as *value in use* and is concerned with overall costs (see List 23, 'Pricing', Figure 23.1). *Value in use* refers to performance and reliability; *perceived value* is the value of the total offer.

There will be as much difficulty getting a generally agreed definition of quality as there has been in relation to defining marketing itself. The critical importance of quality is obvious enough. A reputation for poor quality, which in turn implies that a value-for-money assessment is negative, will always lose customers, who will be disappointed because their expectations – wrongly or rightly based – will not be met. Replacing lost customers is not the only cost of poor quality in products and services. A company in such a situation will tend to spend a great deal of time and money correcting errors, will lose key distributors and will probably have a high rate of employee turnover. A reputation for poor quality will doom a company to continually higher costs for a considerable period of time. Along with product *zero defect* there should be an objective of customer *zero defection*.

It is possible to produce many variants of quality indicators. Appendix 25A provides a range of factors for consideration against which auditors can check their performance. It is not of course sufficient to produce a superlative result for any one component. The customer's reaction will for the most part be based on the totality. Question 25.3 is an early and important starting point.

Question 25.6 concerns the problem of understanding customer perceptions, most particularly of a service. Customers can find it difficult to identify and articulate exactly what they like or dislike about a product or service experience. Often even the vendors, let alone the customers, cannot define each element of the offer. In cases where customers are less than completely satisfied, the problem often lies in a host of obscure peripherals rather than in the more obvious core product/services. Nevertheless, this information updated is vital to maintaining a constant quality performance.

It has been well said that satisfied customers stem from under-promising and over-delivering. At the very least, customer expectations of quality must be met and if such expectations move out of line with reality the cause can always be traced to over-enthusiastic marketing.

From their very first exposure to a company, often through advertising, customers form an image of the product/service. From this image they create expectations of what the offer will be like. Customers whose expectations are met (but not necessarily exceeded) are usually happy ones. It is crucial that all elements of the offer be consistent so that the customer does not develop conflicting expectations. Inconsistency in this respect confuses customers. It takes twelve positive quality attributes to overcome the impact of one negative one. The odds are heavily weighted against the marketer.

In Questions 25.16–25.18 the topic is raised as to whether customers have sufficient knowledge about the product/service to form an accurate assessment of its quality attributes, although this relates back to the answer to Question 25.6. Stemming from this, it must then be asked if better informed customers are more easily satisfied and thus likely to be retained.

The implication of Question 25.22 is that unless there is a quality supremo, seen to have the full support of top management and with authority to act to improve quality and to correct failure, a total quality control system is unlikely to be achieved.

Because the whole question of quality is now a major consideration and likely to remain so, all companies have to deal with the question of Total Quality Control (TQC) and accreditation, for example ISO 9000 and other national standards such as Baldrige (USA). While such accreditation may give an advantage, it could well be that in the future it will be a basic requirement. Questions 25.23–25.26 relate to this topic.

Question 25.27 seeks to force consideration of reality. No matter how well the product is manufactured, there will always be some failures. There is no such thing in manufacturing as perfection, and near perfection can increase total cost and therefore will be inefficient.

Trade-off analysis may lead to lower quality and lower prices but, provided customers are totally satisfied and convinced they have received value for money, the marketing objectives will be fulfilled.

The temptation to cut quality when there are cost over-runs, or delivery schedules cannot be met, is enormous. This must be resisted if the quality perception and reality are to be maintained. Question 25.34 recognizes this risk.

An important distinction is now needed which is raised by Question 25.38. However well a supplier might be rated on any particular aspect of quality, it has little marketing value unless that aspect is of importance to the customer. The distinction to be made is between what the customer regards as significant and how well the company rates on that factor.

Figure 25.1 illustrates this. 'Delivery punctuality' is of considerable importance to the customer, but the actual performance is rated at less than half the importance rating. While the supplier is performing extremely well in terms of 'documentation', this is of relatively little concern to the customer. Thus underperformance in the first case and overperformance in the second make no contribution to the marketing effectiveness. In

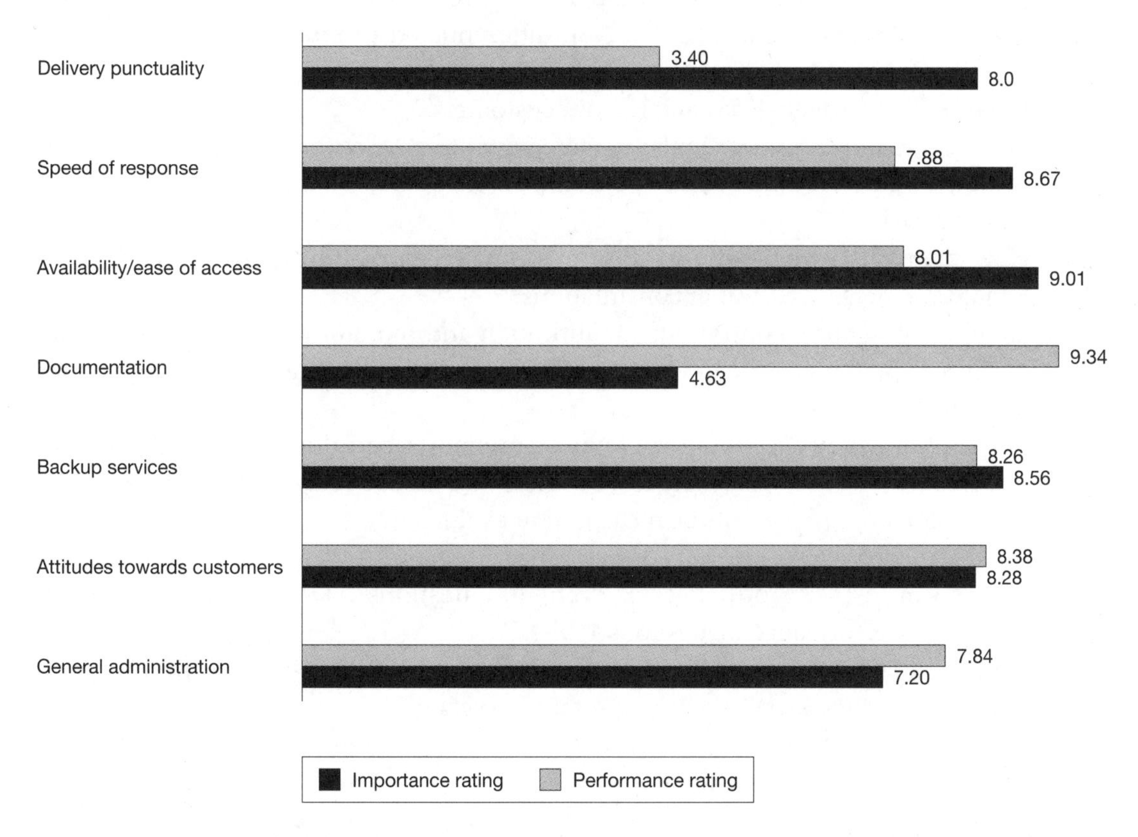

Figure 25.1 Importance/performance comparisons

looking at quality it is always necessary to make the trade-off between performance and importance.

Perhaps a statement once made by the chief executive of Scandinavian Airline Systems (SAS) sums up the quality situation to perfection:

> We don't seek to be one thousand per cent better at any one thing. We seek to be one per cent better at one thousand things. SAS has ten million passengers a year. The average passenger comes in contact with five SAS employees. Therefore, SAS has fifty million 'moments of trust' per year. Fifty million, unique, never-to-be-repeated opportunities to distinguish ourselves, in a memorable fashion, from each and every one of our competitors. My job is to manage the fifty million moments of trust!

25.1 Have we distinguished between 'quality' and 'value'? (See Introduction.)
25.2 Do all our personnel understand this difference?
25.3 Have we clearly stated the components of quality? (Select from Appendix 25A.)
25.4 Are all members of the company aware of these?
25.5 Are there clearly set-down standards of performance for products/services and staff? (See List 10, 'Customer care and support staff's role in marketing', Introduction, and Questions 10.2–10.9; and List 26, 'Non-differentiated products and commodities', Question 26.9.)
25.6 Is our definition of quality similar to our customers'?
25.7 Is our definition of quality similar to our competitors'? (See for comparison purposes List 20, 'Competitive intelligence', Question 20.11.)
25.8 How do we know?
25.9 How far and how frequently are customers involved in setting quality standards?
25.10 Should we increase customer consultations?
25.11 Should a system for continuous identification and monitoring of customer quality needs and preferences be developed? (The question arises again in List 27, 'Service businesses', Question 27.38.)
25.12 Is there an easily accessible customer complaints handling system? (Compare answers with List 16, 'Analysing lost business', Questions 16.2 and 16.32–16.36.)
25.13 Can customer requirements be measured or evaluated?
25.14 What standards can we/do we adopt for measurement? (Quality accreditation is also covered in List 2, 'Product/service range', Questions 2.17 and 2.18; and List 4, 'Company performance', Questions 4.27–4.29.)
25.15 Do all marketing communications state with accuracy physical and performance characteristics, life expectancy, guarantees, servicing?
25.16 How knowledgeable are customers about the quality of our products/services?
25.17 Would better informed customers be easier to satisfy?
25.18 What steps can we take to ensure customers are aware of quality and assess it by appropriate criteria?

25.19 Does our business plan include a policy statement on quality standards? (This should be incorporated within the considerations set out in List 1, 'Marketing strategy and planning', Question 1.3; the answer to 1.17 is also relevant to this topic.)
25.20 Does the plan define the inputs necessary to achieve the standards set?
25.21 Is there any person(s) in the organization responsible for quality development and maintenance?
25.22 Is the authority of that person(s) sufficient to ensure implementation of policy?
25.23 Would quality accreditations give us a market advantage? (This question will have been answered in List 1, 'Marketing strategy and planning', Question 1.36, and again in List 4, 'Company performance', Question 4.29.)
25.24 How likely is it that accreditation will become a precondition for purchasing?
25.25 Should we seek appropriate accreditation?
25.26 Would the cost and changes required to obtain accreditation be offset by any advantages in increased profitable sales and customer loyalty?
25.27 Are there quality sacrifices the customer will make in return for price reductions? (See List 23, 'Pricing', Introduction.)
25.28 Are all service activities within the quality system? (See List 3, 'The service element in marketing', Question 3.15 and Appendix 3A.)
25.29 What aspects of quality differentiate us from our competitors? (See List 20, 'Competitive intelligence', Question 20.8.)
25.30 Where are the gaps between our quality targets and reality and how can they be closed?
25.31 Can we calculate the costs of improving the quality of every component of quality, and to different levels?
25.32 Will any increase in costs be reflected in price?
25.33 Is the customer prepared to pay the price of improved quality? (This and the previous three questions are tangentially connected to List 13, 'Non-personal promotion: methods and media', Question 13.60; and List 26, 'Non-differentiated products and commodities', Question 26.15.)
25.34 Do we compromise quality in order to meet costs and schedules?
25.35 What is the trade-off for doing/not doing this?
25.36 Does all our print and documentation conform to product/service standards? (This question arises in a number of different contexts. The auditor should consult, compare and align answers with those given in List 4, 'Company performance', Questions 4.42 and 4.44; List 9, 'The salesforce and its management', Question 9.117; List 16, 'Analysing lost business', Question 16.40; and List 24, 'Images and perceptions', Question 24.28, which itemizes the components of quality in documentation.)
25.37 How do we and our competitors rate on the following quality indicators? (See also List 20, 'Competitive intelligence', Question 20.10.)

Service quality indicators

- adherence to timetables, schedules
- benchmark against competitors
- completeness of service
- customer participation
- impact on the environment
- number of complaints/claims/returns
- number of items processed over time
- reliability/safety measures
- supplier evaluation
- utilization of service
- waiting time, delays, lead times
- cost of service
- customer satisfaction/evaluation
- incidence of rework
- number of errors, freedom from errors
- reliability of measures
- repeat purchase
- time taken to process items
- utilization of time

25.38 Can we/have we conducted an importance/performance analysis? (See Introduction, Figure 25.1.)

Appendix 25A
Determinants of quality

Component	Attribute	Example
Performance	Primary operating characteristics	acceleration (vehicles) clarity (VDU) station seeking (radio) holding, transferring and providing money products (banks) delivering markets (advertising agencies)
Features	Supplementing basic functions	tamper-proof packaging (food) counselling (life insurance) project viability (leasing)
Reliability	Consistency of performance, dependability and low risk of error	accuracy in billing (credit cards) keeping records correctly strategic supplies (components)
Responsiveness	Willingness to provide a service	sending a transaction slip immediately calling the customer back quickly emergency service
Competence	Possession of the required skills and knowledge, and low risk of error	qualification and experience of the contact personnel knowledge and skill of operational and support personnel research capability of the organization
Conformance	Extent to which product/service meets any established standards	financial audit (accountants) medical tests (doctors) building regulation compliance (architects) tolerance stack-up health and safety human rights

Component	Attribute	Example
Access	Approachability and ease of contact	availability of personnel backup stocks convenient hours of operation convenient location of operation
Durability	Length of utility or relevance	education and training services R & D obsolescence factors
Courtesy	Politeness, respect, consideration and friendliness of contact personnel	consideration for the customer's property (visiting services) clean and neat appearance
Communication	Keeping customers informed in language they can understand	explaining the product/service explaining how much it will cost explaining the trade-offs between quality and cost
Credibility	Trustworthiness, believability, honesty and positioning	company reputation product/service reputation personal characteristics of contact personnel
Security	Freedom from danger, risk or doubt	financial security (insurance) confidentiality statement of safe limits health and safety
Understanding/ knowing the customer	Making the effort to understand the customer's needs	learning the customer's specific requirements providing individualized attention
Tangibles	Physical evidence of the service	physical facilities equipment used to provide any service or deliver and install the product or test
Cost	Clear pricing or accurate estimates	known financial commitment no hidden extras contingency pricing

List 26

Non-differentiated products and commodities

INTRODUCTION

So much in marketing appears irrelevant to a manufacturer of a standard (non-differentiated) product. After all, metals, cables, chipboard, wire fittings, ball valves, industrial fastenings and drills, for example, made to a fixed standard, are identical in every respect. As a result, most companies marketing these types of product tend to fall back on a price response. 'Price-cutting,' it has been remarked, 'is a technique for slitting someone else's throat and bleeding to death yourself.' A price response is a conditioned reaction based on a primitive perception of what customers buy. It is as unnecessary as it is destructive. Companies who feel themselves trapped in a market in which price is the only criterion for purchasing need to view their products and their markets in a much more creative way. There are techniques for removing the price emphasis in favour of values. As proof of this statement, many buying practice studies in the United Kingdom and in other countries have shown that something in excess of 60 per cent of DMUs would not move from their best suppliers for a drop in price of 5 per cent plus.

A study of the problem of standard product and commodity marketing pointed out that technical and commercial parameters of such products may well give an impression of a largely immutable situation which marketing cannot alter. However, before considering differentiation it has to be said that there are circumstances when the introduction of product 'pluses' can generate at least one opposite effect to that intended: a downward pressure in price on the existing products. A new improved chipboard for the furniture industry offered at the same price as the inferior one only had the effect of creating a demand for a lower price for the original material, since the industry did not require a better-quality product for a component which in many applications was not subject to mechanical wear.

Add to this somewhat strange phenomenon the fact that no financial or technical benefits accrue from using one manufacturer's products rather than another's, and that there are no corporate or personal prestige factors stemming from purchase. There seems little opportunity to move away from price as a determinant in decision-making.

Differentiation will come not from observable or measurable product characteristics but from intangible factors which marketing must promote. There is evidence all round in consumer goods marketing that differentiation of similar products can be successful – petrol, detergents, lamps and many food products are all examples.

There are some preliminary screening factors to be considered before tackling the marketing problem. First, there is the need to establish if the product is truly non-differentiated. The early Question 26.1 deals with this point. Second, it is necessary to see, even if it is non-differentiated, whether it would not be possible to adjust it in some way to create a technical or physical differentiation, preferably innovative. The answers to Questions 26.9 and 26.11 are intended to determine whether the standards are preferred or merely accepted. It is not possible to go below a legal standard, but nothing stops a company going above it, or, for non-legal standards, below it. Essentially, the question is: 'Do we know what customers really want, or do they buy what is offered because no alternative is available?' If it is possible to depart from the standard, then there is the chance of a product differentiation.

Third, nothing in marketing can succeed without a knowledge of the buying/selling interface. Since non-differentiated products tend to fall into the 're-buy' class, the strategy to be adopted has to be to force a reconsideration of alternatives (see Introduction to List 15, 'The buying process').

Similarly, there has to be a knowledge of benefits that buyers either seek or would want if they were aware of them. Non-differentiated products and their suppliers do not necessarily produce non-differentiated benefits.

Fourth, one cause of price-cutting, as has been shown already, can be the form of sales remuneration that may encourage the offer of reduced prices. The arithmetic of this phenomenon will be found in List 9, 'The salesforce and its management', Introduction. Before tackling non-differentiated markets, the marketing auditor should look hard at sales representatives' remuneration method.

Consideration of these four factors will remove products that are not truly similar and also ensure that the efforts to achieve a differentiation for products that are similar are not negated by a lack of understanding of the buying process or by encouraging sellers to cut the price.

Question 26.17 draws attention to the fact that what is a standard and very unremarkable product in one industry might well be a new and innovative one in another. It is always a worthwhile exercise to look at the possibility of new markets for old products. The example of the spring balancer, quoted in the Introduction to List 7, 'Market size and structure', shows a successful approach to differentiating a market rather than a product. This essentially is the strategy involved in List 17, 'Introducing new products/services', Figure 17.1 (Square 2) in the Introduction.

From Question 26.18 onwards the questions inherently contain suggestions for differentiation. Appendix 26A lists a number of techniques for differentiating a product. Obviously not all of them will apply in every situation or product/service. Questions 26.20–26.24, for example, call for a re-examination of guarantee policy – usually set by trade practices or tradition and frequently completely out of line with what *could* be given, usually at little extra cost. An examination of guarantee claims and post-guarantee service charges will quickly show how far a guarantee can be safely extended. Apart from the values to the customer of a long and unequivocal guarantee, it is also a public affirmation of a firm's faith in its products.

Inherent in Question 26.24 is the fact that customers frequently are unaware of the value of support services. A technique which can be used is to issue invoices to their value clearly marked 'not for payment'. This identifies a benefit which the customer might have taken for granted.

Question 26.26 highlights a mistake frequently made in the selling of non-differentiated products. Because there is thought to be little to say about products such as ball bearings, minerals, seals, duplicating paper, rivets etc, organizations tend to use order-takers rather than salespeople. But if it is impossible to differentiate the product, it is certainly possible to differentiate the sales team. After all, selling used to be about and continues to be about being liked and trusted, despite claims for a so-called 'scientific approach'.

Reference made previously to establishing 'true' price is of particular relevance in non-differentiated products and services, when it is necessary for customers to see the values inherent in the cluster of customer-satisfying attributes that have been added to the core product. Question 26.35 returns to this topic.

Finally, Question 26.38, which deals with JIT, is particularly apposite as non-differentiated products are especially suitable for just-in-time delivery systems.

26.1 Is our product truly non-differentiated?

26.2 Would an improvement in the product force down the prices on existing products without guaranteeing increased sales on the modified product? (See Introduction.)

26.3 Are there, or could there be, any significant cost or other benefits for the customer in using our product as compared with competitive products?

26.4 If so, have we promoted these?

26.5 Would improved customer knowledge of the product and its use reveal benefits not obvious from the standard?

26.6 If so, can we launch a persuasive educational campaign?

26.7 Is it possible to introduce any prestige factors associated with ourselves or our customers?

26.8 Does our remuneration system for sales representatives encourage price-cutting? (See Introduction; also List 9, 'The salesforce and its management', Question 9.27.)

26.9 Is the standard offered the preferred one? (See Introduction; also List 2, 'Product/service range', Questions 2.17 and 2.18; and List 25, 'Quality in marketing', Questions 25.5–25.7.)

26.10 Do our marketing personnel and sales force understand the buying processes for our product? (See List 15, 'The buying process', particularly Questions 15.1–15.17.)

26.11 What evidence do we have about customer acceptance of and preference for the standard? (This question has arisen on a number of occasions throughout the lists in relation to other topics. The answers given should be consulted and aligned. List 3, 'The service element in marketing', Question 3.33, concerning complaint rectification; List 13, 'Non-personal promotion: methods and media', Question 13.60 on guarantees; List 16, 'Analysing lost business', Question 16.39 on seeking out dissatisfied customers; List 23, 'Pricing', Questions 23.1 and 23.2 relating quality aspects; and List 28, 'Product/service financial information', Question 28.52 on the cost of guarantee and warranty fulfilment.)

26.12 Can we go above/below standard?

26.13 What would the impact on price be?

26.14 Would the improvement in standard be seen by customers to compensate for any increase in price?

26.15 Would a lowering of standards be seen by customers to be compensated for by a decrease in price? (A comparison should be made with responses in List 25, 'Quality in marketing', Questions 25.33 and 25.34.)

26.16 Can we differentiate the product and the firm by a differentiation in marketing?

26.17 Can we differentiate the markets into which we sell? (See Introduction; also List 4, 'Company performance', Questions 4.4 and 4.11; and Introduction to List 17, 'Introducing new products/services', Question 17.9.)

26.18 Would improved delivery methods compatible with customers' handling facilities (or lack of them), commercial requirements, or supply or loan of handling equipment differentiate us from our competitors? (See Appendix 26A, also List 21, 'Physical distribution and packaging', Question 21.11.)

26.19 Would a self-imposed penalty for unreliable delivery or products create a differentiation that would be meaningful to the customers?

26.20 What length are our guarantees and why? (Part of this answer will have been provided in List 13, 'Non-personal promotion: methods and media', Question 13.60; but also the Introduction to that list; List 20, 'Competitive intelligence', Question 20.51; and List 28, 'Product/service financial information', Question 28.52.)

26.21 Could our guarantees be extended in length at nil or low cost to give us a marketing lead? (See Introduction and the answer in List 13, 'Non-personal promotion:

methods and media', Question 13.62; and List 28, 'Product/service financial information', Question 28.52.)

26.22 Would guarantees extended in time and coverage have a value or benefit to the user?

26.23 What would it cost as compared with the image and goodwill trade-off values?

26.24 Are customers aware of the monetary value of services not charged for?

26.25 What is the quality of the competitive salesforce? (See List 20, 'Competitive intelligence', Question 20.46 and Appendix 20A.)

26.26 Could we distinguish ourselves by the employment of a higher-quality salesforce? (A comparison could usefully be made between this answer and List 20, 'Competitive intelligence', Question 20.46.)

26.27 Can we achieve a favourable dissimilarity by a link (acquisition, franchise, solus, trading, etc) with distributors?

26.28 Would consignment selling (stock filling) be a marketing variant that would enhance our sales performance?

26.29 Can we link our product with another, perhaps original equipment, that will distinguish us (eg approvals, recommendations, mandatory use)?

26.30 Are there alternative uses for our product that would create a differentiation? (See example given in List 7, 'Market size and structure', Introduction.)

26.31 Can we distinguish our product/service or the company by promoting a different image? (There should be a consideration of the whole of List 24, 'Images and perceptions'.)

26.32 Have we isolated the technical and commercial attributes of our products and our firm? (This important topic is restated in other lists and the answers should be compared. See List 2, 'Product/service range', Question 2.43; List 16, 'Analysing lost business', Question 16.10; List 20, 'Pricing', Questions 26–28.)

26.33 Can we place a perceived value on these attributes? (See List 16, 'Analysing lost business', Question 16.10; List 20, 'Competitive intelligence', Question 20.58; List 23, 'Pricing', Questions 23.26–23.31 and Appendix 23A.)

26.34 Can we provide add-on services which would furnish a product distinction? (See List 3, 'The service element in marketing', Appendix 3A.)

26.35 Do we know the 'true price' of our product? (Compare with answer to List 2, 'Product/service range', Question 2.23; and see List 23, 'Pricing', Question 23.30, and Figure 23.1 in Introduction. It would also be useful to consider this subject together with the answers given in List 25, 'Quality in marketing', Questions 25.31–25.34.)

26.36 Will official accreditation such as ISO 9000 give us a market 'plus'. (See List 4, 'Company performance', Question 4.29; and List 25, 'Quality in marketing', Questions 25.33–25.35.)

26.37 Can we develop a zero defect system?

26.38 Would a JIT agreement provide us with a market advantage in the form of a favourable differentiation? (See List 21, 'Physical distribution and packaging', Questions 21.16, 21.17 and 21.20.)

Appendix 26A
Adding value to a product or service is to differentiate it

- Ability to serve buyer needs anywhere (Delivery of spares anywhere in the world in 48 hours or 'Cat' [Caterpillar] pays)
- Account queries settled in 10 working days
- Approvals and accreditation
- Cluster of backing services
- Compatible delivery methods and materials
- Consequential loss insurance
- Control of distributive channels
- Credit/claims settled within 10 working days
- Customer training
- Dedicated sales switch board and 'hot' line
- Differentiated markets – application engineering
- Differentiated marketing
- Discontinuance notice
- Emergency service
- Flexible credit terms
- Guarantee manipulation
- High quality selling
- Image development
- In-feeding and reciprocal trading
- Issue non-payable invoices for uncharged services
- Lifetime costs
- Management/market consultancy
- Non-restrictive Terms of Business
- Outcome selling
- Packaging mechanics and appearance
- Price signalling
- Provision of management support and market information
- Reciprocal trading and in-feeding
- Reusable packaging
- Sales process team
- Self-imposed penalties
- Simplified service/maintenance contracts
- Single point for buying and for customer service

- Stock filling service (just-in-time)
- Superior compatibility among products
- Trial use and/or demonstrations
- Twenty-four hour order taking and delivery of spares/supplies
- Waste handling and recovery
- Zero customer feedback time
- Zero offer improvement time

List 27

Service businesses

INTRODUCTION

List 3, 'The service element in marketing', dealt with what services companies provide as backup for their products. This section is concerned with pure service businesses. These range from simple refuse removal to complex financial or technical services. They have much in common with product businesses, but the differences that divide services from products are vital in deciding and applying the marketing approach and method. Among the differences, the main ones are: it is impossible to physically display a service – only surrogates can be shown; there can be no demonstration without actually delivering the service; warranty is always difficult and sometimes impossible; sampling is out of the question; packaging at best is marginal; quality is variable. All these and other issues must be taken into account when devising and executing marketing activities. The fact that there are so few cross-references to this list in the earlier compilations indicates the extent of the differences. Nevertheless, a large number of the questions listed in other sections, suitably modified, can apply. Where there is a link between a product and a service, the text has indicated this by referring to 'product/services'.

With the sale of a service the element of 'hope' is dominant. It is never possible to know precisely what will be received until the service has been rendered. Unlike a product, where the claimed physical and performance characteristics can be checked against specification or sample, a service can only be described, and communication is very imprecise. How quick is 'quick'? How does one rate the 'effectiveness' or 'efficiency' of an accountant's service in absolute terms?

The situation is complicated by the fact that services are rarely pure intangibles, but often contain a physical element, just as products will often contain a service element. Similarly, although theorists may talk of services 'perishing at the moment of their production', the reality is that services and their outcome can have a durability. While auctioneering and hairdressing are consumed as they are produced, R&D services can spread over years. It is a very useful exercise to categorize services, because it is then possible to compare services that are widely different but fall into similar categories to achieve a marketing cross-fertilization. The main categories – durability, tangibility and extent of commitment – are exampled in Appendix 27A. A further category that somehow escaped the earlier classifications is, of course, 'Degree of essentiality'. Clearly some services such as communications and financial are vital for all businesses and the vast majority of consumers. Other services can be considered 'important', 'standard' or 'desirable', but which service fits into which category is perhaps an arbitrary and particularized decision. Questions 27.1–27.5 deal with the categorizations and 27.6–27.7 imply the use to which the data might be put.

So far as professional services are concerned, marketing frequently continues to be rejected because it is seen to be incompatible with the culture of the various disciplines. List 9, 'The salesforce and its management', and List 13, 'Non-personal promotion: methods and media', are totally applicable and auditors in professional service firms would do well to use both lists, but in particular to consider Question 13.3.

Thus, for professional service firms, Questions 27.8–27.10 call for this reconsideration. The major firm of consulting engineers referred to in List 22, 'Industry contacts', lost a two-year marketing advantage by remaining in their association and accepting its ban on marketing when subsequently the profession was deregulated.

Most services comprise a 'core' – the basic purpose of the business or practice – and 'satellites', which are the peripheral and add-on facilities. For example, the core service of a hotel is a 'place to sleep', but satellite services usually include shops, restaurants, room TV, business centres, etc. Some satellite services are indispensable for rendering the core service; others improve the quality of the core service. It is necessary, since the quality and image of a service will be affected by the existence and performance of satellite services, that none should be introduced that will not be compatible or that might affect the core service adversely. This is covered in Question 27.14, but the auditor should return to List 3, 'The service element in marketing', and examine the questions posed there relative to the development of groups of satellite services that give added value to the core offering.

So far as professional services particularly are concerned, but also for many other types of services, the element of 'hope' referred to earlier means that there are many uncertainties involved in purchasing a service that are not present when tangibles are bought. A major part of the marketing task is to identify the sources of these uncertainties, which will vary according to the service, and to ensure that the marketing messages reduce rather than increase the uncertainties. Similarly, professional and many other services are essentially problem-solving. It is necessary to attack the substantive problem and to help customers and clients identify these problems. Finally, in regard to professional services, the client buys professionalism. The marketing auditor must ask the questions concerning how clients define professionalism, and must ensure that the whole organization conforms to these criteria. Answers to Questions 27.15–27.25 examine these points.

Another characteristic of services is that the user is often a participant in its production, ranging from merely specifying requirements to providing technical or physical inputs. Questions 27.22 and 27.23 raise the important issue of how far a customer is willing or can be persuaded to become involved in the transaction.

The interpersonal network (referrals) is a vital source of business for many service companies, but all too many fail to trace the source of such referrals, fail to acknowledge them, and fail to market them. These three monumental omissions can easily be dealt with if they are identified. Most service businesses will find the best sources of new business are satisfied clients, whose value is greater than the revenue they generate. Questions 27.28–27.35 cover these points. Important referrers, that is, those who introduce good quality contacts, require special treatment apart from the usual courtesies. The auditor should record such important members of the network as key clients and treat them accordingly. Thus List 19, 'Key customer marketing', is as applicable in networking as in dealing directly with customers.

The answer to Question 27.40 will often reveal a crucial weakness in service companies and practices where the task of marketing the service is separated from the task of carrying it out. Thus, an accountancy firm or a management consultancy may conduct a marketing campaign above criticism, but when the audit clerks or the practitioners move into the client firm it is not unknown for their attitudes and behaviour to antagonize it. This usually occurs in an attempt to prove they are not 'salespeople' but are highly skilled in other disciplines. Every service company must monitor the attitude of all staff from telephonist to the most senior members who interface with the client. Because a service company sells intangibles, the person is the surrogate for the 'product' and everything the staff say and do will impact on the success of the service company. There is an obvious and important link here with List 10, 'Customer care and support staff's role in marketing'.

Question 27.43 draws attention to the three basic methods by which a company marketing intangibles can approach its market. It is important to choose the correct approach for the service and market and for those who comprise the decision-making unit.

Question 27.51 may be regarded as paradoxical if services are indeed wholly intangible. Even if this were so, most services have an important tangible aspect of which perhaps 'information' is the most ubiquitous. If those resources and functions which enable a service to be delivered can be stored, it reduces lead time to completion, and 'lead time', it will be seen, is one of the marketing tools to be found in the format in List 13, 'Non-personal promotion: methods and media', Question 13.3.

The quality of service delivery is best understood if it is appreciated that customers may gain different perceptions and develop different attitudes to a service company as the various stages of the process of buying a service are reached. The situation has been well illustrated and the marketing actions to make each stage a satisfactory contact can be easily deduced from the process (see Figure 27.1).

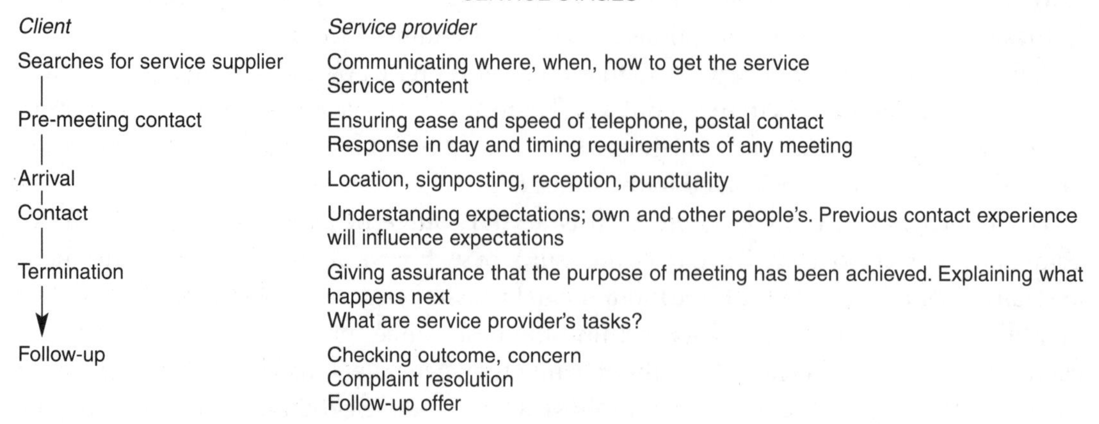

Figure 27.1 Stages in service delivery

(Questions 27.1–27.9 should be read in conjunction with the Introduction to this list and Appendix 27A.)

27.1 How durable is our service? (By way of example: 6 months = perishable; 6 months to 3 years = semi-durable; more than 3 years = durable.)
27.2 How tangible is our service (services providing tangibles, services giving added value to a tangible, services that make a tangible available)?
27.3 What commitment from the purchaser does our service require (long-term or fixed or both; short-term or flexible or both; optional)?
27.4 What degree of essentiality can be ascribed to our service?
27.5 To what extent is the service testable in more than abstract or qualitative terms?
27.6 Do other services that are successful share the same characteristics as ours? (See Introduction.)
27.7 Is there any aspect of their marketing that we can emulate?
27.8 Are we prevented from marketing by the codes of practice or rules of our profession or association, or by law? (See List 22, 'Industry contacts', Question 22.10.)
27.9 What are the 'gains' and 'losses' of not conforming?
27.10 What criteria have been used for decisions on acceptance and rejection of tools of marketing? (See Introduction, and List 13, 'Non-personal promotion: methods and media', Question 13.3.)
27.11 What improved customer/client knowledge would assist in delivering a more efficient service? (See List 10, 'Client care and support staff's role in marketing', Question 10.7.)
27.12 In what ways is customer/client knowledge of the service deficient?
27.13 How can we improve customer/client knowledge?

27.14 Have we a formal policy on the development of satellite services? (See Introduction.)
27.15 Can we identify and list sources of uncertainty among our customers and clients in purchasing our type of service?
27.16 In what way does our sales message attempt to reduce or eliminate these uncertainties?
27.17 Does our salesforce and our non-personal promotion reinforce the messages designed to reduce uncertainty?
27.18 Do we market our problem-solving capabilities and techniques for reaching a problem solution? (This is the service business equivalent of marketing benefits instead of features. The question should be completed using the same format as in List 2, 'Product/service range', Figure 2.1.)
27.19 Would our performance and acceptability be increased by a problem-solving approach?
27.20 How far are our customers capable of identifying their substantive problems?
27.21 Are our staff trained and motivated to assist customers in identifying their substantive problems? (See List 10, 'Client care and support staff's role in marketing', Questions 10.26 and 10.27.)
27.22 How much time are customers prepared to invest in the delivery of the required service?
27.23 In what way would the service be improved by greater customer involvement?
27.24 What criteria do customers and clients use to identify professionalism?
27.25 Do we conform to these criteria?
27.26 Are the skills of the representatives of the company, firm or practice commensurate with those of the clients to whom they are selling?
27.27 What percentage of new business comes from our initiative in approaching potential clients?
27.28 What percentage comes from referrals (interpersonal network)?
27.29 Do we know the sources of referrals? (See comments in Introduction to List 2, 'Product/service range', on indirect marketing, which are relevant to networking.)
27.30 Do we have a formal system for recording referral sources?
27.31 Do we have any contact with the referral source, most particularly to acknowledge and thank them for introductions?
27.32 Is networking one of our marketing targets? (See also answer to List 7, 'Market size and structure', Question 7.32.)
27.33 What percentage of referrals comes from existing clients? (See Introduction.)
27.34 Does an analysis of referrals reveal a disproportionate number emanating from a few contacts?
27.35 What steps can be taken to 'reward' referrers? (See Introduction.)
27.36 Do we have any knowledge of the processes that customers use to select (a) a type of service, (b) the firm to provide it? (See List 15, 'The buying process', where most of the questions on purchasing procedures are applicable to services if appropriately modified.)

27.37 What criteria are adopted by customers for selection of (a) the type of service to be utilized, (b) the firm that is to provide it? (See List 15, 'The buying process'.)

27.38 What evaluation methods will be used after the completion of the service to decide whether it has been satisfactorily completed? (Although mostly referring to products, the answer could usefully be compared with List 6, 'Marketing information: systems and use', Questions 6.44 and 6.45; List 15, 'The buying process', Question 15.42; and List 25, 'Quality in marketing', Question 25.6.)

27.39 Is there a formal method of identifying and dealing with client dissatisfaction? (This point will have been covered in List 3, 'The service element in marketing', Question 3.20; and List 6, 'Marketing information: systems and use', Questions 6.44 and 6.45, with the cross-references; and List 25, 'Quality in marketing', Questions 25.11 and 25.12.)

27.40 Are the service personnel/professionals who will actually undertake the service trained and motivated to deal with clients? (See Introduction.)

27.41 Is there a pattern of dissatisfactions? (See answer to List 10, 'Customer care and support staff's role in marketing', Question 10.13.)

27.42 Is the physical support of our operations compatible with the image we seek to project?

27.43 Is our marketing message based on (a) the methods or techniques of the service, (b) the reputation of the company or its personnel, (c) previous successful assignments, or (d) a mix of these? (See Introduction, and also compare answers to List 9, 'The salesforce and its management', Question 9.64.)

27.44 Is the approach appropriate both to the service and the market?

27.45 Can capacity be readily expanded by hiring more employees?

27.46 Is a buffer possible?

27.47 How much of a buffer should be built into the system for times of peak demand?

27.48 How much impact will idle time have on the efficiency of the service delivery system?

27.49 Is scheduling or the use of time shift techniques possible to avoid times of peak demand?

27.50 What criteria should be used for scheduling?

27.51 Is there a way to 'store' components of the service? (See Introduction.)

27.52 Should the service provider go to the customer or will the customer come to the service provider?

27.53 How many service sites are needed?

27.54 How much geographic distance will customer accept as possible to still permit an efficient service relationship?

27.58 Are branch locations viable?

Appendix 27A
Service classifications

Degree of durability

Classification	Durability	Example
Consumer services	Perishables (less than 6 months)	Cinema shows, hairdressing, laundry, sports events, removals
	Semidurable (6 months to 3 years)	Hire purchase, accountancy, employment agencies
	Durable (more than 3 years)	Education, defence, health, life insurance, house purchase
Producer services	Perishable (less than 6 months)	Plant maintenance, factoring, auctioneering, distribution, linen hire, services, travel, brokerage, computing
	Semidurable (6 months to 3 years)	Advertising, public relations, contract hire, executive search, architecture
	Durable (more than 3 years)	Management consultancy, contract R&D, equipment rental

Degree of tangibility

Classification	Producer services	Consumer services
Services providing pure intangibles	Security, communication systems, franchising, mergers and acquisitions, valuations	Museums, auctioneering, employment agencies, entertainment, education travel services
Services providing added value to a tangible	Insurance, contract maintenance, engineering consultancy, advertising packaging design	Launderettes, repairs, personal care, insurance
Services that make available a tangible	Wholesaling, transport, warehousing, financial, services, architecture, factoring, contract R&D	Retailing, automatic vending, mail order, hire purchase, charities, mortgages

Degree of commitment

Classification	Producer services	Consumer services
Long-term commitments requiring regular expenditure of fixed amounts of money; failure to meet such obligations may result in loss substantially greater than the amount of the missed payment	Insurance, loans, mortgages, R & D, pension schemes	Life insurance, house purchase, private medical schemes, accident insurance
Either long-term or fixed commitments, but not both	Contract hire (vehicles, plant, office communication systems), contract catering, business education, factoring, management consultancy	Accommodation rental, hire purchase, equipment rental, repair and maintenance of consumer durables
Short-term, flexible commitments, where expenditure is often postponable, reducible, or can be eliminated	Contract maintenance, security services, training, advertising	Private education, cleaning, laundering, public transportation, repair, private medicine
Optional services that can be indefinitely postponed	Welfare schemes, microfilming, design consultancy	Recreation, travel, entertainment

List 28

Product/service financial information

INTRODUCTION

There is obviously a very close link between this one and List 3, 'The service element in marketing', and it is helpful to consider them together.

This last list begins with an all too frequently neglected activity – undertaking a customer value analysis (CVA), already referred to in the Introduction to List 18, 'User industries'. It is also an analysis that has its place in the designation of key customers, List 19, 'Key customer marketing'.

Clearly, maximizing marketing operations requires more information than that referred to in List 4, 'Company performance', List 6, 'Marketing information: systems and use', and other calls for data through the book. The questions that follow are related to the two sections referred to above and extend some of the key questions. For example, Questions 4.3 and 4.4. in List 4, 'Company performance', call for annual sales units and/or value of products/services, whereas Question 28.3 below adds information on margins. More importantly, however, this list calls for a review of precisely who within the company gets information. Many marketing aspects have implications for managers and departments not directly involved in marketing. For example, Question 28.46 deals with stocks; and while it clearly concerns the warehouse manager, buying department and, of course, production, it is also of importance to marketing.

This list, perhaps more than any other, treats the firm as a total organism and not as a series of autonomous or even barely related departments and activities. It is recognized that throughout the book the marketing aspect has been dominant – they are, after all, marketing audit questions – but the lists have never lost sight of the fact that the firm is an integrated unit, and no one department can operate efficiently or at all without the others.

Thus, underlying what follows is the question not only of what information shall be gathered, but of who shall have it.

Questions 28.23–28.25 and 28.32–28.40 highlight a frequently occurring position where important financial data, which might well place a totally different interpretation on both the company's and on the marketing department's performance, are hidden by the reporting method.

Question 28.34, asking how data will be used, can and should of course be applied to all information-gathering, whether it be financial, marketing, production, human resources, or other functions. It is expensive in every way to gather data that are not used or used inappropriately. The mirror opposite question to ask is 'what would the effect be of not circulating the information?' Yet another litmus test for the value of information is to enumerate the actions that have been taken as a result of receiving it and that might not otherwise have been initiated.

Credit ratings are important to every company, and all too often remain unchanged despite the vicissitudes that customer companies go through. Few organizations have a regular checking and updating system, which could easily avert bad debts. If the marketing departments and most particularly the salesforce are kept informed of customer ratings, they can adjust their efforts accordingly or, if appropriate, tactfully withdraw. Questions 28.42–28.44 examine these criteria.

In companies where inventory is a vital ingredient of marketing message and operations, there is not infrequently a failure to distinguish the stock content by a number of criteria, such as current, modified and obsolete – and, where deterioration can take place over time, Question 28.46 might highlight a situation needing some adjustment.

As with so much that has gone before, the decision as to what data shall be collected, analysed and distributed is very much related to the firm, its operations and its markets. The questions suggest some items that will be key to most companies, but each organization must devise its own list. It is always important to emphasize the *use* of data rather than their collection.

Appendix 28A contains a summary and a possible format for financial control information. The auditors can extract those items they consider relevant to their needs. The data will in any event give some insight into many of the previous sectors of the marketing audit.

The rule has already been stated and if it is followed information overload will be avoided. *Need to know, not want to know.*

28.1 Do we (should we) carry out customer value analysis? (Answers should be compared with those given and called for in List 14, 'The distributive system', Question 14.58; List 18, 'User industries', Questions 18.77 and 18.78; List 19, 'Key customer marketing', Questions 19.9 and 19.11.)

28.2 Do our financial data provide sufficient, reliable and timely information on customer profitability to enable our targeting and budgeting to be decided with accuracy?

28.3 Are individual products/services and product/service groups, costs, units, sales and margins reported regularly? (See Appendix 28A. The answer to this and the following question may have been given in part in List 4, 'Company performance', Question 4.3.)
28.4 Are product line/service contribution reports produced regularly (eg price reviews, cost analysis, promotions analysis, product additions, product deletions)? (See Appendix 28A.)
28.5 Who receives these reports? (See Appendix 28A.)
28.6 Who decides who shall receive the information?
28.7 When was the circulation list last reviewed?
28.8 What evidence is there that the data are fully utilized by recipients?
28.9 What would be the effect of terminating the circulation of information to any particular manager or department?
28.10 Are annual sales contracts reviewed regularly to determine the impact of cost changes?
28.11 Who reviews them?
28.12 Are the data on which decisions are based complete?
28.13 Do any competitive pricing analyses and rationales available explain the differences? (See List 20, 'Competitive intelligence', Question 20.67 and Appendix 20A.)
28.14 Who produces them?
28.15 Are those who produce them interrogated as to the justifications offered?
28.16 Are variances from list prices controlled by appropriate managers? (Compare answer with that of List 6, 'Marketing information: systems and use', Questions 6.36; and for a departmental example List 23, 'Pricing', answer to Question 23.11 in relation to this; and Questions 28.17–28.25.)
28.17 How are these and other variances reviewed? (See answer to List 6, 'Marketing information: systems and use', Question 6.36.)
28.18 How is the control exercised? (See answer to List 23, 'Pricing', Question 23.11.)
28.19 To whom are variances reported? (See, for one example, answer to List 23, 'Pricing', Question 23.11.)
28.20 Is there a clearly understood policy on variances?
28.21 When was it developed?
28.22 Should it be reviewed?
28.23 Are special pricing arrangements, promotional prices and 'deals' reported as variance from list prices? (See Introduction.)
28.24 If not, how are they treated?
28.25 Does the system permit variances to be classified in a way that may disguise a position? (Compare with answer to List 6, 'Marketing information: systems and use', Question 6.36.)
28.26 Do the benefits of cost control outweigh the benefits of the perceived disadvantages?

28.27 Is cost control information geared to the requirements of responsible personnel?
28.28 Are cost control requirements subject to discussion with recipients?
28.29 Are results measured in accordance with the same unit of measure in which standards are set?
28.30 Do recipients of control information know how to extract the most essential facts?
28.31 Do all involved employees have cost targets?
28.32 Does production/marketing management have detailed cost sheets (including labour, servicing, material, packaging, overheads, guarantee claims, etc.) for all products?
28.33 If not, would there be any value in circulating these?
28.34 How would such information be used? (See Introduction.)
28.35 Is there a standard cost system in use for projecting profits?
28.36 Are prices compared by geographical areas, regularly, sporadically? (See List 5, 'Export marketing'.)
28.37 Are they truly comparable?
28.38 Are receivables monitored by marketing management?
28.39 Are credits/returns collated and detailed on sales, and margin reported?
28.40 If not, how are they treated in control data?
28.41 Are credits and returns monitored according to product and product lines and reason? (This analysis will also reveal information relative to List 6, 'Marketing information: systems and use', Question 6.44; and List 13, 'Non-personal promotion: methods and media', Question 13.62 concerning guarantees.)
28.42 Is there a formalized credit rating system?
28.43 Who is responsible for operating and updating it? (See Introduction.)
28.44 Are sales staff given information on customer credit ratings? (See answer to List 9, 'The salesforce and its management', Question 9.116.)
28.45 Are detailed, accurate and up-to-date inventory reports available to appropriate marketing management?
28.46 Is inventory analysed in terms of current and obsolete products and shelf life and related to short-term forecast sales? (See Introduction.)
28.47 What is current marketing expenditure? (This will have been partly answered in List 13, 'Non-personal promotion: methods and media', Question 13.5.)
28.48 What items are included under 'marketing' in the budget?
28.49 Is expenditure identifiable by product/service, activity, market, customer? (Some information will have been derived from the answer in List 13, 'Non-personal promotion: methods and media', Question 13.13.)
28.50 Are the costs of all marketing activities (including sales team and agents) planned and related to sales objectives? (Part of this call for information will have been satisfied in the answer in List 13, 'Non-personal promotion: methods and media', Question 13.13.)

28.51 Are all marketing activities formally evaluated in terms of effectiveness, cost, performance versus plan? (See List 13, 'Non-personal promotion: methods and media', Questions 13.16, 13.18 and 13.21.)
28.52 Do we know the cost of guarantee claims? (See List 13, 'Non-personal promotion: methods and media', Introduction and Question 13.62; also List 26, 'Non-differentiated products and commodities', Question 26.21.)
28.53 Is there a recognized and enforced monitoring procedure to survey marketing costs related to marketing campaigns?
28.54 Who is responsible for operating it?
28.55 What changes have been introduced as a result of data emerging from the monitoring?
28.56 What does it cost to produce a proposal or tender?
28.57 Can the cost be reduced by adopting standard procedures and by mechanization? (The answer to this question will have been given in List 9, 'The salesforce and its management', Question 9.72.)

Appendix 28A
Model for required information control

Performance information	Report frequency W = weekly M = monthly YTD = year to date	Standard	Variance shown by	Marketing director	Sales manager	Service manager	Chief executive
				Executives receiving reports: C = Control purposes I = Information purposes			
1 Sales							
Total sterling	W or M/YTD	Forecast	Sterling & %	I	C	C	I
By product/service	W or M/YTD	Forecast	Sterling & %	C	C	C	I
By region	W or M/YTD	Forecast	Sterling & %	C	C	C	I
By district	W or M/YTD	Forecast	Sterling & %	C	C		I
By nominated accounts	W or M/YTD	Forecast	Sterling & %	C	C	C	I
2 New accounts							
Total new accounts opened	W or M/YTD	Forecast	Sterling & No.	I	C	C	I
By product/service	W or M/YTD	Forecast	Sterling & No.	C	C	C	I
By region	W or M/YTD	Forecast	Sterling & No.	C	C	C	I
By district	W or M/YTD	Forecast	Sterling & No.	C	C		I
By nominated accounts	W or M/YTD	Forecast	Sterling & No.	C	C	C	I
3 Profits							
Net for company	M/YTD	Forecast	Sterling & %		I	I	
Company return on investment	quarterly	Forecast	Sterling & %		I	I	
Gross margin	M	Forecast	Sterling & %		I	C	
By product/service	M	Forecast	Sterling & %		C	C	
By region	M	Forecast	Sterling & %		C	C	
4 Expenses							
Total sales and marketing	M/YTD	Budget	Sterling & %		C	C	I
By product/service	M/YTD	Budget	Sterling & %	C	C	C	I
By department	M/YTD	Budget	Sterling & %	C	C	C	I
By region	M/YTD	Budget	Sterling & %	C	C	C	I
By district	M/YTD	Budget	Sterling & %	C	C		I
5 Pricing/discounts							
Amounts of variance from planned prices							
By product/service	W or M	Plan	Sterling & %	C	C	C	I
By region	W or M	Plan	Sterling & %	C	C	C	I
6 Sales activity							
Total sales calls and orders ratio	W or M	Plan	No. & %	C	C	C	I
By product/service	W or M	Plan	No. & %	C	C	C	C
By existing/new accounts	W or M	Plan	No. & %	C	C	C	I
By region	W or M	Plan	No. & %	C	C	C	I
By district	W or M	Plan	No. & %	C	C	I	I
By nominated accounts	W or M	Plan	No. & %	C	C	C	I
Non-billable time expenditure[1]	M	Budget	No. & %	I	C	I	I

1 Professional practices and time-based services

				Marketing director	Sales manager	Service manager	Chief executive
Performance information	Report frequency W = weekly M = monthly YTD = year to date	Standard	Variance shown by	Executives receiving reports: C = Control purposes I = Information purposes			
7 Customer accounts							
No. gained by region	W or M/YTD	Plan	No. & %	C	C	C	I
No. lost by region	W or M/YTD	Plan	No. & %	C	C	C	I
Net change by region	W or M/YTD	Plan	No. & %	C	C	C	I
No. gained by product/service	W or M/YTD	Plan	No. & %	C	C	C	I
No. lost by product/service	W or M/YTD	Plan	No. & %	C	C	C	I
Net change by product/service	w or M/YTD	Plan	No. & %	C	C	I	C
Ratio of corporate to private clients	YTD	Plan	No. & %	C	C	I	C
8 Customer service							
Complaints by type	W or M/YTD	Acceptable standard	No.	C	C	C	I
Complaints by product/service	W or M/YTD	Acceptable standard	No.	C	C	C	I
Complaints by region	W or M/YTD	Acceptable standard	No.	C	C	C	I
Refunds and allowances	W or M/YTD	Acceptable standard	No.	C	C	I	I
By nominated accounts	W or M/YTD	Acceptable standard	No.	C	C	C	I
Guarantee claims	W or M/YTD	Acceptable standard	Sterling & No.	C	C	C	I
9 Credit							
No. and value of accounts outstanding			No.				
Over 10/30/60 days	M	Objective	Sterling & %	C	C	I	
By product/service	M	Objective	Sterling & %	C	C	I	
Names of accounts over 60 days				C	C	C	
10 Advertising							
Sterling spent by media	M/YTD	Budget	Sterling & %	C	I	C	C
Sales promotion	M/YTD	Budget	Sterling & %	C	I	C	C
Public relations	M/YTD	Budget	Sterling & %	C	I	C	C
By product/service	M/YTD	Budget	Sterling & %	C	I	C	C
Status reports on functions, literature, etc.	Quarterly	–	–	C	C	C	C
11 Market research							
Project completed	M	Plan		C	I	C	C
Projects pending	M	Plan		C	I	C	C
Sterling spent on research	M/YTD	Budget	Sterling & %			C	C
12 Product development							
Status of each project pending	M	Plan	No. of weeks	C	I	C	I
New projects started	M	Plan	No. of weeks	C	I	C	I
Projects completed	M	Plan	No. of weeks	C	I	C	I
Projects in market test	M	Plan	No. of weeks	C	I	C	I
By product/service	M	Plan	No. of weeks	C	C	C	I
13 Marketing/sales personnel							
No. employed	M	Budget	No. & %		I	C	I
By product/service	M	Budget	No. & %	C	I	C	I
By function	M	Budget	No. & %	C	I	C	I
No. of unfilled vacancies	M	Budget	–	C	I	C	I
No. and type of training courses	M	Plan	No.	C	I	C	I
In process	M	Plan	No.	C	I	C	I
Completed	YTD	Budget	No.	C	I	C	I
No. of personnel attending	M	Plan	No.	C	I	C	I
No. of personnel completed	YTD	Plan	No.	C	I	C	I

Conclusion

The lists are not complete – they never will be. The marketing auditor and others may well extend them beyond this framework and beyond that within which the marketing resource realization technique can be practised. The dangers of an endless list are obvious enough and were pointed out at the beginning. Deletion must be as important as accretion. Self-discipline will always be needed to avoid producing a *tour de force* rather than a down-to-earth practical aid to improving marketing.

It is fitting to end with the three notes of caution that have been reiterated throughout the book.

1. All answers to all questions should be examined critically in relation to the source of information. 'How do we know?' is a vital interrogative. Folklore must be eschewed at all costs.
2. The way data are used is more important than acquiring them. The system fails totally and the time investment is wasted if the data gathered are not applied, are used only partially, or are used badly.
3. No action will occur as a result of the marketing audit unless every task is clearly allocated, tightly scheduled and monitored punctiliously.

With the knowledge that every business has locked-in and hidden resources, waiting only to be identified in order to be used, auditors should start and complete their task with the certainty that success must follow.

Index